Walpole
in Power

'Sir R. Walpole, the Stature of a Great Man or The English Colossus', cartoon 1740.
(British Museum)

Walpole in Power

JEREMY BLACK

SUTTON PUBLISHING

First published in the United Kingdom in 2001 by
Sutton Publishing Limited · Phoenix Mill · Thrupp
Stroud · Gloucestershire · GL5 2BU

British Library Cataloguing in Publication Data
A catalogue record for this book is available from the British Library

ISBN 0-7509-2523-X

For Anthony Musson

Typeset in 10.5/13pt Sabon.
Typesetting and origination by
Sutton Publishing Limited.
Printed and bound in England by
J.H. Haynes & Co. Ltd, Sparkford.

Contents

List of Illustrations

Frontispiece: 'Sir R. Walpole, the Stature of a Great Man or The English Colossus', cartoon 1740. (British Museum)

Plates (between pages 116 and 117)

Sir Robert Walpole, 1st Earl of Orford, *by* Michael Dahl (Wakefield Museum/ Bridgeman)

Houghton Hall, Norfolk, painting by kind permission of Lord Cholmondeley (Jarrold)

George II, *by* Charles Jervas (Guildhall Art Gallery/Bridgeman)

Sarah, Duchess of Marlborough, *by* William Darby (Wallace Collection/ Bridgeman)

'Chairing the Member', *by* William Hogarth (Sir John Soane's Museum)

Charles, 2nd Viscount Townshend, unknown artist (National Portrait Gallery)

Jonathan Swift, *by* Charles Jervas (National Portrait Gallery)

Sir Robert Walpole Addressing his Cabinet, *by* Joseph Goupy (British Museum/ Bridgeman)

Spencer Compton, later Earl of Wilmington, *by* Sir Godfrey Kneller (National Portrait Gallery)

John Campbell, 2nd Duke of Argyll, *by* William Aikman (National Portrait Gallery)

Note on Dates

Unless otherwise stated, all dates are given in old style, the British calendar of the period. Most European countries conformed to new style, which was eleven days ahead. New style dates are marked (ns).

ABBREVIATIONS

Add.	Additional Manuscripts
AE.	Paris, Ministère des Relations Extérieures
Ang.	Angleterre
AST. LM. Ing	Turin, Archivio di Stato, Lettere Ministri Inghilterra
Beinecke	New Haven, Yale University, Beinecke Library
BL.	London, British Library
Bod.	Oxford, Bodleian Library
C(H)	Cholmondeley Houghton collection
CP.	Correspondance Politique
Chewton	Chewton Mendip, Chewton House, Waldegrave papers
Cobbett	W. Cobbett, *Parliamentary History of England* (36 vols., 1806–20)
Coxe, *Orford*	W. Coxe, *Memoirs of the Life and Administration of Sir Robert Walpole, Earl of Orford* (3 vols., 1798)
CRO.	County Record Office
CUL.	Cambridge, University Library
EHR	*English Historical Review*
Farmington	Farmington, Connecticut, Lewis Walpole Library, Hanbury Williams papers
f.	folio
HHStA.	Vienna, Haus, Hof, und Staatsarchiv

HJ	*Historical Journal*
HL.	San Marino, California, Huntington Library
HMC.	Historical Manuscripts Commission
Hervey	R.R. Sedgwick (ed.), *John Lord Hervey, Some Materials towards Memoirs of the Reign of King George II* (3 vols., continuous pagination, 1931)
Lo.	Loudoun papers
NAS.	Edinburgh, National Archives of Scotland
NLS.	Edinburgh, National Library of Scotland
(ns)	new style
PRO.	London, Public Record Office
RA.	Windsor, Royal Archives, Stuart Papers
SP.	State Papers
SRO.	Edinburgh, Scottish Record Office
Sandon	Sandon Hall, archive of Earl Harrowby, papers of Dudley Ryder
Sedgwick	R.R. Sedgwick (ed.), *The House of Commons 1715–1754* (2 vols., 1970)
Walpole corresp.	Correspondence of Horace Walpole and Horace Mann, edited by W.S. Lewis in *The Yale Edition of Horace Walpole's Correspondence* (New Haven, 1937–83)

Unless otherwise noted, the place of publication for all books is London.

Preface

There is not an evening, that there is not some paper cried about the street, good or bad, of Robert hatch, Robert hangman, Robert the coachman etc. or something of this kind, which shows what a spirit he has to defend himself against.

Dowager Countess of Portland, 1730.[1]

So long ago as the days of Sir Robert Walpole, the scarcity of Patriotism was a ground of complaint. Sir Robert used to say he could produce patriotism when he pleased. The means became an object of curiosity. It was asked him how? He good-naturedly answered 'By refusing an unreasonable demand, you shall next day see a man start up a violent Patriot'.

The World, 6 March 1792

The most puzzling aspect of Sir Robert Walpole's political life was the extraordinary longevity of his ministry. Walpole was the leading minister of the Crown from 1721 until 1742 without a break. This contrasted with the periods before and after, which were characterised by ministerial instability. In the distance of history, 1721 to 1742 simply seems a period of dates, but comparison makes the point clear. A winner of three parliamentary elections in succession, Margaret Thatcher was seen to dominate her period in office, but it was only from 1979 to 1990.

The longevity of Walpole's ministry is inextricably involved with the question of the stability of Britain then, and this notion of stability provides the key concept through which various aspects of Britain in this period can be discussed. Walpole's ministry raises the question whether a stability of ministerial personnel necessarily denoted an underlying stability in the economy, in popular politics, religious attitudes, constitutional concerns, and in national and regional relationships. We need to address the questions of how Britain moved from the acute instability of 1679–1721 into a more stable political world, why Walpole held power for so long, and what the Whig Ascendancy meant in practice, in terms of power and the character and purposes of political culture and government. An account of Walpole's acquisition and retention of power provides an understanding of the parliamentary and wider political system which he exploited.

I have been working on the Walpole years since 1977, and my work has benefited both from the stimulus and studies of other scholars and from bodies that have supported my own research. I am most grateful to both. In the case of the latter, I would like to mention the Beinecke and Huntington Libraries for electing me to visiting fellowships, the British Academy, and the Universities of Durham and Exeter. Rather than taking the opportunity to reprint my *Robert Walpole and the Nature of Politics in Early Eighteenth-Century Britain* (1990), I have tried to re-examine my views and to take on board new perspectives derived from my own research and from the contributions of other scholars. Such a re-examination appears particularly appropriate now given the claims that Walpole's ministry followed Tory policies and was centred on Tory principles,[2] a claim Walpole would have rejected. The parallel with the Blair government is interesting.

I have also incorporated insights derived from archival material recently deposited in public holdings. The most important are the papers of Walpole's brother, Horatio, formerly held at Wolterton and acquired for the British Library in 1993,[3] the National Heritage Memorial Fund contributing £200,000 towards the price. These include some of Sir Robert's papers apparently removed from his archive probably in or after 1742 when he fell. Other correspondence of Sir Robert Walpole that was held at Wolterton until 1931 and subsequently became 'the property of a lady' was purchased by the British Library at Christie's in 1986.[4] The process of acquisition continues. Thus in 1998 the British Library purchased a notebook of Walpole's father recording his expenses and receipts in the 1690s.[5]

As a consequence of work on these and other collections, this book can claim to be a study of the Walpole ministry which is based on more extensive archival research than that conducted by any other scholar. Aside from the private papers examined by Archdeacon William Coxe, who produced his masterly study in 1798,[6] there is also a thorough examination of other private collections, as well as of state papers and of foreign diplomatic material, neither of which Coxe had the opportunity to consult. More extensive research is not of course the same as more profound insight, but it does provide the basis for testing assumptions. Furthermore, this study draws on my own work in a number of overlapping fields, including foreign policy, Parliament and the press. Having published a biography of Pitt the Elder, I have deliberately tried not to match that format, but rather to focus on Walpole's political position and what it can tell us about the political system and culture of the period, more specifically, about the development of a degree of stability.

I would like to thank Grayson Ditchfield, Eveline Cruickshanks, Bill Gibson, Bob Harris, and Murray Pittock for their characteristic generosity in commenting on an earlier version of this text.

I have tried to include as many quotations as possible in order to provide a flavour of the political discussion of the period. Spelling, punctuation and capitalisation have been modernised. These were the years of Swift and Johnson, Pope and Gay. They are years of great interest, and studying them has given me much pleasure for over two decades. I hope I can communicate some of the interest in the following pages. I am particularly pleased to be able to dedicate this book to a friend and fellow-scholar who is also a keen walker of Devon's fair byways.

1

The Rise to Power, 1676–1721

In 1688, as in 1485, England was successfully invaded. The political situation, however, was very different in 1688 for a number of reasons, not least the validating role of Parliament in England, and the need to ensure that Scotland and Ireland were brought into line. Nevertheless, there was also a fundamental continuity. Political issues were settled by conflict. Furthermore, the dynastic position was crucial. Political legitimacy could not be divorced from the sovereign and the succession. Both these factors ensure that the elements of 'modernity' suggested by the constitutional products of the 1688 invasion, especially the Bill of Rights of 1689, and the moves towards regular parliaments and elections and a freer press, have to be qualified by reminders of more traditional features of the political structure. The foreign force invading England and the aristocrats rising against the king were reminiscent of the French-supported opposition to King John in 1216 and of Henry VII's French-backed seizure of power from Richard III in 1485.

While the 'Glorious' Revolution was an important advance for a particular view of England, it did not secure that view instant dominance, or allow the nation to unite around it. In fact, the Revolution produced a number of competing strands of patriotism. Alongside praise for William III as a Protestant and providential blessing on the nation, were Jacobite, Tory and 'Country' views of the new king as a usurper and of an England suffering depredations under his tutelage, views that were perfectly viable and that attracted considerable support in the 1690s. These views, however, were marginalised – not because of any inherent absurdity, or necessary incompatibility with English national character – but because the circumstances of William's reign allowed him a political and polemical victory over his opponents. Most importantly, William proved able to win the military struggle over the British succession that followed 1688. He could, therefore, exclude his opponents from power, and condemn critics of his vision of nationality and

1

political destiny as disloyal. In addition, William's military victory coincided with a dramatic expansion of public politics. In the 1690s, the advent of annual sessions of parliament, the ending of pre-publication censorship, and the development of a considerably more active press, meant that polemical politics began to produce more and different kinds of sources. As a result, the particular patriotic discourse associated with the victors of the revolution was widely disseminated, and gained the highest profile in the culture of print, as well as in government records.

The consequence of this victory for Williamite patriotism has been to shape not only Georgian Britons' view of their world, but also later historical understanding of the period. The 'Glorious' Revolution was seen as the source of a 'matchless constitution'. Much of the scholarship dealing with the century after 1688 has been soaked in the sort of Whiggism promoted by that event, with the result that many of the ambiguities and complexities of the period have been lost. Until recently, historians of the eighteenth century were almost as effective as Williamite politicians in marginalising the Jacobite and other dissonant voices of the age. Consequently, the Protestant and Whiggish vision associated with the victors has come to seem natural to the English, and the coherence and potential persuasiveness of alternative world views has been obscured. This threatens to underrate the challenge faced by Walpole.

Similarly, too little attention has been paid to the exclusivity and polemical nature of the eventually dominant patriotism. Its victory has hidden the fact that it was necessarily divisive because directed against critics of William, and that it derived much of its early drive from its partisan character. Civil war in Scotland and Ireland was the first consequence of the 'Glorious' Revolution. It was won by William and his supporters, but the nature of the struggle and the results of the victory affected both Scotland and Ireland thereafter, creating problems that were to affect the Walpole ministry.

In the meantime, the aspiring politician was more affected by another consequence of the 'Glorious' Revolution, war with Louis XIV, King of France from 1643 until 1715. The cost, course and consequences of this struggle were to be greatly divisive, interacting with and exacerbating the tensions between developing political groups. These can be referred to as parties, although that does not imply that they were similar to modern political parties. The Whigs made more of their opposition to Louis XIV than the Tories, while there were also important tensions within the crucial world of religion that helped shape political alignments, and also gave them energy. The 'Glorious' Revolution had loosened the hegemony of the Established episcopal church in England (the modern Church of England) and destroyed it in Scotland. In England, the Established Church was challenged by the Dissenters, many of whom looked back to a long tradition of opposition to Stuart rule. A society that had no positive experience of religious toleration, and indeed regarded it as an alien concept, was not the best background for the introduction of religious pluralism. In England, under the Toleration Act of 1689, Trinitarian Dissenters who took the oaths of Supremacy and Allegiance, and made the Declaration against Transubstantiation, could obtain licences as ministers or schoolmasters, although these had to be registered with a bishop or at the Quarter Sessions. This was found threatening by many members of the Established Church. In addition, to make the situation more volatile, many Whigs were anti-clerical, while non-Trinitarian Dissenters were excluded from the Toleration Act.

Tensions between the Church of England and the newly resurgent Dissenters interacted with different tendencies within the Church of England and, in particular, a division between 'high' and latitudinarian clerics. The former were more hostile to other Protestant groups and more inclined to see a threat in toleration, a threat not only to religious orthodoxy, but also to the moral order and social cohesion that the Church was seen as sustaining.

Dr Henry Sacheverell, an Anglican cleric and a Tory, felt able to argue in 1709 that the Church was in danger under the Revolution Settlement, as interpreted by Whigs. The latter were traditionally associated with Dissenters, especially in Tory propaganda. The Tory ministers who came to power the following year were determined to limit Dissent and also saw action against it as a way to maintain Tory cohesion. The Occasional Conformity Act of 1711 was designed to prevent the office-holding by Dissenters who avoided the ban on non-Anglicans by communicating once a year. The Schism Act of 1714 attacked separate education for Dissenters.

This was the divisive and partisan context of Walpole's rise to parliamentary prominence. He came from a line of Norfolk landed gentry. His grandfather, Edward Walpole, was elected MP for the port of King's Lynn in 1660 and 1661, and created a knight of the Bath in 1661. His eldest son, Robert (1650–1700), was the father of Sir Robert Walpole. A prominent Whig in Norfolk politics, he was elected, for the small Norfolk borough of Castle Rising, to the Parliament that legislated the Revolution Settlement in 1689, and again in 1695 and 1698: he had purchased twenty five burgages in the borough, and the right of election rested with the burgage holders. Robert Walpole also held county office, as a Deputy Lieutenant and a colonel of militia. His more active and ambitious son was to be the leading minister by the age at which his father had died.

Sir Robert Walpole, a fifth child, was born in 1676 and educated at Eton (1690–6) and at King's College Cambridge (1696–8), to which in 1723 he gave £500. With the death of his two elder brothers, the eldest, Edward, in 1698 and the second, Burwell, in 1690 in the battle of Beachy Head with the French fleet, he became the heir. As a result, plans for a clerical career were abandoned, and he began to manage the family estates. In 1700, Walpole married Catherine Shorter, who was a noted beauty and the daughter of a prominent London merchant.

With the death of his father in November 1700, Walpole succeeded to the family estates and began his political career. From the outset, he showed great ambition. At his first general election (1701) he contested one of the two Norfolk county seats, traditionally the sphere of the well-connected and prestigious. Unsuccessful there, he followed his father and was elected for Castle Rising. In 1702, however, in the first election of Queen Anne's reign, Walpole switched to King's Lynn, the seat he was thereafter to represent until he was created Earl of Orford in February 1742. King's Lynn was a prosperous port, whose representation was shared by Walpole and a member of a prominent local family, the Turners. Charles Turner, MP for King's Lynn from 1695 until his death in 1738, had married Walpole's sister Mary in 1689 and was a close friend.[1] Walpole used his position to have another close friend, Charles Churchill, elected for Castle Rising from 1715 on.

Many MPs were not noted for their activity in the Commons, preferring to regard a seat there as due recognition of family position. This was not Walpole's style. Within three days of his first session of Parliament in 1701, he was serving on a committee, and he was prominent as a speaker and a teller. For example, in February 1702 he acted as teller against an amendment that 'persons who take upon them offices shall not depart from the communion of the Church of England'. That December, he moved unsuccessfully for the resumption of all Crown grants made by James II. In 1704, he was active in opposing a bill against occasional conformity. He quickly showed himself indispensable to the Whigs: in 1704 both James Stanhope and Spencer Compton wrote to him to come to the Commons (from his Norfolk residence at Houghton) where his leadership was needed.

The following year, Walpole came into office as a member of the Admiralty Council. This was a reward for his diligence and ability, a recognition of his electoral influence in Norfolk – both at Castle Rising and at King's Lynn, and a product of his links with the Marlborough–Godolphin connection who increasingly dominated the government. This appointment also reflected the disenchantment of the connection with much of the Tory party and their search for Whig support. Walpole found himself acting both as a lightning rod for tensions between Lord Treasurer Godolphin, a Tory by background, and the Whigs; and also as an advocate of a wholesale move towards the Whigs.

His own career prospered, and in 1708 Walpole was appointed Secretary at War. John, Duke of Marlborough handled Britain's strategy in the War of the Spanish Succession, and Walpole's surviving correspondence with him dealt with army commissions rather than strategy,[2] but the problems of supporting a war in which most of the British army was deployed abroad created major administrative and financial burdens for Walpole. In 1708, he was concerned with delays in the supply of 'biskett' for the forces,[3] as well as with the pay and supply of dragoons sent as part of the British army in Spain and, more generally, the army establishment there.[4]

In January 1710, Walpole was appointed to the more lucrative post of Treasurer of the Navy. In both posts he played a role in Britain's wartime success and also learned at first hand about the difficulties of waging war and obtaining success. This role and these lessons are both worth bearing in mind when considering his subsequent opposition to bellicosity. Much of the correspondence he received focused on the need for more resources, whether, for example, naval stores in the Mediterranean in 1708 or more troops in Spain in 1710.[5]

The political situation was to wreck this promising ministerial career. Growing war-weariness sapped support for the conflict, while at court the Marlborough interest was under challenge, not least because Queen Anne (1702–14) had wearied of her favourite, Sarah, Duchess of Marlborough. Walpole was prominently involved in defending the government in the Commons, in the management of which he had been playing an important role. The eventual battleground was Sacheverell's sermon. Walpole was one of the managers for the Commons impeachment of the volatile cleric. His speech of 28 February at the impeachment provides a glimpse of Walpole in action, proclaiming his Whig beliefs and linking High Church views to arbitrary power. It also shows Walpole at his combative best, going straight to the nub of the issue:

The doctrine of unlimited, unconditional passive obedience [to a monarch], was first invented to support arbitrary and despotic power, and was never promoted or countenanced by any government, that had not designs some time or other of making use of it. What then can be the designs of preaching this doctrine now, unasked, unsought for, in Her Majesty's reign, where the law is the only rule and measure of the power of the Crown, and of the obedience of the people? If then this doctrine can neither be an advantage or security to her Majesty, who neither wants nor desires it, to what end or purpose must every thinking man conclude it is now set on foot, but to unhinge the present government, by setting aside all that has been done in opposition to that doctrine; and when, by these means, the way is made clear to another title, the people are ready instructed to submit to whatever shall be imposed upon them . . .

And all that the Doctor alleges in his defence is that in the Revolution there was no resistance at all; and that the King did utterly disclaim any such imputation. But surely, my Lords, it cannot be now necessary to prove resistance in the Revolution; I should as well expect that your Lordships would desire me for form's sake to prove the sun shines at noon day. If then, there was undoubtedly resistance used to bring about the Revolution, it will follow, that all the censures, which are so freely bestowed upon resistance in general, must attend, and will be imputed to the Revolution; and if 'resistance be utterly illegal, upon any pretence whatsoever'; if it is a 'sin', which unrepented of, by the doctrine of the Church of England, carries 'sure and certain damnation'; if, 'upon repentance', there is no 'remission of sins', without a steadfast purpose to amend the evil we have done, and to make all possible 'restitution', or at least to do our utmost endeavour for that purpose; I beg your Lordships to consider what a duty is here professed, upon peril of damnation, upon every man's conscience, that knows, or believes, that there was resistance in the Revolution, and is conscious to himself, of being in any ways assisting, or even consenting to this 'damnable' sin; and what must be the consequence, if these doctrines, without any reserve or exception, are with impunity preached throughout the kingdom.[6]

The Whigs won the case but lost the argument. Now without the support of the Crown, their unpopularity cost them dear in the 1710 election. Walpole had sought to use it to set the seal upon his Norfolk political career, by winning a county seat, and thus to help win both county seats for the Whigs. Instead, he finished bottom of the poll, far below the winners.[7] However, he was still returned to the Commons, as he had been re-elected for King's Lynn, where he had also stood as a safety measure. Dismissed from office by the new Tory ministry at the start of 1711, Walpole became one of the leaders of the Whig opposition in the Commons. The main battleground was peace, and in November 1711 Walpole moved an amendment to the Queen's speech declaring that no peace would be acceptable if Spain and its American colonies be left to a Bourbon, a member of the royal house of France, the very compromise settlement that the Tory government was trying to negotiate. Henry St John, Viscount Bolingbroke, the Tory Secretary of State seeking to negotiate peace, pointed out:

'Those who oppose the Queen's measures know as well as we who pursue them, that the war is becoming impracticable, that the end which they pretend to aim at is chimerical, and that they ruin their country by driving on this vain gaudy scheme which has so many years dazzled our eyes'.[8]

Defeated by the Tory majority, Walpole was, in turn, accused of responsibility for the mis-application of public funds, specifically of receiving bribes whilst making forage contracts for the army in Scotland in 1709–10. This was part of a more general attack on the financial administration of the Godolphin ministry in the 1700s. The Tory Commission of Public Accounts was partisan but their findings not necessarily untrue. What they said about

Marlborough's corruption was accurate; Walpole both spoke and wrote in reply. For example, he drafted the detailed financial calculations on which Arthur Maynwaring's pamphlet, *A Letter to a Friend Concerning the Publick Debts, particularly that of the Navy* (1711) was based.[9]

Voted guilty of 'a high breach of trust and notorious corruption' in January 1712, Walpole was expelled from the Commons and committed to the Tower. Re-elected the following month for King's Lynn, he was then declared ineligible for the existing Parliament. Walpole's imprisonment helped make his name. Ballads, broadsheets and pamphlets appeared for and against, and Walpole himself contributed to the controversy, writing *The Case of Mr Walpole in a Letter from a Tory Member of P–t to his friend in the Country*. This spell in the Tower was referred to when Walpole became first minister, by way of underlining his credentials as a true Whig and Patriot. It was used, for example, by Philip Frowde in the lavish dedication to Walpole of his play *The Fall of Saguntum* (1727).

Although released in July 1712, Walpole was unable to re-enter the Commons until Parliament was dissolved in August 1713 and there were fresh elections. He at once resumed his prominent role in the Whig leadership, criticising the expulsion of the Whig MP, journalist (and fellow Kit Kat Club member) Richard Steele from Parliament, resisting the Schism Act, and claiming that the Protestant Succession was in danger under the Tory ministry. The last was a clear accusation of Jacobitism. Queen Anne had no surviving children and the Whigs supported the exclusion of the male line of the Stuarts (now in the person of James III and VIII, the son of James II and VII), which was central both to the Revolution Settlement and to the supremacy of parliamentary statute; for both had decreed that the succession lay with the Protestant House of Hanover, through the Electress Sophia of Hanover, the granddaughter of James VI and I. The opposition of the Hanoverian house to the Treaty of Utrecht, the peace with France negotiated by the Tory ministry in 1713, also led them to look to the Whigs.

By the time of Anne's death in 1714, Walpole had distinguished himself as one of the leading Whig parliamentarians. His rise had been rapid, and he was, by the standards of the day, a sound party man. The Tory Jonathan Swift referred to 'his bold, forward countenance, altogether a stranger to that infirmity which makes men bashful, joined to a readiness of speaking in public'.[10] A proficient speaker in the Commons, Walpole was an effective political animal, skilled in 'management', the handling of the patronage without which both the political system and government could not operate. Steele replied to press attacks on Walpole as deceitful by stating that he had 'an open behaviour and honest countenance, a noble elocution, and many other qualities which render the gentleman the object of respect and love to all that know him . . . this gentleman is a perfect master in business, and has so clear a head, that he communicates his thoughts as perspicuously as they are placed in his own mind'.[11] Other pamphlets praised his abilities.[12] Not all, however, were so favourable.[13] Walpole's reputation was clearly located in partisan terms.

Given his apprenticeship it might have been expected that Walpole would have played a major role in putting Whig schemes into practice after George I came to the throne in 1714, turned out the Tories and put in a clearly Whig ministry. However, Walpole did not gain the role that had been anticipated. The posts of Paymaster General of the Forces and Treasurer of Chelsea Hospital, to which he was appointed in 1714, were profitable; the former involved much work in the aftermath of a major conflict, and Walpole became a Privy Councillor, but he was not given one of the leading offices of state. Nevertheless, he was powerful because of his prominence in the Commons, while the appointment of his brother-in-law, Charles, 2nd Viscount Townshend, as Secretary of State for the Northern Department further increased his influence. The other Secretary of State, James Stanhope, was in the Commons, but was really an ex-army officer and lacked Walpole's parliamentary skill. Furthermore, at this stage, he was close to Walpole, and regarded as repeating 'Mr Walpole's words'.[14] The First Lord of the Treasury and Chancellor of the Exchequer, Charles, 1st Earl of Halifax, was in the Lords. In May 1715, he died and was replaced by Charles, 3rd Earl of Carlisle, who was also in the Lords.

As a consequence, Walpole played a major role in the parliamentary business of the ministry. This was resolutely partisan. George I had informed his first Privy Council that he wished for the repeal of the Occasional Conformity and Schism Acts, and the Whigs were determined to end the possibility of two-party politics by tarring the Tories as Jacobites and destroying their leadership. When, after the Whig success in the 1715 general election, George I's first Parliament met that year, Walpole moved the Address, which condemned Anne's Tory government; he was also appointed chairman of the Committee of Secrecy established to punish those who had plotted to restore 'James III'. Walpole drew up the resulting report, presented it to the Commons in June, and impeached Bolingbroke, the Secretary of State who had masterminded the Treaty of Utrecht. Walpole was given charge of this impeachment and was also made responsible for those of other leading Tories.[15] His skill at this probably prompted Bolingbroke and Ormonde's flights abroad.

This keen energy was rewarded when the ministry was reshuffled in October 1715. Two months earlier, a commentator had predicted, 'Mr Walpole [will] soon be at the head of the Treasury, for Lord Carlisle does not care for business'.[16] Walpole, in contrast, did. He became First Lord of the Treasury and Chancellor of the Exchequer. Walpole's administrative experience made it clear that he possessed the capacity to manage money, and his defence of Whig finances in 1711 had shown that he fully understood the public politics of money, but this promotion was essentially a reward for his position in the Commons.

It also testified to the alignment of Crown and ministry against Toryism and Jacobitism at a time when the Jacobite rising of 1715 put the Protestant Succession in danger. Walpole was clearly identified with hostility to what he presented as the Tory-Jacobite nexus. Once the rebellion was suppressed, he pressed hard for firm action against its leaders. In the face of considerable popular pressure in February 1716 for a reprieve for the young James, 3rd Earl of Derwentwater, Walpole defended the death penalty in the Commons, and Derwentwater was beheaded on Tower Hill. Walpole had claimed in the Commons that he had been offered £60,000 to secure a reprieve, but this public show of ministerial probity was somewhat undermined by the corrupt practices that surrounded the sale of part of the Derwentwater estates, although Walpole himself was not personally involved. In addition, in 1716 Walpole was granted a lucrative place in the Customs for the lives of his two elder sons.

In the Commons, Walpole also attacked the Tories:

'Walpole . . . set forth the carriage of one set of men among us, who tho' ty'd by the strongest obligations of religion as well as by their interest and their country's welfare to support the King against the pretender, had yet in all their conversation and behaviour affected to express an indifference for the success of the rebellion which sort of men (he said) differed from declared rebels only in that they wanted courage to draw the sword'.[17]

Having acted against the claimant to the throne, Walpole was soon to discover that the favour of its occupant was fickle. Aside from reversing many of the acts of the Tory ministry and establishing Whig hegemony, the Whig leadership was also faced with a foreign ruler whose knowledge of British conditions was limited, but whose expectations, especially in the field of foreign policy, presented difficulties in terms of domestic politics. For most of the previous reign, political debates on foreign policy had been subordinated to the needs of the war with France. A new situation emerged with the dual developments of the accession of a Hanoverian ruler with German and Baltic interests of his own, and the negotiation, by James Stanhope in 1716, of an alliance with France. As a result of George I's interests, British politicians were now forced to define their attitudes towards states they knew little about, such as Russia, in the context of a rapidly changing international situation. Hanover's close involvement in the Great Northern War of 1700–21, at this stage a struggle to partition Charles XII of Sweden's Baltic empire, meant that George I expected from his British ministers a greater commitment to Hanoverian interests than he was subsequently to require or receive in the early 1720s. Differences of opinion over foreign policy were treated as tests of loyalty.

Matters were made worse by tensions in the royal family and the Whig élite, and the relationship between the two. George was suspicious about the links between Townshend and Walpole, and George, Prince of Wales, while the increasing favour that the king showed to Stanhope and to Charles, 3rd Earl of Sunderland, exacerbated strains. As a member of the Whig Junto (leadership) of Anne's reign, Sunderland was senior to, and better connected than, Walpole. Whig unity had ebbed as soon as the dangers posed by Toryism and Jacobitism had receded.[18] Walpole wrote to his brother, then an envoy in The Hague, in March 1716, 'I don't well know what account to give you of our situation here, there are storms in the air, but I doubt not they will all be blown over'.[19] This was not to be. The government was widely thought to be unstable. 'It has been much talked for some time that we are to have great alterations at Court', an observation in a letter of Charles Cathcart in August 1716,[20] was a frequent theme in the correspondence of the period.

Townshend and Walpole were reluctant to support the fiscal, political and diplomatic consequences of George's Baltic policy, specifically to move Britain into clearcut opposition to Sweden. George responded by trying to reconstruct the ministry in December 1716. He promoted Stanhope to the crucial Northern Department, responsible for relations with northern Europe, and demoted Townshend to the Lord Lieutenancy of Ireland. This failed to produce either harmony or a smooth parliamentary session in 1717.

A political crisis ensued in April 1717. The ministry had exposed the 'Gyllenborg Plot', a conspiracy which committed Charles XII of Sweden to help the Jacobites, in return for Jacobite money, and were determined to use it in order to secure a definite parliamentary commitment to support George's anti-Swedish policy.[21]

Walpole and Townshend split openly with Stanhope and Sunderland over this issue. In parliamentary terms, this was a sensible decision as support there for a war against Sweden was weak, and suspicion of Hanoverian designs behind British foreign policy acute. It was, however, hardly the issue to divide over if the purpose were to increase the King's favour for Walpole and Townshend. The brothers-in-law probably hoped to force George to recognize that parliamentary support for his foreign policy could only be obtained by coming to terms with them,[22] and making concessions over foreign policy. The net result, instead, was to drive George further into the arms of Stanhope and Sunderland. One of the striking aspects of the 'Whig Split' was George's unequivocal support for his ministers and his determination to use all royal patronage to this end.

On 8 and 9 April 1717, Parliament was asked for funds to enable George to concert measures with his allies against hostile Swedish designs. The opposition countered by accusing George's Hanoverian ministers of using British money to support Hanoverian territorial aggrandisement. Though Walpole voted with the ministry, his supporters voted against, and Townshend opposed the measure in the Lords. Townshend's dismissal was followed by the resignation of most of the Walpolites, including Walpole himself, and the reconstitution of the ministry. George I was very sorry to lose Walpole and tried to persuade him to stay.

The remainder of the session was very troublesome for the Court. Walpole supported the passage of the scheme, that he had played such a large role in devising, for the rescheduling of the national debt in order to reduce interest payments. This saved nearly £326,000 per annum, the savings being known as the 'Sinking Fund'. In other respects, however, his actions justified the contemporary claim that he was 'doing ev'rything to make the Parliament impracticable'.[23] On 13 May, the Tories supported by Walpole, pushed through by a majority of ten a motion to choose a High Churchman to preach before the Commons, and on the 30th the opposition pushed through a motion that the preacher should have the thanks of the House and that his sermon should be printed.[24] On 4 June, an attempt to charge Cadogan, a close associate of Stanhope and Sunderland, and a favourite of George I, with embezzling the funds entrusted him for bringing over Dutch troops to help suppress the '15 was defeated by only ten votes.

The situation was exacerbated by the deteriorating relations between George and his son. The existence of a reversionary interest was in itself a cause of instability. George I, aged 57 in 1717, was fairly fit, although there had been recent fears about his health. He was disinclined to allow his son any real political role, and this led to a curtailment of the Prince's powers during George I's absence in Hanover in 1716. George was equally determined to curb his son's patronage. Efforts to effect a reconciliation between father and son after the 1717 session failed, and many of the Prince's supporters, led by John, 2nd Duke of Argyll, lost their places.

In the next parliamentary session, which opened in November 1717, opposition attacks concentrated on foreign policy and the army, issues on which it was possible to unite opposition Whig and Tory views and to present British foreign policy as being distorted for Hanoverian ends.[25] There was a revival of a traditional 'Country' platform, with both Tories and opposition Whigs objecting to the large size of the army. The French alliance was also widely unpopular. Walpole supported the Tory proposal for a reduction by a quarter in the size of the army. The debate on 4 December was highlighted by a highly provocative speech by the Jacobite MP, William Shippen. The second debate on the army (on 9 December) was of a more technical nature. The issue of whether the army should be maintained in separate corps or not, was presented by Walpole as a means of effecting a cash saving of £100,000 by a more efficient method of military organisation. The government again won the division, although with a smaller majority. There was tension within the opposition. Walpole condemned Shippen's anti-Hanoverian speech on 4 December, while the support given by the opposition Whigs to the land tax angered the Tories, many of whom therefore proved unwilling to co-operate with Walpole.

When Parliament reassembled after the recess, many more Tory MPs attended. On 22 January 1718, in a debate in a Committee of the Whole House, the Tory/opposition Whig group scored their first victory. Walpole and the Tory Archibald Hutcheson maintained that the lists of half-pay officers included many who had no right to be on them, and a ministerial procedural motion was defeated. Two days later, Hutcheson and Walpole succeeded in having officers from the 13 regiments which had been reduced in Ireland struck off the half-pay lists. On 25 January, there was a debate on the ministerial request for £115,000 for the half-pay list. Walpole again displayed his political skills. The opposition proposed £80,000 instead and, after some debate, the £94,000 suggested by Walpole 'was readily accepted on both sides without any opposition'.[26]

No progress had been made in bringing about a reconciliation between George I and the Prince and, as Lord Perceval noted, the 'Walpolites' were increasingly seen as 'the Prince's party'.[27] On 17 March 1718, the Commons received a message from George I requesting additional supplies to equip a fleet, with no indication as to where that fleet was to be sent. Only two MPs spoke against the address to provide the additional expense necessary: Walpole and the Tory Joseph Herne. They complained that no previous notice had been given to Parliament and that the ministry had waited till the very end of the session before raising this issue. They argued that war must be avoided, as it would lead to increased taxation and contracting new debts, and went on to suggest that the ministry try and pay off the national debt first, and that Parliament should examine treaties concluded with the Emperor to ascertain whether support for Austria was in the national interest; the implication being that it was intended to use the fleet to win Austrian backing for Hanover. Walpole and Herne, however, were not supported, and the address was carried without a division.[28]

Walpole's speech tends to discredit rumours that he was moderating his stand in order to effect a reconciliation with the Court, as suggested by his voting with the ministry on 12 February on the third reading of the Mutiny Bill.[29] Furthermore, on 17 March, when the government sought a supply for a naval expedition to the Mediterranean in defence of Austrian possessions in Italy against a possible Spanish attack, Walpole opposed the measure, although he failed to enlist much support.[30] Ministerial supporters were in no doubt of Walpole's hostility, Cadogan reporting:

'The play of Mr Wa-le and his cabal is to create a jealousy of the ministry, by spreading a thousand extravagant stories, and to give Mr Wa-le his dues his genius is as productive and fertile in this way, as ever that father of lies the honest Earl of Oxford was', the last a reference to Robert Harley, a leading Tory of Anne's reign.[31]

Many Tories were deeply suspicious of Walpole, who was suspected of being engaged in negotiations for a reconciliation with the Court. *The Defection Consider'd*, a ministerial pamphlet, had predicted in 1717 that the alliance between Walpole and the Tories would not succeed:

'The Tories had done too much against him, as well as he too much against them, ever to be forgiven, much less trusted; and that after they have made all the use they can of him, they will throw him by, as a tired traveller does his dirty boots, and have no more regard to him than he has to his master'.[32]

Walpole's vote for the third reading of the Mutiny Bill, an important item of government business, on 12 February 1718 had aroused anger among the Tories,[33] while Walpole was also held responsible for advising the Prince of Wales to abstain on the issue in the Lords, instead of voting against, as the Tories advised.[34]

Yet Walpole also helped fulfil Tory goals by thwarting the ministry's legislative intentions. This was important as it gave a more moderate character to the Whig regime, and thus set the context for Walpole's period in office. Whiggery was neither an ideology nor a policy, but, instead, a tendency capable of different definitions and developments.[35] Under George I, the Whigs came to power with a monarch who was not a member of the Church of England: George I was a Lutheran, although he conformed to Anglican liturgy in his Chapel Royal. Furthermore, after electoral victory in 1715 and the Septennial Act of 1716, there was no need to fear an election for another seven years. This provided the opportunity to press on to make a fundamental change in the political system. Such changes had become a pattern, with the 'Glorious' Revolution of 1688–9 and the parliamentary Union with Scotland in 1706–7.

Now, it was the turn of the religious settlement in England. The position of the Church of England as the Established Church, and England as an Anglican political community was to be weakened with the repeal of the Occasional Conformity and Schism Acts. Furthermore, George I, Stanhope and Sunderland envisaged in 1717 the repeal of the Test Act and the passage of an Act to limit the independence of Oxford and Cambridge, where most of the clergy of the Church of England were trained.[36]

13

Many Whigs were worried by such plans. In May 1717, Rapin de Thoyras, the Whig historian, had defended the justice of a repeal of the Occasional Conformity Act, but warned that it would be opposed by some Whigs and might enable the Tories to revive their cry of 'the Church in danger'. Five months later, John, 2nd Earl of Stair, put forward a similar argument and, while reaffirming his loyalty to Stanhope and Sunderland, urged them to abandon the repeal of that act, as well as any legislation against the universities, since he thought Parliament would not support them:

'By attempting things, even right things, which you are not able to carry, you expose yourself, in our popular government, to the having the administration wrested out of your hands . . . if heat and impatience will make you go out of the entrenchments, and attack a formidable enemy with feeble forces, and troops that follow you unwillingly, you will run a risk to be beat'.[37]

This was a position akin to that of William Wake, the Archbishop of Canterbury.

However, unable to win the support of the Tories because of their views on foreign policy, and, anyway, disinclined to take this option, the ministry pressed on in late 1717 with plans to aid the Dissenters. They were under pressure from them, and also concerned to gain the support of the electorally significant Dissenting interest in many constituencies. Alarming rumours began to circulate that the Dissenters would demand the abolition of bishops, or that they had 'desired to be put on an equal foot with other subjects'.[38] However, negotiations to find a 'Declatory Test' acceptable to both the Dissenters and those bishops willing to support the ministry over the issue, failed, and this made it less likely that the ministry could risk a parliamentary debate on this issue. Several bishops began to show greater independence, voting with the opposition and signing protests. Archbishop Dawes of York and four bishops signed the protest against the Mutiny Bill.

It was thus understandable that the ministry did not introduce legislation favourable to the Dissenters in the 1718 session. Walpole's co-operation with the Tories had helped to shape the contours of the subsequent decades. At the same time, it raised the always fluid and uncertain confluence of principled stands and the political tactics of the moment, and threw light on the difficulties confronting opposition.

The crisis of 1718 foreshadowed the political developments of the subsequent quarter-century, the 'Age of Walpole'. An alliance between the Tories and government Whigs had been made impossible by differences over foreign policy and ecclesiastical issues. In foreign policy, although most Whigs sought to limit the personal role and Hanoverian aspirations of George I and George II, they were willing to comply with the monarch's wishes. The Tories showed no such inclination, and harped incessantly on the theme of a

Hanoverian policy. Walpole's failure to use the Tories either to create an effective opposition coalition or to force himself back into office, prefigured the failure against him as minister of the more famous 'Patriot' opposition platform, the Bolingbroke–Pulteney scheme, which was as unoriginal as it was unsuccessful. Forced to oppose British foreign policy, and thus to anger the King, the opposition Whigs of the late 1720s and 1730s reaped only failure from their Tory alliance.

The 1718 crisis also underlined the centrality of foreign policy issues to the political and parliamentary history of the period. The need for increased taxation to finance a controversial foreign policy created parliamentary difficulties for the ministry, who were indeed fortunate that the war with Spain in 1718–20 proved so short and successful. Had it not done so, it is difficult to conceive how the ministry could have maintained itself in Parliament. Some of Walpole's disinclination to take a marked role in European power politics can be attributed to the legacy of the late 1710s. Walpole's success in influencing government policy in 1718 did not take him into office, but it did challenge the cohesion and confidence of the ministry. Walpole made it clear that a Whig government could not necessarily expect, still less command, the support of Whig parliamentarians, a lesson that his own years in office were to show that he had learned well.

The complex means by which Walpole subsequently returned to power in 1720 were effectively described and analyzed by J.H. Plumb,[39] and his account largely stands. As the subject of this book is Walpole in power, not his rise to office, there is no need to repeat his account, but several themes are important for his subsequent career. First, Walpole's skill in the Commons was not simply dependant on his deployment of the fruits of patronage. He was shown by his years in opposition to be an effective parliamentarian – as speaker, leader, organiser and tactician – without such fruits. Secondly, he knew how to benefit from the play of circumstance in years that were indeed particularly volatile. Subsequently, Walpole was to be presented by some critics as an essentially immobile beneficiary of his control over patronage. This was misleading, and in 1719 and 1720 he certainly showed himself as anything but immobile.

As Walpole was still in opposition, his activity was necessarily focused on responding to government moves. In 1719, Walpole opposed both the introduction of the Peerage Bill and the repeal of the Schism Act, a measure whose introduction he had opposed in 1714. The Peerage Bill, a product of George I's feud with his son, was an attempt to restrict the membership of the House of Lords, and thus to prevent the future George II from creating fresh peers when he came to the throne in order to buttress a new ministry that he might appoint. Walpole stirred up opposition to the measure both in the House of Lords and in the Commons, the latter a body from which new peers would have been recruited. He also published *The Thoughts of a Member of the Lower House . . .* on the Bill. Having prepared the ground, Walpole spoke forcefully against the Bill in the Commons, asking MPs if they would 'consent to the shutting the door upon [their] family ever coming into the House of Lords', and helped secure its defeat on 8 December 1719.[40] Legislation to increase government control over Oxford and Cambridge was dropped because of the strength of likely opposition.[41]

Later in his career, Walpole and his apologists sought to contrast his conduct in 1717–20 with the supposedly disloyal conduct of later oppositions. A ministerial London newspaper, the *Daily Courant*, claimed on 19 January 1734:

'he withdrew from office without withdrawing from his duty. He declined serving his late Majesty as a minister, but persisted in the most submissive obedience as a subject; he betrayed no private conversations; he entered into no combinations; he aimed not at disturbing the government, after he had quitted his share in it. Such a conduct failed not of obliging even those from whom he differed, and the concurring voice of all parties acknowledged his virtue was without stain, and his management without reproach'.

These claims, made in response to opposition criticisms of Walpole's inconsistency, were inaccurate, and reflected a subsequent unease over his opposition to a Whig ministry in 1717–20. Indeed, Walpole's methods then were factious, and he did not hesitate to adopt every possible means to bring down the ministry. An opposition pamphlet of 1731 suggested that Walpole had written a scandalous ballad during the Whig split, adding 'about that time he laid down his employments, and spurned as much against the government (as his champions are pleased to call the ministry) and distressed them as much in their measures as ever' Walpole's opponents had done since. Spencer Compton, a political ally of Walpole in the late 1710s, secretly urged the Spanish envoy, Montéleon, to encourage Spain to resist British diplomatic moves, whilst Walpole was accused, with some reason, of hoping that the dispatch of a British fleet to the Mediterranean in 1718 to resist Spanish schemes would lead to difficulties for the British government.[42]

In Parliament, Walpole's oratory was violent. A critic, Charles Whitworth, envoy at The Hague, wrote in April 1718, 'All the world here are extremely surprised at Mr Walpole's conduct; they blame his impudence as well as his animosity'.[43] When motions for the repeal of the Occasional Conformity and Schism Acts were introduced in December 1718, Walpole joined the Tories in attacking the ministry's plans, comparing George I and Sunderland with James II and the latter's adviser, Sunderland's father. Lord Perceval noted:

The eldest Walpole gave offence to many by the free manner of his speaking. He told them he was turned out for not consenting to the repeal of these Bills; run

16

parallels between King James and King George, declaring at the same time that, although they were not justly drawn, the Jacobites would persuade the people they were; they have been told (said he) that King James recalled the Penal Laws and Tests, will they not be told King George recalls the security of the Church? They have been told King James set up a high commission court, will they not be told his present Majesty is now upon appointing commissioners for a royal visitation? . . . They talk of the dissatisfactions of the people, and the disorders this Bill will probably produce in the country, which he affirmed is against the judgement of even half of the Whigs, he said he had one comfort still and that was although His Majesty had been led into such ill measures they were not hereditary in the royal family for that he had a son who not only voted against the Bill but entered his protest . . . he added that this consideration would keep the people quiet.[44]

The Duke of Montrose, who heard the speech, thought it 'the most impertinent one I ever heard and I must own to you I am one of the very many that was surprised he was not taken up for it in an other manner than he was'. Walpole was also criticised on the grounds that he had formerly opposed the Acts. An anonymous verse pamphlet of 1718 asked:

> Can the fanatick schemes of Tories find
> Reception in your penetrating mind?
> Can such a genius as yours believe
> The wild, and senseless notions they receive?
> But if, (as sure I think) you still disdain
> The visionary systems, which they feign;
> How can you join with them, and act a part
> Repugnant to the dictates of your heart?[45]

In 1719, the Duke of Newcastle wrote to Stanhope:
'the great point I think we ought to aim at is, that there should be but two parties that for and that against the Government and I cannot but think that by a new election, Mr Walpole and the few friends his party will be able to bring in, will be so incorporated with the Jacobites, that we shall have but little difficulty in dealing with them'.[46]
Yet in 1720, Walpole returned to government. This reflected both the weaknesses of the latter and Walpole's own desire to play a major role in a Whig ministry. Temperamentally, he was not an opposition figure, as, for example, William Pitt the Elder was to be. It is appropriate to stress the matter of temperament as it is all too easy to present Walpole as being drawn to office by a desire for its perquisites, in short by corrupt motives. This was to be the refrain of opposition criticisms, and it is true that Walpole was not averse to the benefits that could flow from office. Yet, he also enjoyed being in power for

other reasons, not least an ability to direct affairs and put ideas into practice. In office, Walpole did not display the temperament of opposition that Pitt was to show while in power during the Seven Years' War. Blocking the Peerage Bill was not the sum of what Walpole sought to obtain.

The process by which reconciliation occurred is obscure. It is possible that Walpole and Townshend benefited from tension between Stanhope and Sunderland, and George I's German confidants, especially Bernstorff, and possible that they deliberately accentuated this tension. This can be linked to differences of opinion within the government over Britain's Baltic policy, as well as to concern over how best to support the cost of military and diplomatic preparations. As a related issue that may also have driven the pace of reconciliation, there was the matter of the end to the rift between the king and his heir, in which Walpole played a part through the offices of Caroline, Princess of Wales. This again could be related to the state of the Civil List, the parliamentary grant to the Crown. Ending the Whig Split, would help ensure that the accumulated debt would be paid off.[47]

In the spring of 1720, the Court was the sphere in which reconciliation took place. On 23 April, the Prince of Wales made his submission to his father, and, next day, the opposition Whigs followed. Walpole played a major role in arranging the parliamentary dimension of the reconciliation. On 6 May, he steered the bill for tackling the Civil List debt through the Commons. This demonstrated both his consistency with his submission on 24 April, his value to the new government, and his place in the new political system. He had not only been reconciled with the government Whigs but also publicly broken with the Tories.

Walpole's position in the Commons was anchored with office, which also increased his value to the ministry. On 11 June 1720, Walpole was made Paymaster-General with the agreement that he should become First Lord of the Treasury at the earliest opportunity. The Paymastership was less prestigious than the Treasury, but, nevertheless, a lucrative post. It was later held by Henry Pelham, Henry Fox, and Pitt the Elder. Townshend became Lord President of the Council.

This was not equivalent to a gain of power, and Walpole's new office was what he had gained in 1714, not the more senior post he had been promoted to in 1715. Stanhope and Sunderland were still in office, and relations between Sunderland and Walpole remained poor. However, Walpole was now a more central figure than he had been in 1714–16. He had shown his importance in Parliament. When he returned to office, he was also able to bring in connections. His friend and fellow King's Lynn MP, Charles Turner, who had followed Walpole into opposition in 1717, was now rewarded with a Lordship of the Treasury, as was Richard Edgcumbe, another Walpole ally. Walpole himself gained control of the secret-service money, part of the Civil List and not subject to parliamentary control, which was very important in electioneering, and also provided a source of political payments.

Walpole was helped by the culling among Whig leaders. Several who had been prominent in the 1710s, such as Marlborough (strokes 1716, died 1722) and Earl of Halifax (died 1715), had died or lost their health. Others were to be disgraced as a consequence of the bursting of the South Sea Bubble and the subsequent political fall-out. The rise in the shares of this finance company had been seen as a way to private wealth and public stability: it was presented as a way to help pay off the national debt and this plan was steered through Parliament in February 1720. Walpole had attacked it as financially unsound and also because it was then a policy of a ministry of which he was not a member.

The collapse of the Company's stock in September 1720 ruined the finances and hopes of many, and led to accusations of fraud against the directors and the ministers close to them. Some of the latter had indeed been rewarded with large amounts of stock, and several had been implicated in the very dubious financial practices of the directors. As Bank of England and East India Company stock also fell heavily, there was a danger of a widespread financial collapse. The crisis led to pressure for George I to return early from Hanover and for an early meeting of Parliament. George was Governor of the Company, and the crash of what had basically become a fraudulent financial conspiracy was seen as a crisis that reflected the corruption of the governing order. George had not paid for the South Sea shares he held and, like other prominent people, had taken them as bribes to promote the company.

Walpole was a major beneficiary of the crisis. Indeed, Countess Cowper observed, 'We have had a report in the country that Mr Walpole is immediately to be at the head of the Treasury. I suppose that has been spread to raise credit'.[48] The ending of the Whig Split provided sufficient parliamentary support to underpin the reorganisation of public finances. On 8 December 1720, the government won the Commons debate on the Address by 261 to 103.

Walpole played a central role in producing a plan to deal with the financial results of the collapse, and, more particularly, defending it in the Commons. Walpole's scheme was presented to the Commons on 21 December; he was described as speaking 'with the greatest skill imaginable'.[49] His complex plan involved the rescheduling of the inflated debts of the South Sea Company and a writing down of its capital. The government acquired a liability on which it paid interest until the capital was redeemed in 1850. Annuitants who had exchanged their government securities for South Sea stock were left with much lower annuities. Subscribers to the stock who had paid for their initial investment in cash now found it worth far less, although they were not obliged to complete their subscriptions. There were many losers, but fewer and for less than had seemed likely prior to Walpole's restructuring. He helped to restore confidence both in the financial system and in the government's financial activity, probity and prospects.

Although criticised for defending ministerial colleagues implicated in the Company, and termed the Skreen-Master, Walpole benefited from the problems that affected the latter. Charles Stanhope, Secretary of the Treasury, who had been given a lot of stock, lost his post, although, thanks to government pressure on critical MPs to abstain, he was acquitted of the parliamentary charge brought against him. His cousin, James Stanhope, was not guilty of fraud, but a stressful exchange in the Lords about relations between the government and the Company, led to his death from a cerebral haemorrhage on 5 February 1721. John Aislabie, the Chancellor of the Exchequer, who had negotiated the crucial agreement with the Company, resigned on 23 January, and was expelled from Parliament for corruption. James Craggs, one of the two Secretaries of State, who had helped Aislabie, died of smallpox on 16 February; his father, who had been heavily involved in the South Sea Company, committed suicide a month later.[50]

Sunderland remained in office, but had been badly tarnished by the crisis. Walpole had to help defend his governmental colleague on 15 March 1721 – George I would expect no less – but he was able to gain the key post; after all, Walpole had also to defend George I who had received free stock. On 3 April, Walpole became First Lord of the Treasury and Chancellor of the Exchequer; while Townshend replaced Stanhope as Secretary of State. Walpole faced problems aplenty, not least Sunderland's continued role at Court, but was now as clearly the dominant figure in the ministry as he had been in the Commons since his return to office in 1720.

An account of his rise to office throws light on Walpole as a political animal, on his resourcefulness, energy, determination, talent and abilities, but it is also worth drawing attention to some other aspects of his life. First, it is clear that he had a major advantage in that he was generally healthy, robust and energetic. Yet, at the same time, like his contemporaries, he was subject to the ailments of the period and affected by the limited effectiveness of the cures and panaceas available. In 1710, he suffered a serious bout of ill-health. Walpole's career was certainly stressful, and, at times, this was revealed. In May 1716, he wrote to his brother Horatio:

'I have been here about ten days and find so great a benefit from the air, that I gather strength daily and hope as much time more will recover me from the lowest and weakest condition, that ever poor mortal was alive in, and I shall be able to get to town and do business again'.[51]

In late 1721, Walpole was believed sufficiently near death as to lead to speculation about his likely successor. Destouches, the French envoy, reported that Carteret, an ally of Sunderland, would have become First Lord, allowing the latter to dominate the government.[52] In 1723, ill-health led Walpole to seek relief in the fresh air and country pursuits of Houghton.[53] The following year, he was reported as ill with colic again,[54] and in early 1735 with gout, sufficiently so to be absent from the Commons.[55] Of his younger brothers, Horatio (1678–1757) survived him, but Galfridus (1683–1726), a naval officer who had lost an arm in action in 1711, did not.

In part, ill-health reflected over-exertion. Another sphere of such over-extension was expenditure. Walpole's accounts reveal a degree of conspicuous consumption that does not accord easily with any description simply in terms of a fox-hunting squire, the politician who first opened his letters from his huntsman, and who attributed his strength to hunting.[56] Walpole did indeed enjoy hunting. In 1722, he wrote to his brother about the Atterbury Plot: 'We are in trace of several things very material, but we fox-hunters know, that we do not always find every fox that we cross upon, but I doubt not but this matter will come out so as to shame all gainsayers'.[57] Walpole indeed kept a pack of harriers at Houghton, where, each November, he held a 'hunting congress' of friends and local gentry. In October 1723, he entertained the Duke of Devonshire and Lord Godolphin at Houghton: 'I made them both go both fox and hare-hunting'.[58] In 1731, Sir Thomas Robinson hunted six days in the week he was there.[59] In 1738, Walpole's trip was delayed by the sensitive state of Anglo-Spanish relations, but he still got to Houghton.

Walpole was not only in Houghton in the autumn. The following May, Stephen Poyntz noted, 'My brother and I passed the birthday very pleasantly at Houghton where there were three tables full of company'. He spent that Christmas there as well.[60] The summer could also see him at Houghton, for example in July 1723, July 1731, and July 1735, although the 1731 trip was delayed by fears about a possible French invasion after the collapse of the Anglo-French alliance.

Walpole also kept a pack of beagles in Richmond. His recovery from gout in early 1735 (not yet complete) was shown when he went hunting in Richmond.[61] His expenditure on hunting was not that of any ordinary fox-hunter. Aside from his massive spending on the stables at Houghton, Walpole also spent very heavily – allegedly £14,000 – on Old Lodge, his hunting lodge in Richmond New Park. This itself reflected Walpole's patronage, for in 1727 his eldest son, Robert, Lord Walpole had been appointed Ranger of Richmond Park. The senior Robert first hired and then built a house in the Park. This was also an investment in his career as George, Prince of Wales established a summer residence there: he bought Richmond Lodge from Ormonde's confiscated estate in May 1718.

Elsewhere, Walpole also spent heavily on accommodation, most fabulously so at Houghton. He also had two houses in London in the 1710s, one on Arlington Street, the other, with more land, at Chelsea. In 1722, Walpole purchased another house at Chelsea for £1,100. This took him out of the bustle and smell of London and gave him some semi-rural calm. Chelsea was also near both the royal palace at Kensington and, easily reached by boat across the Thames, the hunting pleasures of Richmond. Walpole tended to spend the summer there, being 'interrupted in my diversions' in August 1725 by a courier from Hanover with the news of Roxburgh's dismissal by George I.[62] He also travelled in England. Thus, on 25 August 1724 he visited Exeter with his heir, as well as Dodington, William Yonge, Edgecumbe and Charles Churchill, dining at the bishop's palace and being presented with the freedom of the city, a sign of his popularity and presence reported in the press, for example the *Post Man* of 1 September 1724. Walpole never visited Scotland, Wales, Ireland or the Continent, but, within England, he was better travelled than George I or George II. An official residence in Downing Street was offered by George II in 1731, but Walpole did not occupy it until 1735. When he fell from office in 1742, Walpole left Downing Street for his town house and returned to Arlington Street.

The maintenance, furnishing and decoration of these properties was a constant strain, of sums both large and small: £3 1s for 'twenty flower pots for the garden at Chelsea' on 25 May 1715, ten shillings to the watchmen at Chelsea on 24 April 1716 for 'ten weeks watching', £32 on 12 May 1716 'to Mr Wintles ironmonger for work done at your Honors Lodgings in Chelsea', £42 18s 6d four days later for coal delivered at Chelsea, and £98 to Mr Story the gardener at Chelsea the same day. A new copper in the brewhouse at Walpole's Chelsea property cost £11 13s in September 1716. There was expenditure at Houghton before the new house went up: £135 on 8 September 1716 'to Mr Turner linen draper in full for sheeting etc. sent to Norfolk', and £6 2s three days after 'for making nineteen pair of Holland sheets and three dozen pair of pillow cases sent to Houghton'.

The accounts also show considerable expenditure on alcohol, clothes, and goods. Six gallons one pint of arrack in August 1714 were followed by sixteen gallons, one quart and one pint a year later, fifteen gallons in September 1716. Hogsheads of wine were also purchased,[63] and in 1733 Walpole had his wine supplied from France.[64] At a less potent level, in the autumn of 1716, £14 10s was spent on tea, coffee and 'the finest sugar' sent to Norfolk, and £19 6d for 'a hundred of lemons sent to Houghton', and in July 1718 16s 3½d for 'the freight of Bath waters'.[65]

Walpole's Norfolk 'congresses' were to be criticised by opposition writers for their alleged luxury and for a preference for foreign food. The *Norfolk Congress*, a prose squib that appeared in November 1728, with a ballad version the following month, made much of food imagery. Before the guests depart for the hunt they receive a breakfast of foreign dishes and after the hunt a dinner of the same that does not agree with their 'English stomachs'. Walpole's policy was linked to his appetite: 'But now French sauces will go down . . . so much a Frenchman he is grown'.[66]

Clothes listed in the accounts included thirty six ells of Holland and six yards of cambric which were made into twelve shirts and cuffs and neckcloths respectively in August 1714. In the same month, £11 was paid for a brocade waistcoat and 6s 9d for gloves, hatband, buckles and buttons. In September, £17 10s was spent on lace for a neckcloth and two pair of ruffles, and £2 9s for twelve pair of cambric ruffles. Expensive objects also clearly pleased Walpole. In October 1715, there was a goldsmith's bill for £84 16s and the following March £68 was spent on a gold repeating watch for Horatio. Money had to be spent on animals, whether the bay gelding bought from Colonel Charles Churchill in June 1716 for £50, or the 9s on 'goldfinches and bullfinches for your Honr.'s Vollery at Chelsea' the following January. Paintings were a particular interest of Walpole's and he went on spending on them when in opposition. In August 1717, £86 was 'paid to Mr Richardson painter for drawing your Honors and Sir Charles Turner and brothers pictures' and the following April £13 5s was 'paid for two pictures at Mr Graffier's auction'.

This expenditure was met in large part by rents from his estate (the rent roll of which in June 1700 had been £2,169), official sources, and share dealing, but could only be covered by borrowing. In April 1716, Walpole paid the interest on three loans which amounted to £1,500. There are suggestions that Walpole's delay in meeting the subscription calls for the Royal Academy of Music indicated financial problems.[67] He died £40,000 in debt. This was far larger a sum than could be justified as anticipation of income.[68] Debt was scarcely unique to Walpole. Despite receiving legacies and private and government annuities, William Pitt the Elder borrowed from friends, was forced to raise mortgages on his property, and died £20,000 in debt. William Pitt the Younger also had substantial debts, and even so wealthy a man as Newcastle was forced to sell lands and to borrow in order to pay off the enormous debts he had incurred through electioneering. The government itself was heavily in debt.

Far from sharing the values of prudence, thrift, and restraint advocated for the urban middling orders and shown by many of them, Walpole displayed the characteristics of landed society, such as concern for display, living in debt, feeling the draw of the 'paternal oaks',[69] and relying on friends and connections. Nevertheless, the widespread nature of debt did not lessen its impact. It must have encouraged Walpole to seek office, although ironically his lack of popularity and the manner of his departure were such that he did not benefit, as Pitt the Elder was to do, by a parliamentary vote to pay his debts. Without the benefits of office, the Walpole estate was so burdened by Robert's expenditure and the resulting debt that his grandson, George, 3rd Earl of Orford, had to sell Houghton's splendid picture collection.

Aside from the specific encouragement that Walpole's personal circumstances gave to his gaining and benefiting from office, they can also, albeit more tenuously, be related to his quest for power and the character of his rule. The assurance that Walpole displayed, and his show in the Commons were part of his personality as much as of his politics.

2

A Political Narrative

This chapter is designed to provide an anchor for what follows. It is introductory and does not seek to be comprehensive, not least because much is better tackled in the analytical chapters. Nevertheless, it is valuable to have a narrative introduction, as certain problems, features and responses of Walpolean government are best seen in such a context. Furthermore, the congruence of problems was an important aspect of their seriousness. The narrative concentrates on the period down to 1738. By then, Walpole was being affected by a political re-positioning, linked to a somewhat different political world: the death of the Queen in 1737 altered the Court, there were new tensions in the ministry, the opposition had changed, and new issues were coming to the fore. Walpole's last period as minister and his fall is covered in chapter 10. Naturally, any narrative is highly selective. What follows should be read in conjunction with the subsequent chapters.

Having risen in a political world of ministerial rivalry, court division, and parliamentary warfare, Walpole was well aware of the precariousness of office. After all, he himself had already fallen twice, once as the consequence of Tory triumph and a second time as a result of Whig factionalism and its relationship with royal views. To avoid a repetition of either fate would require skills and good fortune. More specifically, Walpole would need a coherent ministerial group that the king would accept, and, hopefully, support, an ability to lead the Commons, and a set of policies that did not undermine either.

This was the political challenge throughout his ministry, and his success was in part co-terminus with what has been seen as the stability of his years in office. This success initially rested on the factors that had taken him back into office in 1720, but his ability thereafter to strengthen these factors was important. Walpole's response to circumstances was crucial. His active role in thwarting and exposing the Jacobite Atterbury Plot in 1722 underlined his zeal for the

Hanoverian Succession and commended him greatly to George I. That spring, Walpole and Townshend had an army camp prepared in Hyde Park to overawe London, summoned troops from Ireland, and requested that the Dutch hold 3,000 troops ready to be sent if required. This firm response made the plans for a revolt inappropriate. In April 1722, the French government provided crucial information on the conspiracy, and also alleged that the recently dead Sunderland had had links with the Tories.[1]

Walpole set out to find out the details of the conspiracy. The Jacobite leaders in London were placed under surveillance and all foreign mail intercepted at the Post Office. Walpole made other ministers appear less zealous and active. In May 1722, he wrote to his brother Horatio about the use of postal interceptions to expose the plot, adding 'it appears to me so very difficult to believe enough with regard to Spain, without believing too much, that I am inclined to carry my apprehensions from that quarter a great deal further than I think it proper for any of us as yet to own, or than either of the Secretaries of State will agree with me in'.[2] In September, the details of the conspiracy were discovered when a clergyman, Philip Neynoe, who had already been selling Walpole items of information on the plot, was arrested and incriminated the leaders. Habeas Corpus was suspended the following year, and action was taken against the plotters. With the exception of Francis Atterbury, Bishop of Rochester, who was banished as the result of a parliamentary Act of Pains and Penalties, the prominent Jacobites were not prosecuted in Parliament, presumably because Walpole had taken note of the failure to impeach Oxford successfully in 1715–17. However, Christopher Layer, a Norfolk lawyer who was Lord North's agent, was possibly tortured and certainly imprisoned in harsh circumstances before being hung, drawn and quartered for high treason on 17 May 1723, a brutal reminder of the issues at stake. Lord North and the Earl of Orrery were imprisoned, and North was driven into exile.[3]

Walpole continued thereafter to demonstrate his anti-Jacobite credentials. In 1724, John Freind, MP for Launceston, was unseated on petition after a bitter debate about the conduct of his election. As Freind had been arrested the previous year for his role in the Atterbury Plot, this enabled Walpole to show his zeal: 'Mr Walpole and his creatures made great merit, and intended to arrogate the whole credit of turning him out to themselves'.[4]

Walpole's successful use of the Atterbury Plot helped hinder the parliamentary opposition. The latter had negotiated with Sunderland in 1721, as he sought to outmanoeuvre Walpole. The failure of these negotiations led in the autumn of 1721 to a regrouping by the opposition. This produced an alliance between the Tories and a group of dissident Whigs led by Earl Cowper and the Duke of Wharton. In November 1721, this group began a bitter parliamentary assault on the ministry, with Cowper being particularly active in mounting attacks on British foreign policy in the Lords. There was little hope that the government could be defeated in Parliament, but the opposition hoped to discredit it in the eyes of the electorate. Thanks largely to Walpole, the opposition failed. In addition, Cowper was not helped by the weakness of his supporters.[5]

Resisting opponents outside government was linked to supplanting rivals within. Walpole and Townshend acted to remove those of different views and to put in their place people they could trust, a process eased by Walpole's role as master of government patronage in the 1722 general election. The political settlement of 1720–1 had not been accepted by Sunderland and, both then and thereafter, he and Walpole struggled for dominance. This struggle involved ministerial patronage and was also linked to the financial settlement. One commentator observed in January 1722:

'These two persons are the heads of the two great branches of the same party and are praised or cried down in all companies . . . The two great bodies of people that appear for them are the Bank for Mr Walpole and those concerned in the South Sea for my Lord Sunderland. I mean as Companies'.[6]

The struggle ended when Sunderland suddenly died of pleurisy on 19 April 1722. His former adherents were removed from office, although the process took several years. Sunderland's most important supporter was Lord Carteret, Secretary of State for the Southern Department from 1721; his promotion had been seen as a blow to Walpole. After a struggle for control with Walpole in 1723, that was decided by George I, Carteret was sent in 1724 to Ireland as Lord Lieutenant in what was, with reason, regarded by many as a form of exile, and which Walpole hoped would wreck him: 'we shall at least get rid of him here'.[7] Walpole was seen as the clear victor, by friends and foes alike. Arthur Dillon, the Jacobite agent in Paris, reflected, 'so the victory is declared in Walpole's favour'.[8] Stair reported from London:

'. . . the king's favour is entirely declared on the side of Robert Walpole. The king has pressed him to continue as Secretary of State which Mr Walpole has declined. Lord Carteret and the Duke of Roxburgh have made great submissions to Mr Walpole'.[9]

Walpole benefited from the resolution of the complex interaction of court and ministerial politics with foreign policy and with divisions in the French and Hanoverian ministries. The specific issue at dispute in 1723, which was minor in itself, was exploited by Townshend and the Walpole brothers in order to claim that Carteret and his protégé Sir Luke Schaub, the envoy in Paris, were harming the Anglo-French alliance.[10] As this was largely resolved during George I's visit to Hanover in 1723, a visit on which George was accompanied by both Secretaries of State – Carteret and Townshend – Walpole played a less direct role than Townshend. However, his management of domestic politics and finances was important in strengthening his position. In the first session after the 1722 general election, Walpole displayed his mastery of the Commons. On 26 October, there was a majority of 71 (236 to 165) on a motion to increase the size of the army:

'Mr Walpole spoke with such extraordinary strength and weight that [John] Trenchard sent him this day to let him know he was so entirely convinced by his speech, that if he could have prevailed with himself to speak, he would have stood up and owned his conviction . . . and he has desired an audience of Mr Walpole'.[11]

The following August, Walpole congratulated himself on the flourishing condition of public credit and on having accurately predicted to George I the price of stocks, adding, 'I think it is plain we shall have the whole supply of next year at 3 per cent . . . and I flatter myself that the next session of Parliament will bring no discredit to those that have the honour to serve the King in his revenue'.[12] His financial acumen led George I's mistress, Melusine von der Schulenburg, the Duchess of Kendal, to seek his advice on share dealings.[13] Stair noted in 1724, '. . . we are like to have a very quiet session of Parliament . . . Money is very plentiful at 4%, the government pays but 3. Walpole has the sole credit at St James'.[14]

Changes to the Treasury Board ensured that in 1724 it became a body very much under Walpole's influence. Aside from Walpole, there was his Norfolk ally Charles Turner (1720–30), another ally, William Yonge (1724–7, 1730–5), George Dodington, then an ally of Walpole, (1724–40), and only one member, George Baillie (1717–25), who, while wishing well to him, was not an ally; Baillie was replaced the following year, bought out as he was given a pension equal to his salary.

In 1725, the Earl of Macclesfield, the Lord Chancellor, was impeached successfully for corruption in a move which some blamed on Walpole, and Roxburgh, Secretary of State for Scotland, was dismissed for failing to keep Scotland quiet. Diplomats closely associated with Carteret, such as Schaub and the Earl of Marchmont, were denied posts. This process led to what has been seen as ministerial quiescence. Hatton referred to 'the consensus among ministers achieved by the Townshend–Walpole coup . . . the absence of factional strife made for relative ease of cabinet business'.[15]

Nevertheless, as George Baillie had pointed out in 1723, 'Walpole doubtless has secret enemies'. The conduct of several ministers in 1727, when George Dodington and the Duke of Dorset, the Lord Steward, deserted Walpole for his challenger Spencer Compton, confirms this view. Within the Council, there was a superficial air of unity concealing envy and tension. Many hoped that the accession of George II would lead to the removal of Walpole.[16] Furthermore, the failure to appoint William Pulteney Secretary of State led him to go into opposition in 1725, creating an articulate and active opposition Whig group. Walpole, however, still enjoyed substantial majorities in the sessions of 1726 and 1727. The majority against an opposition motion of 9 February 1726 for an inquiry into the national debt was 262 to 89, and, eight days later, the government majority on a motion promising backing for Hanover if it was attacked was 285 to 107. The majority on the vote of credit on 25 March 1726 was 270 to 89, on the Address on 17 January 1727, 251 to 85 and on the increase of the army on 25 January 1727, 250 to 85.

Walpole had returned to office with Townshend who remained his brother-in-law until 1726 when Walpole's sister died. Their relations continued to be good. Tension has been detected between the two brothers-in-law, especially in 1725, when Walpole was displeased by the financial consequences of Townshend's expensive attempt to recruit foreign allies by means of subsidies.[17] These tensions have probably been over-emphasised in light of future rivalry between the two ministers. Townshend was quite aware of the political difficulties of persuading Parliament to grant peacetime subsidies to foreign powers. Any attempt to define respective spheres of interest, with Townshend dealing with foreign affairs and Walpole with the House of Commons and fiscal matters, needs to cope with the interdependence of these spheres.

Plumb suggested that tension between the two men steadily increased, that Walpole acquired sufficient self-confidence to challenge Townshend's control of foreign policy, that Townshend resented Walpole's growing strength in Norfolk politics, symbolised by the building of his grandiose seat at Houghton, and that the death of Walpole's sister helped to weaken the links between the two men.[18] Against this, must be set the continued successful partnership of the two men and the relative absence of contemporary suggestions of division between them. George I's ministry, when he set out for Hanover on his last journey in the summer of 1727, was a successful administration. The leading ministers were united, and the jealousy of them that existed within the ministry was held in check by governmental success and royal favour. Nevertheless, Walpole, aware of opposition within the ministry, was conscious of the need to maintain royal support. Bolingbroke was foolish to believe that George was going to dismiss Walpole.[19] George had honoured Walpole publicly, with the newly-created Order of the Bath in 1725 and that of the Garter the following year. Walpole, the sole commoner with that honour, and the first to be promoted to it since 1660, found his Garter a cause of anger and criticism.

Walpole's relations with George, Prince of Wales were not particularly good. During the mid-1720s the Prince had played little part in politics and had led a rather retired life. The spectacular disputes with his father had been replaced by a mutual coldness. There is little sign of any difference of opinion over policy, but there was tension over the Prince's position, although the ministry sought to smooth matters.[20] Nevertheless, he had a distinct group of friends and confidants, while his mistress, Henrietta Howard, Countess of Suffolk, had links with the opposition. After George II came to the throne she enjoyed little power, but this had not been predicted, and George's earlier favour for her had been seen as a sign that Walpole would not survive the change of monarch.[21] Walpole did not make the mistake of some ministers and courtiers of assuming that Henrietta Howard was the power behind the Prince of Wales. Instead, close to George's wife, he claimed to have 'the right sow by the ear'.

Given the significant political shifts that had followed the accession of recent monarchs, it was understandable that the fall of the Walpole ministry was anticipated. On 3 June 1727, *Applebee's Original Weekly Journal*, a London weekly newspaper, printed a letter warning 'all designing statesmen and unwary politicians' that:

'as their power only depends upon the breath of their sovereigns, an angry blast of that flings them at once from the summit of their glory and the height of their ambition; or at most their authority generally determines with the life of their Prince, it being very rarely found that the most expert statesman can continue a favourite to two Princes successively'.

George I died at Osnabrück en route for his beloved Hanover on 11 June (22 June ns). On Wednesday 14 June, towards 3 pm, the news reached Whitehall. Walpole gave orders to double the guard throughout London and then left for Richmond to inform the Prince of Wales that his father had died. A myth at the time had it that he rode two horses to their deaths in his determination to be the first to bring the news to George. That evening, George came to London and the following morning was proclaimed King.

On the day that George was proclaimed, the Duke of Newcastle, since 1724 Secretary of State for the Southern Department and then a key ally of Walpole, wrote of 'the concern and distraction we are all in here . . . we can make no judgement of affairs here, in all probability the Speaker will be the chief man',[22] the last a reference to Spencer Compton, Speaker of the Commons and Treasurer to the Prince of Wales. Arthur Onslow, MP for Guildford, who was in London at the time, noted:

'that everybody expected, that Mr Compton the Speaker would be the Minister, and Sir Robert Walpole thought so too, for a few days . . . the new king's first inclination and resolution, which was certainly for Mr Compton . . . who had long been his Treasurer, and very near to him in all his counsels. It went so far as to be almost a formal appointment, the king, for two or three days, directing everybody to go to him upon business . . . but, by the Queen's management, all this was soon over-ruled'.[23]

Onslow's interpretation was shared by many others, not least because it was generally believed that George was heavily influenced by his wife. In 1727, Walpole, telling the Lord Chancellor, Lord King, 'of the great credit he had with the king', attributed it to 'the means of the Queen, who was the most able woman to govern in the world'. The contrast between Caroline's bright, sparkling, witty nature and George's more dour, boorish demeanour greatly influenced contemporaries, such as Lord Hervey, who was close to her. Later, Coxe regarded George as a puppet manipulated by his wife. It was thanks to her reputation as a shrewd intriguer that contemporaries and historians have largely attributed Walpole's continuation in office to the Queen.[24]

This influence, however, has been exaggerated, and there were other reasons for Walpole's continuance in office. Caroline and others overestimated her influence,[25] and the picture of George as a headstrong, blinkered boor is overdrawn. Lord King's account does not mention Caroline, but suggests that George was persuaded to continue Walpole in power by personal experience:

'. . . by his constant application to the king by himself in the mornings, when the Speaker, by reason of the sitting of the House of Commons, was absent, he so worked upon the king, that he not only established himself in favour with him, but prevented the cashiering of many others, who otherwise would have been put out'.[26]

The accession of a new monarch meant that Parliament had to be summoned, the Civil List (annual grant paid to the Crown by Parliament) settled, and elections held for a new Parliament. With his proven track record as a parliamentary manager, Walpole was needed for these purposes. Parliament sat from 27 June to 17 July, and during this time Walpole made himself extremely useful, securing an enlarged Civil List of £800,000. This was an unprecedented sum for the start of a reign. Walpole's command of the Commons was of direct value to George, who had a reputation for avarice and meanness and had accumulated considerable debts as Prince of Wales.[27] Walpole also obtained the largest jointure any queen had ever enjoyed for Caroline.

The Saxon envoy suggested that Walpole was given an opportunity to display his skill and that George had decided to delay any governmental changes until after the elections, in order to be in a state to gratify those who had helped with the elections, and those whose help would be needed in the subsequent Parliament. If this was so, Walpole passed the test with flying colours. He made full use of government interest in boroughs such as Plymouth, as well as of the secret-service money. After the election petitions were heard, the new Commons consisted of 415 ministerial supporters, 15 opposition Whigs, and 128 Tories, a government majority of 272, the largest since George I's accession. The comparable figures after the 1722 election were

389 Whigs and 169 Tories, a majority of 220.[28] Walpole was again elected unopposed for King's Lynn.

Other reasons were advanced as to why it was against the king's interest to change the government. First, Walpole's influence with Parliament and with the great chartered corporations – the Bank of England, the East India Company, and the South Sea Company – was held to be very important for the credit-worthiness and stability of the government. Secondly, to change the government was held to be inadvisable for British foreign policy. The French *premier ministre*, Cardinal Fleury, pressed George to maintain the Walpoles in power, and opposition supporters blamed Fleury for Walpole's continuance in office.[29]

This was clear within a fortnight of George's accession but was subject to two questions: first, whether Walpole would be forced to accept many changes in the ministry, and, secondly, whether George would follow the advice of his ministers. In the event, George's aristocratic friends did not gain high office, while Carteret, the opposition Whigs and the Tories were kept at a distance, and ministers who had fallen out with Walpole, such as William Chetwynd, a Lord of the Admiralty, lost office. The dismissal of Viscount Malpas, Walpole's son-in-law and the Master of the Robes to George I, the day after the accession, had led many to assume there would be major changes, but, instead, Malpas became a Lord of the Admiralty. On 27 June, Hervey, having dined the previous night with Walpole, was able to inform Stephen Fox that 'the political world rolls on just as it did'.[30]

The major challenges of that autumn were outside Walpole's control: a severe and protracted bout of ill-health on the part of Townshend and the difficulty of persuading Spain to end a cold war with Britain preparatory to an international peace congress. Walpole's task was that of delivering a supportive Commons, and he did so in the 1728 sessions with significant majorities on key issues such as the army estimates: 290 to 86. Townshend wrote to British envoys that 'the grand affairs of session have been dispatched in less time than ever was known in any Parliament, and with a greater majority than was ever remembered in any reign'.[31]

The impetus offered by this success was dissipated that summer and autumn as the Congress of Soissons failed to settle European differences and as diplomatic problems instead mounted. This led to criticism in the press, especially of the Anglo-French alliance. The government was attacked for its failure to protect British commerce from Spanish depredations, for the threats posed by the developing strength of the French nation, and for signs of French commercial and maritime activity, ranging from repairs to the harbour at Dunkirk, to colonial activities in North America and the West Indies. The difficulties affecting trade and industry were blamed on the international situation, and the uncertainty in European affairs on the government, which was accused of being subservient to the French and unduly tolerant of Spanish activities.

In the 1729 session repeated opposition attacks on foreign policy cut Walpole's majority, leading to the inaccurate rumour that he had asked George II for permission to retire to the Lords.[32] French ministers were uncertain about the stability of the government, the Jacobites in Paris spread a rumour that Walpole had been replaced, and George II was reported to be personally inclined to Pulteney.[33] Walpole was forced to defend the Anglo-French alliance against strong attacks, and did so by claiming that France was a good ally as a result of the international situation: 'we were to consider that states govern themselves by their interest and that the close alliance of Austria, the ancient enemy [of France], with Spain made them as entirely sure to our alliance as heretofore they were enemies when they aimed at universal monarchy'.[34] He also criticised the opposition for encouraging Britain's enemies with the hopes that Parliament would not back government policy.[35] Although the majorities were cut during the session, falling as low as 35 (180 to 145), the ministry did not lose its majority.[36]

By the following winter, the Anglo-French alliance had won the support of Spain, but Walpole faced greater problems within Britain not only because of continued doubts about the alliance but also because of a serious clash with Townshend over foreign policy. The 1730 session witnessed a determined effort by the opposition to use foreign policy issues to ensure the removal of Walpole: there was a degree of Tory-opposition Whig co-operation that posed a real threat. This coincided with Walpole's continued lack of control over the ministry: Dodington, Dorset and Wilmington were unreliable and the government lost the support of Carteret, Townshend and Winchelsea.

Walpole was concerned about the cost, in money and time, of Townshend's policy. He wanted a swift settlement of European problems, an end to heavy British military expenditure, and extensive subsidy obligations, and a reduction in taxation. The political cost of the French alliance, in providing ready issues for the opposition, was also serious. Aside from policy disputes, there was also tension over the composition of the ministry, including, allegedly, an attempt by Townshend to replace Newcastle by Chesterfield that was blocked by Walpole in concert with the Queen.

The crisis blew up in Parliament over Dunkirk. Since 1725, the port, a former privateer base, had been restored, despite specific prohibitions in the Treaties of Utrecht (1713) and The Hague (1717). The British government had complained in 1727, 1728 and 1729, but took no real precautions to prevent parliamentary attacks. On 10 February 1730, the Tory leader in the Commons, Sir William Wyndham, advanced Dunkirk as a proof of the government's failure to protect national interests, and the ministerial speakers lost control of the House. After two days of attacks, it was resolved to address George II for laying all correspondence about Dunkirk before the Commons. In order to give time for this to be prepared, the debate on the state of the nation was adjourned for a fortnight, but, in the meantime, on the 16th the government lost a Commons division on an opposition bill to prevent placeholders or those in receipt of government payments from being MPs. Lord Perceval claimed that Walpole 'it is probable may date his fall from this day'.[37]

However, successful British diplomatic pressure led the French to order the demolition of the Dunkirk works and the government won a comfortable majority (270 to 149) when the issue was re-introduced in the Commons. Thereafter, the ministerial position in Parliament improved.

This prepared the way for a solution to the governmental crisis. Perceval recorded in his journal a story of Lord Lovel arriving in London at the start of the session, and telling Chesterfield that he did not know how to vote. When the Earl replied 'with the Court', Lovel retorted 'the Court is so divided that I don't know which way it leans'. Perceval also claimed that Compton, now Lord Wilmington, was 'forming a party in the House of reasonable Tories and discontented Whigs, to rise upon the ruins of Sir Robert Walpole', in short that the crisis was a new version of that in 1727.[38] The composition of this party is a mystery, although it is probable that it included Dodington and Dorset, and may have comprised former members of the court of George II, as Prince of Wales, such as Chesterfield and Scarborough.

This was unrelated to Townshend's differences with Walpole. The two had fallen out over foreign policy, but Walpole could do nothing until Townshend resigned: George did not dismiss him. Townshend appears finally to have decided to resign because of his frustration at the constant opposition of Walpole to his plans, rather than because of his anger over any particular issue. The Prussian envoy, Reichenbach, in despatches intercepted by the British, reported that Walpole wanted everything to depend uniquely on his will and that Townshend did not wish to be treated like a small boy. He also claimed that George did not want Townshend to go, but was obliged to maintain good relations with Walpole in order to obtain money.[39]

Walpole had clearly succeeded in making life difficult for Townshend, and by May 1730 Townshend was refusing to do anything involving co-operation with Walpole. Delafaye stated that a resignation was essential 'to make the service easy'.[40] Personal disagreements arising from policy differences had become crucial. An undated letter by Townshend's grandson, Thomas, 1st Viscount Sydney, probably to Philip, 2nd Earl of Hardwicke, although written many years later, possesses an immediacy missing from other sources, and makes abundantly clear the court context of ministerial politics, the importance of royal favour, and the role of personal honour in court and ministerial relationships:

It was not at a Cabinet meeting that the quarrel arose between Sir Robert and him but at my grandfather Colonel Selwyn's house in Cleveland Court, where the Duke of Newcastle, Mr Pelham, Colonel Selwyn and Mrs Selwyn were the only persons present. The *immediate* cause of dispute was a foreign negotiation, which had, at Sir Robert's desire, I believe, been dropped. Lord Townshend after having given up the point, still advanced an opinion, that the *design of the negotiation* ought to be mentioned in the House of Commons at the same time that the House should be acquainted that the measure was given up. Sir Robert took offence at this last proposal, and I believe, thought, that Lord Townshend's reason for working for the mention of a measure, which was not to be pursued, was that it might give him a disagreable and troublesome day in the House. Lord Townshend then said, since you object to it, and the business of the House of Commons is your concern more than mine, to be sure I shall not persist in my opinion, but now I have given it up, I can not help saying, that upon my honour I think it would be the more adviseable step. Sir Robert Walpole answered to this effect, My Lord, there is no man's sincerity which I doubt more than your Lordship's and I never doubt it so much as when you are pleased to make such strong professions. A less warm man than Lord Townshend must have been provoked by these words, and accordingly Lord Townshend called him a brute and seized him by the collar: Sir Robert took hold of him in return, and they then quitted each other, and laid their hands on their swords. The company immediately parted them, and stopped Mrs Selwyn, who in her fright was sending her servants to call the Guards . . . The way in which I have heard this unusual want of temper in Sir Robert accounted for was this; the two ministers had some secret, which they had agreed to keep to themselves, but they had both imparted it in confidence to the Queen. Her Majesty was unfortunately jealous of the too great cordiality, which subsisted between those, who were to carry on the public business, and thought that a little jealousy of each other might make both more manageable; she therefore thought proper to let each of them know, that the other had trusted her. Sir Robert was just come from making this discovery. The Queen was much concerned and mortified at the effect of her own manoeuvre, never intending or suspecting that matters would have been carried to any violence. She was very sorry to be reduced to choose between them, but had no hesitation in making choice of Sir Robert when she was forced to decide.[41]

Exasperated and unwell, Townshend resigned even though he still enjoyed the confidence of the king. The crisis, however, was not a defeat for George. Though he did not make Chesterfield Secretary of State, George's protégé

William Stanhope, recently ennobled as Lord Harrington, replaced Townshend. It was claimed that Walpole and the Queen had attempted to gain the post for Horatio Walpole, but had been thwarted by George. In addition, Newcastle, Harrington and the Walpoles were forced to consider Hanoverian interests and to press the French to support Hanover. George could not have hoped that the ailing Townshend would continue as Secretary for many more years. He succeeded in gaining a pliable successor whose tenure of the northern Secretaryship was marked by very few disagreements with the king.

The governmental reshuffle at the end of the session settled not only the Secretaryship, but also the crisis within the government. Wilmington was given an important post, that of Lord Privy Seal, and created an Earl, helping to divide him from the opposition. Newcastle's brother, Henry Pelham, replaced Wilmington as Paymaster-General of the Forces, and Dorset succeeded Carteret as Lord Lieutenant of Ireland. Carteret turned down the Stewardship and this helped keep from court office a major rival of Walpole. Instead, Horatio Walpole was made Cofferer of the Household.

The ministerial team that was to dominate the 1730s was now in place. By keeping Chesterfield from a Secretaryship and Carteret from Court, the crisis created by parliamentary and ministerial opposition in 1730 strengthened Walpole's position. Nevertheless, Dorset, Wilmington and others ready to oppose him remained in office, and the Excise crisis of 1733 was to show that difficulties would encourage these opponents to raise their head.

However, in the meantime, Walpole was given an opportunity to dominate policy and to consolidate his position. The settlement of differences with Austria in 1731 by the Second Treaty of Vienna was one important consequence, because he wished to cut taxes. In 1732, the Hessian troops, whom Britain had subsidised in order to help defend Hanover, were paid off. Walpole intended to enjoy a peace dividend. The land tax fell to two shillings in the pound in 1730 and 1731 and one shilling in 1732 and 1733, and this was doubly welcome as it was a period of falling agricultural prices.

Parliamentary majorities varied in 1731 and 1732, but were generally comfortable. In 1731, the Hessians were carried by a majority of 85, the army estimates by 104, the length of soldiers' service by 98. In 1732, the session opened far more quietly than recent sessions.[42] The majority on the army estimates was down to 70, but Walpole's control of the Commons was not seriously contested.

Ironically, the situation deteriorated sharply the following year over what Walpole had not seen as likely to cause a major political storm, a proposal to extend the excise to wine and tobacco. He saw this as a technical financial measure, designed to build on the changes in regulation that had affected the sale of coffee, tea and chocolate introduced in 1724 and to make revenue raising more efficient, not least by cutting smuggling; and was to defend it as such.[43] Instead, it proved a major challenge, with the opposition exploiting fears that the government was going to press on to tax other commodities and that it would deploy an army of excise officers to raid homes and control elections. Both were crucial issues. The threat of excise duties on food seemed to move Britain closer to the image of a heavily-taxed and regulated Continental state. The nature of excise powers challenged suppositions about the constitution and the character of British liberties. Excise officers and commissioners were seen as arbitrary figures unconstrained by jury trials. Contemporaries could not believe that Walpole would not use the right to search by excise officers in elections as he used customs officers in elections, for example in Liverpool. The critical Master of the Rolls, Sir Joseph Jekyll, whom Walpole had not backed for the Lord Chancellorship, 'said he was sorry a Whig ministry would bring in a Bill, a Tory ministry never durst attempt'.[44] Walpole had not learned the lesson of the malt tax disturbances in Scotland in 1725.

Anti-excise material had appeared in opposition newspapers towards the end of 1732, and it was clear that the legislation would be challenged, but it was not felt that there would be any more trouble than had occurred in previous years over such issues as Hessian subsidies. Initially, it seemed as though the session was going well,[45] but, at the same time that the government passed its other measures, public criticism of the Excise Scheme rose. On 6 February 1733, Henry Goodricke wrote from London:

'The rising tempest of an excise makes a furious roar in this town . . . people have taken a general and violent prejudice to Sir Robert's proposal even before they know what it is; and elections being so near at hand many members will be cautious how they vote full against the bent of their electors; this makes many of opinion that Sir Robert will find this point more difficult than any he has lately attempted; yet every body believes that his skill in these affairs will make him not bring it out without a certainty of carrying it'.[46]

From March, Walpole was faced first by growing opposition in the Commons and then by division within the ministry. On the first division when the Bill was introduced on 4 April, the government majority was 237 to 176, but the majority fell to 17 (214 to 197) on 10 April. This was against an opposition motion to hear by counsel a petition from the City of London critical of the Excise Scheme. The petition was a testimony to the unpopularity of the Excise Scheme and to the opposition's skill in orchestrating a public campaign of criticism. Other constituencies were following London's lead with petitions and instructions.

A number of ministers and courtiers, including Chesterfield, intrigued against Walpole, and Harrington was among others who took an ambiguous position. At the same time, there was a new-found degree of popular hostility to Walpole and the government. The despatches of the French, Sardinian and Spanish envoys all presented a country on the brink of civil war. The Genoese resident, Gastaldi, wrote of the possibility of 'una generale rivoluzione'.[47]

On 11 April, the Commons returned to the Excise Scheme, only to be greatly surprised by Walpole:

> Upon a motion that the House (according to the order of the day) should read the Excise Bill a second time, Sir Robert thought fit to prevent a debate upon it, by a very long speech, in which he declared that though he was still convinced, in his judgment, that the Bill was not obnoxious to those censures that had been passed upon it, but would be truly serviceable to the Public; yet, observing that an universal clamour had been raised against it, he was willing, for his part, it should no longer be insisted on, but entirely dropped for the sake of the public quiet and tranquillity. And thus this Excise Bill, which had put this kingdom into such a flame, came to an untimely end, and perhaps will never meet with a minister that has courage enough to revive it.

Opposition efforts that day to have the Bill rejected by a vote of the House, rather than simply dropped, failed.[48] London was illuminated to mark the failure of the Bill, and Walpole burned in effigy, but, by withdrawing the legislation, Walpole survived the parliamentary crisis. His majority rose at once: in a division on 20 April on an opposition petition against the existing excise regulations for coffee, tea and chocolate, the government had a majority of a hundred. More immediately, on the 11th, Walpole was protected by his supporters from the brawling crowd in the lobby which tried to attack him.

George II's backing was crucial to ending the crisis. A number of prominent Whig peers, the Dukes of Bolton and Montrose, the Earls of Marchmont and Stair, and Viscount Cobham, were dismissed for voting with the opposition in the Lords. Chesterfield lost office, not Walpole. The dismissals were a public show of royal support, but they helped lose Walpole the backing of the clients and allies of those dismissed who sat in the Commons. Walpole was responsible for the royal speech proroguing Parliament on 11 June 1733 in which those who had sought 'to inflame the minds of the people, and by the most unjust misrepresentations, to raise tumults and disorders' were attacked.

The following year, Walpole saw off opposition attacks in the last session of the Parliament. The opposition sought to exploit the international crisis caused by the War of the Polish Succession. Beginning in 1733 with a Russian invasion of Poland, this had broadened out to include French, Sardinian and Spanish attacks on Britain's ally Austria. Walpole was pressed hard on the causes and likely consequences of British neutrality, but won divisions on 25 January 1734 by 202 to 114 and 195 to 102. There were also good majorities in the Lords. The ministry also saw off challenges to the dismissal of opposition army officers, specifically Bolton and Cobham, after the Excise had been withdrawn the previous year, and pushed through an augmentation in the army estimates on 6 February by 262 to 162.

After the session, Walpole demonstrated his political skill in the third general election he had conducted for the government. The Excise certainly handicapped ministerial candidates: 'The excise scheme is made a handle of everywhere' noted a leading newsletter, while in Kent Sir George Oxenden, one of the Lords of the Treasury, 'had a most terrible weight to struggle with, that of the Excise'. One commentator claimed that 'there has not been such a cross-grained medley of an election for the last 50 years' and that Oxenden, who was defeated, was a bad candidate, 'it should have been one not liable to the excise clamour'.[49] The government spent heavily. Mary Caesar, wife of the Tory MP for Hertfordshire, claimed, 'A vast expense attended the Court in making good their elections, it having raised such a fire in the counties against the voters for it, that only money could quench'.[50] Walpole's majority fell from 272 to 102: 330 ministerial supporters, 83 opposition Whigs and 145 Tories were elected. However, the results were better than had been expected,[51] the majority was sufficient to enable him to govern easily, and, under the Septennial Act, the next election was not due until 1741, which gave time for place and patronage to do their work.

Walpole himself was re-elected unopposed for King's Lynn and his brother topped the poll at Norwich; Robert played a major role in Horatio's success, visiting the city in 1733 to present him as a candidate, and to be sworn in as a freeman,[52] and being present on election day in 1734.

A harshly critical opposition pamphlet presented Walpole as having recovered from a serious crisis although it under-estimated the resilience he had displayed:

'. . . the Excise Scheme, which had like to have proven the ruin of the projector. It is certain, that in the progress of it he lost ground upon every question, in so much, that his usual confidence quite forsook him. He talked of submission and resignation . . . but it soon appeared that though he was frightened, he was not converted: The dog returned to his vomit, and he recovered his usual confidence, superciliousness, and obstinacy'.[53]

The failure to overthrow Walpole helped demoralise the opposition. Although, thanks to the election results, opposition votes were higher than in the previous session – 185 against the Address (29 January 1735), and 208 against an increase of the army (14 February), government majorities were still substantial, 80 and 53 on these divisions, and 92 on subsidies for Denmark. Newcastle felt able to claim that the Commons had 'owned the greatest satisfaction in the prudence of His Majesty's measures'.[54] The majorities in the Lords were substantial.

The opposition was not able to mount a strong challenge in the session of 1735. Instead, Walpole was most concerned about preserving British neutrality during the War of the Polish Succession (1733–5) and thus keeping taxes low. He succeeded in this objective, and thus helped ensure that the session of 1736 went better for the Crown than it might otherwise have done. Land tax remained at two shillings in the pound, to which it had been raised in 1734 in response to the failure of the Excise Scheme and the need for military preparations in case Britain entered the war. In 1736, the session opened under favourable circumstances, not least the return of peace to Europe,[55] and it was another unexpected piece of legislation that caused a major crisis. Walpole's support for the Quakers' Tithe Bill, a far from crucial item designed to help a group of Dissenters, led, however, not only to the opposition of the Tories, but also to that of the clergy, led by Bishop Gibson of London.[56] The Bill was defeated in the Lords, a nasty blow for Walpole, but one he could survive by abandoning the measure. At the last moment, Walpole ordered government leaders in the Lords to vote against the Bill in order to avert further damage.

In 1737, the major challenge facing Walpole was not parliamentary attempts to exploit the Porteous Riot in Edinburgh the previous year, but, instead, the death on 20 November of one of his key supporters, Queen Caroline. Again, Walpole, with George's support, survived the crisis. He had further commended himself to George by supporting him in his dispute with his elder son, Prince Frederick.

In 1738, however, death hit Walpole again. His relations with his wife, Catherine, had for long been poor, and indeed he was rumoured not to be the father of her last son, Horace, who was born in 1717, although Walpole was complaisant towards his wife's affairs. Neither partner was noted for fidelity. Horace recounted a tale that underlined his father's enjoyment of women:

'Sir R. Walpole being asked why he suffered Lord Bolingbroke to come home, and yet would not restore him to the House of Lords, replied, "I was once with a lady at a critical minute; she desired me to lock the door; I answered, nobody will come in; she said, do lock it, and then they can't come in".'[57]

In 1724, Walpole became very attached to Maria, or Molly, Skerrett (*c.* 1702–38), like his wife, the daughter of a London merchant. She was accomplished in several respects, including as a singer, and, once she became his mistress, he seems to have been faithful to her. He installed Maria in his house at Richmond, where he spent the weekends. Walpole allegedly paid her £5,000 to establish the relationship, and she certainly became wealthy.

After Catherine died in Chelsea in August 1737, Walpole swiftly married Maria and gave her prominence. Queen Caroline was persuaded to receive her at Court. Walpole had two daughters by Maria, but one died young. The other was painted with the recently married couple, and Walpole's children by Catherine, in a family portrait attributed to John Wootton and Charles Jervas, fashionable painters of the age. When Maria died on 4 June 1738, she was pregnant and her death was probably the result of a miscarriage. Walpole was very badly affected by his loss. The domestic peace and family life he had enjoyed with Maria were gone.[58]

From 1738 the political situation also deteriorated. The opposition enjoyed a new-found vigour, in part because of new leadership, not least the support of Frederick, Prince of Wales, who had fallen out with his father George II and his ministers in 1737, and been banned from court that September. Frederick formed a rival court at Leicester House, and pursued in Parliament his quarrel with his father about receiving a fixed allowance out of the Civil List, instead of being dependent on George's generosity. Although motions for a fixed allowance of £100,000 were defeated in both houses, in the Commons by 234 to 204, Frederick was now clearly associated with opposition to Walpole, who had been obliged to take George's part.

In the summer of 1737, Frederick made a young opponent of Walpole, William Pitt, a Groom of the Bedchamber. Pitt's early career showed how Walpole's position was not popular with talented young parliamentarians. A protégé of Cobham, Pitt's maiden speech of 22 April 1735 was against the Walpole ministry on a bill seeking to debar placemen from sitting in Parliament. The following year, Pitt criticised George II in the Commons when the King was congratulated on Frederick's marriage, and he was dismissed from the army. This was seen as an abuse of power, and, also, an attack on property rights. Walpole's response in the Commons on 18 February 1737 suggested a rigidity that threatened to lose him support. Pitt accused Walpole of violating the privileges of the Commons:

> he produced his own case, as an instance, whose commission, as cornet of dragoons, had been taken from him for no other reason, than he could guess, but for the liberty of speech he had used in Parliament. Sir Robert took fire at this, and after a long complaint of the ill treatment the ministry had met with from licentious tongues, his passion transported him so far, as to raise his voice with a loftier air, and then, as a True Englishman (he told them) he would now speak his mind, and in that Honourable Assembly of English Gentlemen, he would venture to utter his thoughts freely: that whoever might be his successor in the administration, he must be a pityful fellow if he ever suffered any officers in the army to dictate to him, or censure his actions with an unbecoming freedom, and yet suffer them to continue in their posts. But finding he was not rightly understood by some

gentlemen, he explained himself immediately; that it was not his meaning that any member of that Honourable House could justly be deprived of any office or employment, for any liberty of speech they should there use; but he thought those officers who talked with a saucy freedom of the government, out of that house, would not be unjustly used if they lost their places.

This was a Walpole again on the defensive, and, as in 1733, having to persuade the Commons that he was not arbitrary, a charge Pitt returned to in February 1738.[59]

The revived energy of the opposition was seen in the launch of new papers, especially the *Champion*. Furthermore, Walpole suffered not only from divisions within the former Court bloc, which included the defection of Argyll in 1739, but also from tensions within the ministry, especially between Hervey and Newcastle. The latter ceased to be a reliable colleague, and, instead, became a major source of discontent.

The government's failure to produce an acceptable and lasting settlement to Anglo-Spanish commercial disputes served to revive opposition claims that Walpole was unable and unwilling to protect national interests. The Spanish treatment of what was claimed to be contraband British trade in the West Indies led to an emotive concern with national interests and reputation. This was taken up in print and caricatures, on the stage and in public demonstrations, and was exploited by the opposition. The government had showed themselves vulnerable to the charge of failing to protect national interests in the late 1720s, and the opposition returned to the attack, forcing a call of the Commons in March 1738. Opposition charges of humiliation at the hands of the Spaniards were used to make the government appear craven. Contrasts were drawn with past glories especially under Queen Elizabeth (1559–1603). In a Committee of the Whole House on 28 March, Pulteney accused the ministry of doing nothing to protect trade. The government proved unable to counter these arguments effectively and to regain the initiative in the public debate.[60]

More generally, Walpole and his government had run out of steam and the loss of dynamism contributed to disunity and a sense of lack of purpose. Divisions, policy failures and a revived opposition ensured that the 1741 general election was accompanied by a sense of crisis. The election results crippled Walpole's Commons majority and led directly to the fall of the government.

3

Walpole and the Spheres of Power

Walpole is generally described as the first Prime Minister. This was not his formal title – he was First Lord of the Treasury and Chancellor of the Exchequer – and an understanding of what this description was held to entail is important to an appreciation of his career. A powerful minister was scarcely an innovation and indeed Walpole was 'positioned' in opposition press criticism by being compared with unpopular former royal advisors, especially Henry VIII's Cardinal Wolsey and James I and Charles I's Duke of Buckingham, as well as foreign counterparts, particularly the Roman Emperor Tiberius's Sejanus. Such comparisons were not intended to suggest any legitimacy in Walpole's position; far from it. They were intended to underline the corruptibility of power and the inevitable unpopularity and fall of those who wielded great power. They were also very much part of the critique of Walpole in moral terms.

This critique is of limited value in understanding the minister's position, other than serving as a reminder that the governmental implications of effective parliamentary monarchy – that monarch, ministry and Parliament would require an effective interlocutor who would thus exercise great power – were unwelcome to many. Such a minister seemed to break with the anti-authoritarianism of opposition to the Stuarts, which was seen as having been central to the Revolution Settlement. Walpole's position could be seen as new because he was a royal minister who also controlled the post-Revolution state. To many, the power Walpole wielded was as illegitimate as his policies, and each served to demonstrate the other.

These policies cannot be separated from Walpole's position as Prime Minister, both because they sustained it and because a characteristic of Parliamentary monarchy was its dynamic character: there was an annual pattern of activity and legislation that was integral to it. Yet Walpole's official position as First Lord of the Treasury did not ensure the governmental cohesion understood by the term Prime Minister. He was head of the Treasury, but not the government. Instead, it was the monarch who appointed and dismissed all the ministers. This right was not qualified by a concept of collective cabinet responsibility, although in 1744 and 1746 a sense of ministerial solidarity was to help force George II to abandon his support for Carteret.

Fortunately for Walpole, he was able to benefit from a degree of solidarity as a consequence of his role as a party man. Walpole's policies were less strident than those of the Stanhope–Sunderland ministry and less offensive to the Tories, but he was in no doubt that he was a Whig and presented himself thus, not least in crises, such as that after the withdrawal of the Excise legislation in 1733 and that over the parliamentary motions to remove him in February 1741. Walpole's attacks on the Treaty of Utrecht negotiated by the Tories in 1713, for example in the Commons in 1734 and 1739, can also be seen as an attempt to rally the Whigs, as can his frequent denunciation of the Jacobites, for example in the debate on the Address in January 1727. In the 1733 debate on the size of the army, Walpole 'told the House, whatever they might think of it, the Pretender was very busy with his agents here, and was sending dispatches continually to them'.[1]

Furthermore, Walpole's successful handling of the Atterbury Plot in 1722 helped to consolidate his position. His response to the crisis was more intelligent and more successful than the previous Whig attempt to capitalise on the attitudes of a Tory cleric, the Sacheverell trial. Walpole's loyalty to George I was publicly affirmed, as was the danger of co-operating, or considering co-operating, with Tories, a policy with which Sunderland and his followers had been associated. Walpole was no longer associated with such co-operation, as he had been in 1717–20.

Walpole's appointment and promotion policies were resolutely partisan and there was no recurrence of the non-party practice or ideology of earlier decades, nor anything to match Bolingbroke's attempt in the late 1720s and early 1730s to move beyond party distinctions in order to create an inclusive opposition. It was government policy under Walpole to emphasise the importance of party. In contrast, after 1760 it was in the opposition interest to do so in order to maintain the coherence of the resistance to the ministry.

The party character of Walpole's position helps to differentiate him from earlier first ministers: Walpole's party was the Whigs, not a king's party. So also did his parliamentary position. Walpole rose to power because he could lead Parliament, and because, with the Revolution Settlement, Parliament had become a regular and central feature in the political system. Thus, for example, Walpole's skills were more important than those of Danby, because, although the latter managed Parliament for Charles II in the 1670s, he did not have to face the prospect of regular elections that followed first the Triennial (1694) and then the Septennial (1716) Acts. Of the other leading ministers who followed the Revolution, Godolphin was not a party leader and Harley, although Tory, preferred to see himself as a minister above faction. Acute divisions within the Tory party also encouraged him to seek the support of others. In addition, Harley's power did not last long, and his position did not rest on the Commons as that of Walpole was to do. Walpole recognised the political importance of that House and thus of the socio-political character of a broadly-based élite that was in no way confined to the peerage. It was easier to manage the Commons from that House, and Commons management gave Walpole a role and position that other first ministers had lacked. Furthermore, Walpole helped to gain the title of prime minister, one he rejected, by his longevity in office, which suggested a major political change.[2]

Walpole certainly focused the attention of foreigners. The Alsatian jurist Johann Daniel Schöpflin, who was in Britain from September 1727 until January 1728, reported on the country for the French government. He saw the government as a 'triumvirat de Robert Walpole, Myl. Townshend et du Duc de Newcastle', but it was the former who received most attention:

> Robert Walpole est un esprit supérieur et peut être le plus capable de toute l'Angleterre pour la charge qu'il exerce. Étant chef de la trésorerie, il a la direction des finances du royaume, dont il connoit le détail en perfection. Personne n'est mieux au fait du fort et du foible de l'Angleterre que luy. Il ne connoit pas si bien les affaires étrangères, cependant rien ne se fait a son insceu; en sorte qu'il exerce la charge de premier ministre, sans en avoir le titre. On ne doit pas être surpris s'il est fort haïs des Anglais. Comme il dispose de toutes les charges et que le Roy ne fait rien sans luy, il donne non seulement l'exclusion aux Torys, mais aussi aux Whigs, qui ne sont pas de son parti, ce qui fait crier la nation, qui l'accuse outre cela d'une espèce de peculat. . . . Walpole se soutiendra malgré ses ennemis. Il a une grande autorité et parti dans la chambre basse. Son eloquence soutenue par une longue experience et connoissance solide des affaires du Royaume le rend toujours redoutable et superieur à la cabale de ses ennemis.[3]

The very way in which Walpole's career in government is discussed by modern scholars offers an implicit assessment of what is held to have been most important to him. This is seen most clearly by the positioning of the discussion of his policies. To place this after an assessment of his political power and the means by which he retained it, and, more specifically, of his use of patronage, is to suggest that for Walpole the holding of power was more important than his use of it, that his use of it for patronage was more significant than that for the furtherance of policy, or that his policies stemmed from the holding of power and were designed to maintain it. There is some truth in this assessment, and we will return to it, but, in this case, the reason for considering Walpole's position in the different spheres of power before his policies is that the latter have to be understood in light of the former. In particular, it is necessary to appreciate how far Walpole was dependent on others and how much he required continual effort to maintain his position. This casts light on his independence and thus on the extent to which he was free to introduce policy.

The spheres of political power interlocked and interacted, and any separation is somewhat artificial. Nevertheless, it is reasonable to distinguish Crown, Parliament and ministry. Again, the order in which these are discussed appears to imply a prioritisation that is potentially misleading. To put Parliament before Crown is to underrate the importance of the latter, and the authority, power and influence for Walpole in Parliament that stemmed from royal support. Yet as Parliament, specifically the House of Commons, was the sphere in which Walpole made his name, in which he was most important, not least within the ministry, and also in which he was the public face of government, it is there that we should turn first. Contemporaries would have made the same choice.

WALPOLE AND PARLIAMENT

In 1739, Walpole told the Commons:

'I have lived long enough in the world to know, that the safety of a minister lies in his having the approbation of this House. Former ministers neglected this, and therefore they fell! I have always made it my first study to obtain it, and therefore I hope to stand'.[4]

The minister devoted a lot of time to Parliament, both as a speaker and as the prime lobbyist for the government. Sir William Gordon MP described in 1715 how Walpole, 'with a strength of reasoning and power of eloquence peculiar to himself, opened up a charge of high treason against the Lord Bolingbroke'. Five years later, Thomas Brodrick, an independent Whig MP, referred to Walpole as speaking 'with the utmost skill' and again 'with the greatest skill imaginable'.[5] In 1722, he was described as speaking with 'extraordinary strength and weight'. Chesterfield described him as: 'the best Parliament man, and the ablest manager of Parliament, that I believe ever lived. An artful rather than an eloquent speaker, he saw as if by intuition, the disposition of the House and pressed or receded accordingly'. In 1730:

'Sir Robert being provoked by coarse attacks from Shippen and Pulteney, as that rubbing pewter or brass made them brighter, but as to ministers rubbing them made them winch, a sign they were sore; and such low stuff; spoke up for himself an hour, telling the House that as he should not entertain them any more upon that subject he would at once let them hear all he had to say; and he was extremely well heard by everybody, and no reply made'.

Later in the same session, 'Sir Robert thought it necessary to go into a very long justification of all his own conduct from the beginning, which he did with very great temper, and with so much decency, that it gained applause even from Pulteney'.[6]

Philip Yorke MP, later 2nd Earl of Hardwicke, wrote of Walpole that he was 'the best House of Commons man we ever had'.[7] George II and Queen Caroline regarded him as: 'by so great a superiority the most able man in the Kingdom, that he understood the revenue, and knew how to manage that formidable and refractory body, the House of Commons, so much better than any other man, that it was impossible for the business of the crown to be well done without him.'[8]

Sitting in the Commons for 41 years, Walpole became one of the most experienced parliamentarians. He was a good speaker, impressive on most topics and outstanding on fiscal matters, a topic few MPs could speak on with authority. This reflected hard work. In September 1724, Newcastle wrote to Horatio, 'Your brother Walpole is preparing his Treasury politics'. In the 1737 debate over the rate of interest to be paid on the National Debt, Walpole spoke for an hour and three quarters at one time, and 'it was allowed that there was never a finer speech made, and that he had even outshined himself it was so glorious a performance'.[9]

As a lobbyist, he combined his control over most ministerial patronage, and his engaging, affable personality, with an appreciation of what Parliament might be willing to grant. Meetings of his supporters at the Cockpit were used by Walpole to maintain unity. Mrs Caesar noted, 'no man ever had his followers at more command than has Sir Robert'. The correspondence of John Campbell of Cawdor throws light on Walpole's leadership of his followers. Campbell was a valuable supporter of Walpole and an active speaker in the Commons who was selected to move the Address in 1731, 1734 and 1735. Appointed a Lord of the Admiralty in 1736, he lost office on Walpole's fall. In 1739, his correspondence with his son Pryse indicates that parliamentary tactics were discussed at meetings at Walpole's. In March, having been well-prepared, Campbell seconded a crucial motion on the Spanish Convention: 'I was obliged to be at Sir Robert Walpole's this evening by seven, and stayed there till after nine, and I must go by nine tomorrow morning to secure a place in the House'. That November, Campbell went to the pre-sessional meeting which was used to explain policy:

'I am just come from Sir Robert Walpole's where we heard the speech that is to be made on Thursday, there is nothing new in it, nor indeed could it be expected there should be. . . . Sir Robert at the same time informed us that the

King has given his servants leave to declare his intention to distribute the prizes already taken from the Spaniards between the captors, and the merchants who were sufferers by the Spanish depredations, but the several proportions cannot be settled till the value of the prizes is known.'

In 1743, Campbell offered a somewhat different account of parliamentary life: 'On Monday some gentlewomen in our gallery, not being able to hold their water, let it run on Mr Dodington and a Scots member who sat under. The first had a white duffel frock spoiled, the latter almost blinded'.[10]

A pamphlet of 1744 stated that 'though the power of the late minister had a very broad and deep foundation, he knew his influence on the House of Commons was the content which held all together'.[11] In 1739, Frederick William I of Prussia instructed his envoy in London to approach Walpole over a commercial matter, as the latter's credit was so great in the Commons that he alone was capable of determining the fate of the affair.[12] However, although there were those whose support the ministry was certain of, the 'Dead Men for a Ministry', those allegedly 'ready to vote that black is white',[13] they were not sufficient to ensure a majority.

Walpole himself was modest about his strength. In a ministerial meeting in 1738 to discuss Spanish depredations – the Spanish attacks on British commerce in the West Indies that helped to cause the Anglo-Spanish war of 1739–48 – 'Sir Robert said it was necessary not to attempt to extenuate or alleviate the depredations; the temper of the House would not bear it'.[14] He was careful to press supporters to attend the House. A sense of control was captured in a letter from Sir James Lowther of December 1740:

'Sir Henry Hoghton applied to Sir Robert to excuse him from coming to town this session as the only way to secure Mr Reynolds election, Sir Robert refused him at first but I suppose has given him leave since as he is not yet come'.[15]

In fact, both Hoghton and Francis Reynolds were defeated by two Tories at Preston the following year. Despite his constant attention to the Commons, Walpole could be frustrated in its management, as in 1726 when 'Sir Robert grumbled cruelly at our dilatoriness, and was very desirous of putting an end to the session, but that the Speaker never taking the chair till after one, he did not see how we could possibly go through the private business before us'.[16] The skilful placing of supporters also helped management. In 1728, one of Walpole's closest allies, Sir Charles Turner, became Chairman of the Committees of Supply and Ways and Means, posts he held until his death in 1738. He replaced William Farrer, a Whig loyalist rather than a Walpole ally, who held the posts in 1708–10 and 1715–27, thus serving the Stanhope–Sunderland ministry as well as Walpole. Other key allies in the Commons included Newcastle's brother Henry Pelham, a reliable deputy for Walpole, and Thomas Winnington and William Yonge, noted orators.

Walpole's lobbying was not restricted to the Commons. He was also very active in persuading particular peers to support government policy, arranging, for example, payments to Earl Coningsby in 1723 when he switched from opposition to government. It was to Walpole that Townshend turned that year to probe the 'inclinations' of the new Earl of Bradford. Walpole's patronage 'system' – his careful interweaving of considerations and rewards – fully encompassed the peerage. Thus, in 1736 the Queen told Walpole to support the appointment of Thomas Villiers as envoy to Dresden. She had been pressed by Villiers, the Earl of Jersey. Recommending this to George II, then at Hanover, Walpole reflected 'Lord Jersey very much deserves this mark of His Majesty's favour, his behaviour in all respects is what His Majesty must approve'. Villiers got the post, but the striking aspect of the episode was the key role of Walpole and patronage considerations, not of the relevant minister, Lord Harrington, Secretary of State for the Northern Department, and issues of appropriateness for the particular post. Walpole was also careful to manage the proxy system by which absent peers could send proxy votes. In January 1734, for example, he persuaded the Earl of Carlisle to sign a blank proxy.[17]

If it was considered inexpedient to block opposition legislation in the Commons it could be defeated in the Lords, where the government had the support of most of the Whig lords, the Scottish representative peers and the bishops, as well as poor lords dependent on government patronage. Countess Cowper sardonically noted, 'My Lord Radnor stays in town to prorogue the Parliament next Tuesday, for which he hopes his Christmas box should be remembered without doubt'.[18] Grander peers also sought Walpole's support, the Duke of Somerset seeking his help in 1723 in order that his son become Marquess of Hertford and Earl of Northumberland.[19]

When a bill against bribery was considered in 1726, one MP noted, 'Sir Robert Walpole gave us to understand that nothing would come of it, intimating the little likelihood of its going through the Lords'. In 1731, the Pension Bill was defeated in the Lords (97–48); and in 1741, the Place Bill was flung out there as the government thought opposition to it in the Commons unwise on the eve of an election.[20] Peers did not have constituents to consider and the smaller House of Lords was a less volatile body than the Commons.

On the other hand, Walpole had a much tougher time with the House of Lords in the 1730s than the other two ministers of comparable ascendancy that century, Lord North and the Younger Pitt. There were closer divisions and a much narrower gap between government and opposition proxies in the 1730s than in the 1770s or 1783–1801. The most dangerous rise in opposition activity in the Lords during the Walpole ministry occurred in 1733. However, the seriousness of the crisis was swiftly lessened when the ministry's victory in the election of Scottish representative peers in 1734 destroyed the opposition group of Scottish peers which had, the previous year, risen to half the Scottish representation. In 1739, during the debates over relations with Spain, government majorities in the Lords again fell, and many of the peers on whom the government had relied abstained. Nevertheless, Walpolean management of the Lords was more effective than that of Harley had been in 1711–14. Then the crucial parliamentary debates on foreign policy occurred in the Lords, because the Whigs forced the debates on Harley.

Thanks to his activities, Walpole was well aware of the likely response of Parliament to particular proposals, and this, as much as his manipulation of patronage, explains his success in retaining control of the legislature. This success helped to make Britain a functioning parliamentary monarchy, one in which Parliament and the Crown operated in harmony. This was a considerable achievement, and helped to ensure that Britain with its high levels, by contemporary standards, of personal and religious freedom, was praised by many continental intellectuals. To writers such as Montesquieu, who visited London in the 1720s, the British constitution was worthy of praise and deserving of imitation in some respects.

Not all foreign commentators were equally enthusiastic, however, some being influenced by Bolingbroke's portrayal of the Walpolean system as corrupt and unpopular.[21] Scepticism was expressed from a different perspective by British officials and ministerial writers who felt that excessive freedom for criticising and opposing the government existed. George Tilson, a long-standing Under Secretary, complained in 1722 that the election for the parliamentary seat of Westminster revealed: 'a good deal of what is called English Liberty that is licentiousness. The same spirit of the elections often gets into the House among the elected. Only 500 are not so unruly quite as 5000.' Philip Yorke, who before he was 21 had received the lucrative life sinecure of the Tellership of the Exchequer and was returned by his father as MP for Reigate, wrote in 1742 of 'the natural fickleness of our dispositions, our readiness to find fault if everything does not succeed at the very juncture we wish it should, and the effects of a constant opposition which our annual sessions will always contribute to keep up.'[22]

Ministerial newspapers and pamphleteers argued that their opposition counterparts were seditious in both intent and effect. They were accused of spreading lies about government policy, and of encouraging faction, an imprecise term by which opposition could be castigated and which revealed the fundamental ambivalence deeply engrained in contemporary thought about the notion of loyal opposition. The ministerial press based its constitutional arguments on the sovereignty of Parliament, denying that extra-parliamentary views should be heeded if rejected by Parliament, and claiming that most of them were manipulated and/or self-interested. The popular appeal of the opposition was not usually denied, but their supporters were commonly presented as a fickle and foolish 'mob',[23] a group that was differentiated from the 'people'. Ministerial papers stressed the self-interest of opposition writers, the declamatory manner and appeal to the emotions of their writing, their creation of domestic division,[24] and the impossibility of ministerial perfection.[25]

An effective parliamentary monarchy, with parliamentary control over the finances of the State, had been the aim of many of the critics of the Stuarts in the seventeenth century. The Revolution Settlement of 1688–9 had created the constitutional basis for such a monarchy, but the instability of the ministries of the years 1689–1721 suggests that the political environment within which such a monarchy could be effective had not been created. Two major wars with France (1689–97, 1702–13) had been financed successfully, albeit with considerable difficulty, in contrast to the debacle of the last Stuart war, the Third Anglo-Dutch war of 1672–4; but policy formulation and execution had been handicapped, and the confidence of allies sapped, by the frequent changes in government.

At one level, these changes were an indication of stability: power remained the monopoly of the highest social groups, and, despite Tory claims to the contrary, the Whigs were a party primarily of great landowners, not of bankers and Dissenters. At another level, the political instability of 1689–1721 revealed the grave limitations of the Revolution Settlement. A parliamentary monarchy could not simply be legislated into existence. It required the development of conventions and patterns of political behaviour that would permit a constructive resolution of contrary opinions within a system where there was no single source of dominant power. The slow development of these patterns was, particularly serious given the fact that Britain was at war for much of the period (1689–97, 1702–13, 1718–20) and that Jacobitism was a significant force.

Walpole emphasised parliamentary considerations when he discussed policy. Thus, for example, in a draft of 1730 about foreign policy he wrote:

'In what a light will the friendship of France stand in our Parliament, if they do not only fail in the execution of the Treaty of Seville, and appear at last to desert us there, but at the same time violate their own treaties and act so infamously with regard to the demolition of Dunkirk? . . . France must give England satisfaction, ample satisfaction in the affair of Dunkirk, if they hope to continue the union betwixt the two Crowns'.[26]

WALPOLE AND THE TWO GEORGES

Never was the King I believe better pleased with his servants than he is at present or more enraged at their enemies . . . Sir Robert though daily attacked by those only who envy his abilities and his power, is I am persuaded in the situation his best friends could wish him, both as to his master's affections and the opinion of our friends in Parliament.

Duke of Newcastle, 1729.[27]

Parliamentary monarchy required a monarch willing to work with Parliament, and thus focused attention on the character and intentions of the ruler. The existence of a Jacobite claimant to the throne directed additional attention to both. It was Walpole's job to make parliamentary monarchy work and that required the careful cultivation first of George I (1714–27) and then of George II (1727–60). The Walpole ministry was of great importance in the development of an effective constitutional monarchy. Irresponsible opposition, such as that which Walpole himself had conducted in 1717–20, and which his propaganda subsequently distorted, persisted. Opposition leaders, such as Pulteney, Wyndham and Bolingbroke, intrigued with envoys of powers hostile to Britain in order to harm the ministry. A sizeable portion of the Tory party continued to consider Jacobitism as an option and some conspired actively for that cause. Walpole managed, however, to show the Crown that a parliamentary monarchy could help it to achieve most of its aims, and the political nation that it could provide stability, continuity, peace and lower taxes. He also helped ensure that the political and governmental system worked despite frequent lengthy absences by George I and George II in Hanover. This gave the ministers more independence, but also posed the problem of developing attitudes and practices to minimise disagreement.

The education of the monarchs was of particular importance. William III and George I had created considerable difficulties by their determination to use British resources to further their own extra-British foreign policy goals, and to favour those ministers, such as Stanhope and Sunderland, who would support them in this aim. Walpole's ministry saw a tempering of this habit. George I and George II were able to influence policy in favour of Hanover, but not to direct it.[28] Ministers whom the Crown had favoured, largely for their views on foreign policy, fell because they did not enjoy the support of Walpole, and because their policies were not likely to gain parliamentary approval. Whereas Stanhope and Sunderland had not fallen in 1717, Carteret was demoted in 1724 and Townshend resigned six years later. The very fact that two Secretaries of State, the ministers concerned with foreign policy, should depart in accordance with the wishes of the First Lord of the Treasury indicated the willingness of the Crown to accept the implications of parliamentary monarchy, although, in each case, Walpole only obtained his goal with considerable difficulty.

For similar reasons, George II maintained Walpole in power in 1727 and did not appoint his 'favourite', Compton, in his place. This was one of the key crises of Walpole's career, but one that generally receives insufficient attention because the focus of the crisis was the Court, not Parliament. To have made this change of minister would have been to follow usual practice, particularly on the Continent, but George accepted that Walpole's command of a parliamentary majority made him indispensable to the Crown.

Had Compton been given control of ministerial patronage, he could have sought to maintain the harmony between Crown and Parliament that had been so evident in recent sessions. Despite his considerable parliamentary experience (as Speaker of the Commons since 1715), this might have been very difficult had Walpole gone into opposition. Much would have depended on the policies that George II and Compton might have adopted, of which there is no indication. Walpole's move into opposition in 1717 had been so dangerous because George I, Stanhope and Sunderland supported contentious constitutional, ecclesiastical and foreign policies. Even then, determined royal support of Stanhope and Sunderland, ministerial skill in gaining opposition leaders such as Argyll, and a ministerial willingness to abandon contentious legislation, prevented Walpole from overthrowing the ministry in 1717–20. It is possible that the age of Walpole could have been truncated in 1727 had George II supported Compton. However, the political crisis that might have developed might also have put paid to any notion of an age of parliamentary stability.

George II was a firm believer in defending his personal position and in the 1740s he showed himself capable both of supporting a minister who did not possess a secure parliamentary position (Carteret) and of seeking to follow a personal, secret foreign policy, a British version of the French *secret du roi*. This was to cause considerable instability, both within the ministry, where the Pelhams and the retired Walpole resisted Carteret, and within the political nation, where the Hanoverian issue was pushed to the fore, as it had not been in the 1720s and 1730s.[29] The latter was particularly dangerous as war brought French support for Jacobitism.

Care was necessary in the handling of George II, as Richard Grenville MP noted after his patron Cobham accepted military office in the summer of 1742. Grenville wrote to his naval brother Thomas:

Lord Cobham bid me tell Mr Haddock that if either of his sons were for the army, everything in his power should be done, and swore by God he'd jump over the moon if possible to serve him. However things must subside before the new servants can have any great weight, none of us should like to have coachmen, stewards, chamberlains, cooks etc. enter our house by force, and turn out those old ones we have long had confidence in. They must at least convince us that they have put our estates, kitchens, stables etc. into better order than the old ones kept them, before we should appoint every postilion, scullion etc. by their direction.[30]

Walpole's success during the 1720s and 1730s owed much to his ability to persuade George I and George II to accept the consequences of parliamentary monarchy, and it is in part to this that he owes his description as first Prime Minister. This achievement has appeared more impressive of late as recent scholarship has stressed the continued vitality, influence and power of the eighteenth-century British monarchs, and their ability to achieve many of their aims despite significant domestic opposition. There was also considerable respect for the royal position, although this respect did not prevent opposition. In August 1717, General Thomas Erle, long-standing MP for Wareham, explained his views to James Craggs:

The King is certainly master of choosing who he thinks fit to employ. Those who would force others upon him, would think it hard usage to be treated so themselves in their particular concerns. I am under no apprehension but that both him and the public will be well served by those who are now in the administration. No one doubts their capacity. But there are so many who will be judges of their own, that the contention here, who shall have the power and the profit, will never be at an end. It is always happy for England when the people are possessed, that the King governs them himself. They have always had, and always will have submission – for the Crown which they never will have for one another, whilst we are divided into parties as we are. No honest man will come into measures to compel the King to employ anyone, let his capacity be what it will, nor to distress those employed, out of peevishness to the person. But if the Public is apparently in danger by evil counsels the cry will then be general; and there are many instances how fatal it has been to our Kings when they have been tenacious of a favourite, who has justly incurred the odium of his subjects. God be thanked that cannot be the case now. We are governed by a wise and experienced Prince who knows how to choose and when to dismiss, according as he is served.[31]

However, Erle's support for Walpole, then in opposition, led to his being forced to resign all his posts in March 1718.

As the role of the monarch, and, therefore, of the Court, in eighteenth-century politics has been re-evaluated, this has led to the need for a more sophisticated appreciation of the nature and workings of the political system. The avoidance of a clash between Crown and ministry during the Walpole period cannot simply be explained by reference to Walpole's success in meeting the Crown's financial needs through obtaining parliamentary support for a generous Civil List, though this was of great importance for the avaricious George II.

The Crown was constrained in its freedom of political manoeuvre by the consequences of the party conflict. This made it very difficult for William III and Anne to create mixed ministries of Whigs and Tories, for the growth of party loyalty led party leaders to resign from or refuse to accept office because the monarch employed men of another party. As a result, Clayton Roberts argued that 'in later Stuart England the power of party overwhelmed the power of patronage'.[32] This argument is of considerable importance for the early Hanoverian period. Though Linda Colley claimed that the Tories were keen to serve the Crown and that George I and George II were willing to turn to the Tories, there is little evidence after 1715 for the second contention and the first probably underrates the role of Jacobite sympathies. Both kings detested the Tories as the party whose ministry had negotiated the Peace of Utrecht in 1713, ending the War of the Spanish Succession and abandoning Britain's allies, including Hanover. The Utrecht issue was used by the Whigs to great effect throughout the period 1713–40 to discredit the Tories. George I and George II suspected, and were urged to do so by the Whigs, that the Tories were inclined to support Jacobitism. The monarchs were opposed to the 'little Englander' stance of the Tories: their opposition to continental commitments, an isolationism that threatened Hanover, and their hostility to continental Protestantism. In these areas Tory prejudices and ideology, as well as Tory policies, conflicted with royal interests.

Given this situation, it is not surprising that George I and George II had little time for the Tories. In 1714, the French envoy reported that George II, then Prince of Wales, would 'not suffer the sight of any Tories, regarding them all as Jacobites'.[33] In July 1721, Newcastle wrote that:

the report of the Tories coming in, having reached the King's ears, he has been so good as to declare to me and many other of his servants the concern he has at the report, and has assured us that he neither has or ever had any such thoughts, and is determined to stand by the Whigs, and not take in any one single Tory. He is very sensible the Whig Party is the only security he has to depend on, in which he is most certainly right, for it is impossible for his Government ever to be supported by any other Party. . . . Could I imagine there was any design to introduce the Tories I should be as much alarmed as anybody for I shall always think it destructive to the King and the Government.[34]

At times of political tension, as in 1717 and the mid-1740s, when the monarchs risked the defeat of their favoured ministers, Stanhope and Carteret, they were prepared to threaten that they would turn to the Tories for support, but there was little substance to these threats. When George I and George II sought Tory help they did so only in order to serve Whig ministries and measures. The inability and unwillingness of Tory leaders to offer their support helped to make discussion of such schemes abortive, as in 1716–18. For practical purposes, George I and George II were party monarchs, whose wish to have Whig ministries represented a constraint on their political freedom of manoeuvre.

However, it did not oblige them to have a particular set of Whig ministers. The divisions within the Whig party, accentuated from 1714 onwards by political success and the consequent struggle for office and dominance, gave the monarch considerable freedom in his choice of ministers. There were essentially two types of Whig internal dispute. Disputes within the ministry were very significant, and usually involved disagreements over both policy and patronage. The conflict between Walpole and the former Sunderland group, led by Carteret and Cadogan, in 1722–4 related to disagreements over foreign policy as much as to a struggle for pre-eminence. They were inextricably intertwined as both involved an attempt to win royal support. Walpole's success in this struggle was important to the consolidation of his power.

The second type of dispute was usually a consequence of the first. It was a formal parliamentary opposition by Whigs to the Whig ministry, such as that mounted by Walpole in 1717–20 and by Pulteney in 1726–42. These oppositions often looked to the Tories for parliamentary support, but they differed fundamentally from Tory opposition, both in that there was a good chance that the opponents would be taken back into office, and that they were linked often to ministerial factions. The great failure of the Pulteney opposition to Walpole was not the inability to defeat him in Parliament, but the failure to unite effectively with those ministers who were opposed to Walpole. In 1730, Walpole would have been in particular difficulty had Carteret, Townshend and Wilmington supported Pulteney. Their failure to do so allowed Walpole to tackle the parliamentary and ministerial crises of 1730 separately.

In 1733, the situation was more serious as Bolton, Chesterfield, Cobham and Stair, riding a wave of popular opposition, proved willing to co-operate with the Whig opposition in pressing for the removal of Walpole. This led in that session to the ministry facing a serious crisis in the Lords. Of the seventy-five peers who voted for the government on 24 May 1733, Walpole's first defeat in the Lords as chief minister, only ten were without office or place. He was saved by George II's determination to support him, which helped to divide the court opposition to Walpole, for Harrington, Scarborough and Wilmington were unwilling to push their opposition in the face of royal disapproval. In August 1733, John Drummond MP wrote of 'the destruction of Sir Robert, which is not like to happen, for I never saw him easier at Court'.[35]

Thus, despite being restricted to Whig ministries, George I and George II possessed considerable freedom as a result of Whig disputes. The Crown was the arbiter of these disputes and the Court the principal sphere in which they were conducted. The constitutional and political customs of the period ensured that royal support for Whig measures and ministers, did not necessarily lead to ministerial stability. Furthermore, if royal support was a condition of Whig ministries, it also affected them. The absence of a clear party leadership, and, thus, of coherent party leadership reflected in part a political world in which ministers were the king's and rising politicians sought the favour of the Crown. This did not mean sycophancy, but it did mean that Whig politicians regarded royal support as desirable. The clear identification of the first two Georges with the Whigs ensured that royal favour was seen as a natural attribute of the Whigs. Those who lacked such favour were pushed into obscurity, subservience to Walpole, or tactical alliance with the Tories.

Ministers needed royal support, and, as a result, the Crown was able to obtain considerable benefits: an enhanced Civil List, a larger army than would probably have otherwise existed, and support for Hanoverian interests, such as the subsidy treaty with Hessen-Kassel, by which Hessian troops destined for the defence of Hanover were paid by Britain and not by Hanover.[36] Walpole was expected to find money for George I's female German connections.[37] He also had to spend time as a courtier, attending on the royal family, as on 3 July 1724 when he was present at George I's review of the Foot Guards in Hyde Park. Furthermore, the monarchs did not always heed ministerial wishes concerning patronage. In one such matter, in 1738, the Earl of Malton was informed that, although Walpole had pressed George II, 'he had the misfortune and concern to find that he could not prevail'.[38]

Given this situation there was potential for a serious conflict between Crown and ministry. Neither possessed sufficient strength to dominate the other and the constitutional guidelines that sought to define their relationship, such as the Act of Settlement of 1701, were vague, providing scant guidance for most political eventualities, and dependent upon mutual good-will. There was as yet no received understanding of such central issues as the collective responsibility of the Cabinet, the particular responsibility of the departmental head, the special role of the first minister, and the notion that the king should choose his ministers from those who had the confidence of Parliament.[39]

Crown–ministry relations were a significant source of political instability, in ministerial and parliamentary terms, in 1716–20 and 1743–6.[40] Walpole's success in avoiding this situation was a testimony to his political skills, his attention to Court intrigue, his personal good relations with Queen Caroline and George II, and to the political responsibility of George I and George II. Hatton's biography of the former has taught us to be aware of George I's political skills and sense of responsibility, but there has been scant appreciation of George II. Too often assessments of this monarch, particularly for the Walpole period, are based on the hostile views of Hervey, a courtier who disliked the king personally and wrote of him as if he were a boorish fool.[41] Recent work would suggest that this was not the case and that George, if no intellectual, was nevertheless a monarch of considerable shrewdness and political skill.[42] An incompetent and unyielding monarch might well have led to the end of Hanoverian rule in Britain, just as James II had done for the male line of the Stuarts.

The role of the Crown in politics and in patronage ensured that Walpole's position as leading minister was not identical with what was subsequently to become understood as the position of Prime Minister. Walpole was not supported by collective ministerial responsibility or party discipline. Ministers often saw the king individually, and, if they followed royal orders, could hope for the monarch's support against the criticism of their colleagues. The ministry and the Court usually contained members who were opposed to the leading minister and whom it was impossible for him to discipline, such as the Wilmington–Dorset–Dodington group. Dining with Walpole in December 1731, Hervey noted that Dodington always contradicted his host. In January 1733, the government was able to intercept and decypher an instruction from Frederick William I of Prussia to his envoy in London to thwart the intended marriage of William IV of Orange and the Princess Royal. To that end, Frederick William sought to play on animosities within the government which were clearly no secret:

'the jealousy which Robert Walpole has conceived against Lord Chesterfield may be improved by you, if you dextrously insinuate to the former what an overmatch of credit the effecting of that proposed marriage would give to the said Chesterfield with the King and Queen'.

Chesterfield indeed wished to overthrow Walpole. In 1739, it was believed that Scarborough and Wilmington would join the opposition.[43] This helped increase Walpole's reliance on those who were close to him, such as Horatio. The latter was sent, instead of Harrington, to accompany George II to Hanover in 1736. Robert was able to send him an ostensibly private letter that could be shown to the king, as well as an additional private one that was not to be shown.[44]

Given the opposition to Walpole within the Court and ministry, and the large areas of patronage over which he had little control, it might appear surprising that Walpole's position was seen by contemporaries as a new development or that he has been regarded subsequently as the first Prime Minister. This partly reflects the vitality of opposition propaganda. Walpole paid dearly for the fact that his cultural appreciation and patronage were directed towards paintings rather than literature. The disgruntled literary talent that supported the opposition presented his ministry as an aberration, a unique concentration of power reflecting evil intentions and corrupt practices.

In fact, Walpole's power was not unique. There had been other great ministers before him who had combined great influence at Court, control over royal patronage and responsibility for parliamentary management. The term Prime Minister, and others of a comparable nature, were applied to two of Anne's leading ministers, Godolphin and Harley.[45] Walpole's position seemed novel largely because his longevity, his ability to survive the accession of a new monarch, and the degree of his influence in Court and Parliament and over patronage were outside the experience of all living commentators, and because so much attention was devoted to it. The claims that Walpole's position represented a new departure ignored the absence of any institutional change affecting his position as minister. Early eighteenth-century Britain was not an age of administrative revolution. Such innovation as took place was largely in fiscal matters and in the government of Scotland after the Union of 1707, and not in the reorganisation of ministerial responsibilities. Just as there was no simplification of the system by which two Secretaries of State shared responsibility for foreign policy and for law and order until 1782, so there was no clarification of the role, powers and responsibilities of the leading minister.

This was not surprising, given the widespread hostility to the idea of such a position, but it left unclear such matters as whether the leading minister was supposed to sit in the Commons or the Lords, be a Secretary of State or the First Lord of the Treasury. There were benefits from such a flexible, inchoate system, but the absence of definition served to increase greatly the scope for ministerial strife, and this was to be particularly serious after the fall of Walpole. It would, therefore, be mistaken to suggest that Walpole created the office of Prime Minister, or that he created a prime ministerial system. The bases of his political system, namely the attempt to control as much patronage as possible and to retain the support both of king and Parliament, were far from new, though Walpole's determination to remain in the Commons rather than going to the Lords, as Harley and Stanhope had done, was an important development (and seen as such), reflecting his belief that the Commons were both more influential and harder to manage. The inchoate nature of the system left considerable power with the monarch.

CROWN AND MINISTERS

As a consequence both of the nature of Court politics and of the limitations of representation, the principal threat to a minister came not from the electorate, but from those who might contest his control of ministerial and royal patronage: his colleagues and the king. Much about Walpole's ministerial longevity can be explained by reference to his relations with these men. Walpole was not George I's favourite minister, and in 1721 Carteret kept up his spirits and sought to preserve Newcastle's support for Sunderland by informing him that 'The King is resolved that Walpole shall not govern, but it is hard to be prevented'.[46]

Walpole's early ascendancy and George I's need for him, owed much to chance: the financial crisis of 1720 and the deaths of Stanhope and Sunderland in 1721 and 1722. His success in the session of 1721 in performing the difficult task of defending Whig involvement in the South Sea Company consolidated Walpole's position as the leading ministerial spokesman in the Commons. He was to maintain this position until 1742, thanks to his refusal to follow the usual course of successful politicians, such as Harley, Bolingbroke and Stanhope, and obtain promotion to the Lords. Instead, his eldest son was created a peer, Lord Walpole of Walpole, in June 1723.

As government manager and principal spokesman in the Commons and a skilled finance minister, Walpole was invaluable to George I, though it is unclear whether the king would have supported him against Sunderland in the rift that was prevented only by the latter's sudden death from pleurisy. In July 1723, Townshend claimed that the recent successful parliamentary session and the revival of credit had helped Walpole and himself with George. The following month, Walpole congratulated himself on accurately predicting financial movements for George and on the flourishing condition of public credit, 'I think 'tis plain we shall have the whole supply of next year at 3 per cent'. In 1721, Bishop Gibson had claimed that 'as long as our great men go on to agree among themselves, all is like to go very well'.

However, this was not to be.[47] Walpole had to struggle hard in 1724–5 to remove from power his opponents within the ministry, Cadogan, Carteret,

Macclesfield and Roxburgh. Townshend warned Walpole not to offend George I by seeming to triumph in ministerial disputes. In late 1723, Carteret had 'great hopes from Cadogan and Roxburgh's being able to form a party', but, in practice, the removal of Walpole's ministerial rivals did not lead to problems at Court or in Parliament.[48]

With time, Walpole appears to have earned the respect of George I. Commenting in early 1724 on the political situation in London, Stair had no doubt that George's support for Walpole was crucial: 'the King's favour is entirely declared on the side of Robert Walpole . . . his Majesty confides entirely in Mr Walpole for the management of his affairs. There is not the least struggle in that matter . . . it looks as if before the end of the session of Parliament everything was to be modelled to be of a piece as far as Mr Walpole cares to have it so'.[49]

However, Walpole cannot be described fairly as the prime minister in George's last years: he never enjoyed sufficient influence with George, and Townshend's authority in the field of foreign policy was clearly independent of Walpole. There is, nevertheless, no truth in the reports which circulated in 1727 that George I had planned to disgrace Walpole shortly before his death.[50]

George II's accession threatened to bring about Walpole's fall. It was very rare for the leading minister of one monarch to be retained by his successor. Indeed, in 1726, one Jacobite commentator claimed that the future George II would disgrace and execute Walpole and, urging that the Jacobites should therefore approach Walpole, suggested Shippen for the task.[51]

George came to the throne determined to be his own master. Walpole managed to survive the crisis, partly because of Compton's lack of political skills; but, despite his success, Walpole's position was weakened by the fact that George II's accession led to the entry into office of courtiers with whom the king was closely associated, especially Compton, ennobled as Earl of Wilmington, and the Earls of Chesterfield and Scarborough. Further difficulty was created in 1729, when the two Secretaries of State, Townshend and Newcastle, fell out, whilst Townshend and Walpole seriously disagreed over foreign policy. These ministerial difficulties were resolved in two crises, one in 1730 which saw the resignation of Townshend and the loss of office by Carteret,[52] the other in 1733, when Chesterfield, Wilmington, Scarborough and other ministerial Whigs failed to drive Walpole from office during the Excise crisis. Instead, he was able to force them into opposition, as with Chesterfield and Stair, or acquiescence, as with Wilmington and Townshend's replacement, Harrington.

It has been suggested that the expulsion from the ministry of men of talent weakened it. This may well be true, and one can note Sarah Marlborough's barbed comment of 1740: 'Sir Robert . . . never likes any but fools, and such as have lost all credit . . . I cannot reckon above two in the administration that have common senses.'[53] However, the expulsion also served to increase the stability of the ministry. The presence of figures such as Chesterfield, who had been willing to intrigue actively with sections of the opposition, had been a disruptive force. The political tensions of the periods 1714–17, 1720–1 and 1742–4, when no individual minister wielded power comparable to that of Walpole in the 1730s, suggest that his determination to dominate the government should not be seen as a source of ministerial instability.

Walpole was probably at the peak of his power at Court and in the ministry in 1734–8. He survived the Excise crisis of 1733, the high point of the opposition campaign against him, to win the general election of 1734. Despite differing with George II over British policy in the War of the Polish Succession (1733–5), Walpole retained the support, indeed the affection, of the king. The attempt to create a country party encountered increasing difficulties due to tension and differences of opinion between the Tories and the opposition Whigs, and in 1735 Bolingbroke left the country in despair. There was little co-ordination of parliamentary tactics between the two groups. Walpole was clearly the dominant force in the ministry. The Austrian diplomat Wasner reported in 1734 that he was the minister on whom all the others depended absolutely, and, two years later, that he governed the country alone, the Secretaries of State simply executing his orders. In 1735, the Sardinian envoy Ossorio wrote that he was the sole source of all that was done in the kingdom, although the following year he noted Walpole's unsuccessful wish to get rid of Harrington.[54]

The opposition were disappointed in their hope that Walpole would fall after the death of Caroline in 1737. In 1731, Pulteney had in the Commons 'alluded to the report that Sir Robert Walpole is only supported by the Queen'.[55] Five years later, Walpole got Caroline to press George against an alliance with Denmark and Sweden.[56] The *Craftsman* of 15 September 1733 described politics in terms of chess with Walpole as the knight: 'see him jump over the heads of the nobles . . . when he is guarded by the Queen, he makes dreadful havoc, and very often check-mates the King'. However, Walpole's support from Caroline had its limits. During the War of the Polish Succession, she was more favourable to British support for Austria than Walpole.

The contrast between Caroline's bright, sparkling, witty nature and George's more dour, boorish demeanour greatly influenced contemporaries and led commentators such as Hervey to present George as manipulated by Caroline and Walpole. In 1720, Lady Cowper observed that the future king 'is governed by the Princess as she is by Walpole'.[57]

George appreciated Walpole's ability and his skill in 'the management of his affairs'.[58] After he came to the throne (and again after Caroline's death),

George promised Walpole his continued support[59] and gave it until the end of the ministry. This was seen for example in the disposal of army patronage, which was closely guarded by George II and employed to help Walpole. Thus, in 1740, Sir James Lowther observed, 'Colonel Mordaunt has got a regiment, they give almost all of them to young colonels that are in the House'. John Mordaunt, a Walpole loyalist, had indeed received army promotion. However, the Walpoles could not take George for granted and he could be very stubborn in resisting patronage demands, as in 1739 when he did not want to appoint Robert Trevor Envoy Extraordinary and Plenipotentiary at The Hague. Robert Walpole broke the news to Trevor's patron, Horatio:

'it is impossible for you to leave the Hague before somebody or other is there to relieve you, and at this juncture it can be nobody but Mr Trevor that can do the business, but this consideration will just now have no other effect upon the King, but to make him very angry with Mr Trevor, and order us to think immediately upon somebody else'.[60]

WALPOLE AND THE ALTERNATIVES

It is unclear whether any of the other politicians of the period could have governed with more success. Some were better informed on foreign affairs (Bolingbroke, Carteret, Chesterfield, Harrington), but none enjoyed Walpole's mastery of the arts of political management and of fiscal affairs, and few possessed his administrative competence and parliamentary skills. It is probable that other ministers would have pursued different policies. Some would have followed a more pugilistic foreign policy. Carteret, Pulteney, Harrington and Newcastle would probably have taken Britain into the War of the Polish Succession. Lacking any real interest in fiscal matters they would have been unlikely to have introduced the Excise Bill. Some, such as Newcastle, would have sought a Whig-only ministry, others, such as Carteret, would probably have been prepared to turn to the Tories had they been faced with a strong opposition Whig grouping. Before his death, Carteret's patron, Sunderland, had moved in this direction. All would have sought to use Walpole's methods of patronage and parliamentary management, although, as most were in the Lords, the latter would have been more difficult. All the Whig alternatives to Walpole would have been accused of corruption, although Carteret, a patron of the arts and a friend of Swift, or Chesterfield might well have enjoyed a better literary reception than Walpole, at least to begin with. The Whigs would probably have fared less well without Walpole. None of the alternative leaders was as adept politically, and entry into the War of the Polish Succession, though possibly initially popular, might well have been disastrous.

On the other hand, Walpole endangered the ministerial position in the 1734 elections by his espousal of the Excise scheme the previous year, whilst the chances of success in the 1727, elections were increased for any ministry by the relative popularity of the new king and by his keen support of the Whigs. Had Walpole fallen earlier than 1742, for example in 1727 or in 1733 over the Excise, and been replaced by an alternative Whig ministry, as many thought likely, much would have depended on whether he would have been willing to lead an opposition in Parliament, and whether, as seems unlikely, the Tories would have been prepared to co-operate with him.

George II's support was crucial to Walpole in 1733, but George chose well. Walpole's unwillingness, other than in 1733 and 1736, to rock the boat by introducing contentious legislation may well have helped to produce an atrophy of the legislative process, always a danger in a political system unwilling to anger powerful interests and based on a complex and sensitive balancing act. However, his lack of enthusiasm for innovation reflected an awareness of the nature of the system. As the *Northampton Mercury*, a pro-ministerial newspaper, noted on 28 October 1723: 'The first safety of princes and states lies in avoiding all counsels or designs of innovation, in ancient and established forms and laws, especially those concerning liberty and property and religion'. This was also the first safety of ministers, and Walpole's longevity as first minister owed much to his realisation of this.

It is unfashionable today to ascribe much influence to individuals, but the continuation of the Walpole ministry, the political stability that this represented and fostered, and the peaceful economic, social and religious developments for which it provided a framework, or which at least it did not impede, owed much to Walpole's political skills. Lord John Russell, then an MP and later Prime Minister, wrote in his *Memoirs of the Affairs of Europe* (1824) that Walpole was 'one of the wisest statesmen Great Britain ever possessed', adding, 'It is astonishing to see after twenty years of power, how little could be brought against Walpole even when his enemies were in power'.[61]

Writing in the centenary year of the Excise Bill, Sir Robert Peel, a Tory who was soon to become Prime Minister, took exception to the view of Viscount Mahon, later Earl Stanhope: 'You have not made sufficient allowance for the difficulties with which he had to contend; you have not given him sufficient credit for the complete success with which he surmounted them; and you have attached too much weight to the accusations which party rancour and disappointment preferred against him.'

Peel went on to give his opinion. He noted one of the keys to Walpole's success in Parliament, his charm – 'he first convinced, and then dined with them' – and wrote:

64

'Of what public man can it be said with any assurance of certainty, that, placed in the situation of Walpole, he would in the course of an administration of twenty years have committed so few errors, and would have left at the close of it the House of Hanover in equal security, and the finances in equal order? – that he would have secured to England more of the blessings of peace, or would have defeated the machinations of internal enemies with less of vindictive security, or fewer encroachments on the liberty of the subject?'[62]

4

Walpole as Manager of Patronage

To many contemporary commentators, Walpole was synonymous with corruption. Such criticism was scarcely unique, but Walpole was more clearly depicted as corrupt than recent first ministers. His nicknames included Baal and Satan.[1] Aside from the political opposition, most of the leading literary figures of the period, including John Gay, Samuel Johnson, Alexander Pope and Jonathan Swift, attacked Walpole, alleging that he governed through corruption and that his attitudes were debasing British public life and society.[2]

These arguments were reiterated in the press. In its issue of 25 May 1728, the *Craftsman* stated that 'what are commonly called great abilities, in this age, will appear, upon enquiry, to be nothing but a little sordid genius for tricks and cunning, which founds all its success on corruption, stockjobbing and other iniquitous arts'. On 27 January 1727, the paper had condemned Walpole for corruption. Under the guise of a description of Cardinal Wolsey, the *Craftsman Extraordinary* of 30 December 1726 launched a bitter attack:

'This saucy Minister, who, by the way, could never get rid of the scoundrel habits of a low education, had some knowledge, more wit and much more impudence; the fortune he made was equally exorbitant and rapid. The use he made of this fortune was extravagant, and ostentatious to the highest degree. He seemed industrious to erect the trophies of his folly, and to furnish the truths of his rapine wherever he went. He adorned villas, he built palaces; and his train outshined his master's so much, that when he retired into the country, on a party of pleasure, the Court became desert'.

The comparison with Wolsey was also used in William Hogarth's print of *c.* 1728–9, *Henry VIII and Anne Boleyn*.

Fog's Weekly Journal claimed on 1 August 1730, 'in all public places you shall hear them ask, Did he ever yet encourage or prefer one man of parts? What man of wit or genius ever tasted of his beneficence?' *The Knight and the Prelate*, a ballad of 1734, proclaimed:

In the Island of Britain I sing of a k-t [knight],
Much fam'd for dispensing his favour aright,
No Man could he but what's palpable see,
And he judged of Men's Worth by the Weight of their Fee.

The strength of the literary opposition to Walpole has consistently impressed posterity, but it reflected both wider pressure for cultural revival (some of it nationalist in character) and his neglect of the literati of the age, rather than any particular faults of his administration. Gay abandoned his support of the government when he was denied the promotion he felt he merited. As John Andrews, a later writer, noted in 1785:

'Sir Robert Walpole, by neglecting men of letters, drew the whole load of their odium upon him. Hence it is, that no mercy hath been shown to his character; and that he is, according to the representations of the majority of writers, accounted the chief author and modeller of that regular system of corruption which has nearly subverted the constitution'.[3]

This reputation stuck, although Johnson in his later years, like Pitt, thought more favourably of Walpole. The *Gazetteer* of 3 July 1770 referred to Walpole as 'that patron of venality'. On 10 August 1786, the *Daily Universal Register* reported, without any evidence, that:

'Sir Robert Walpole . . . who brought the system of venality and corruption to a more alarming excess than had ever been known previous to his time . . . shamefully declared that to make the people quiet and submissive to his measures, he found it his best policy to keep them poor, and work upon what he facetiously called the consumptive plan – He publicly argued in support of that corruption which he had practised secretly; and indeed too many of later date have not blushed openly to adopt his principles'.

When, in 1768, Philip Thicknesse wrote in praise of Walpole he was conscious that this was an unusual position:

'I own I am such an enemy to my country, as to wish Sir Robert Walpole among us again; he was a staunch Whig, not absolutely destitute of abilities, and what money he idled away, was among his friends at home; not in fruitless fantastical expeditions on the coast of France',[4] the last an attack on Pitt's strategy during the Seven Years' War. This response to the contrast between the two men was different to that drawn by most commentators. In general, the contrast was to the disadvantage of Walpole, who was accused of corruption and of pusillanimity in the face of France and Spain. Walpole did not play to the gallery, did not appeal to the wider political nation to the extent that Pitt was to do, and his reputation suffered as a consequence. In 1758, during Pitt's ministry, the *Monitor*, a leading supporter of Pitt, invited its readers to:

look back to the administration of Sir Robert Walpole. Did not the Chancellor of the Exchequer, that he might be allowed to govern without jealousy, connive at every abuse of power and every breach of trust in those who had it in their power to thwart his measures? Did not his measures expose the dignity of his master to contempt and his country to shame and disgrace? for which he suffered the fate of a bad minister: the people cried for justice, and the wrath of the king went out against him: he was disgraced.

Under such an administration the council became a cabal; where a few private men, without the least regard or esteem for one another, mutually combine to support the share they have usurped amongst themselves in the government of the kingdom.

Other mid-century press descriptions included 'that grand corrupter' or 'the arch-corrupter'.[5]

However, in 1785, Horatio Walpole pointed out that his father had found 'at least a great majority of every Parliament ready to take his money'. The same point was made by James Porter in 1742: 'surely if one side hath bribed, the other has done so likewise, and therefore one is as guilty of corruption as the other. As long as men are men in England, and corrupt ones too, they certainly will take money, if others will give'.[6] The demand factor in corruption was noted by Sir James Lowther MP, when he complained in 1742: 'People are so sordid and rapacious there is hardly anything but corruption from the highest to the lowest. It has been Sir Robert's masterpiece to make it . . . universal'.[7]

Maybe so, but Walpole did not invent corruption and much public office rested on a blurred boundary between private and public income and expenditure. Nor was Walpole the originator of the system of ministerial patronage. Any such argument would insult the intelligence of predecessors, such as Harley and Sunderland, whose capacity for intrigue and for manipulating the patronage structure was substantial. Walpole was different because the longevity of his ministry – a product of political circumstances and of his more skilful and ruthless use of patronage – permitted him to be more systematic and thorough in his control of government patronage, and because this longevity and the minister's seeming invulnerability itself aroused outrage.

There was a dark side to Walpole's manipulation of power. Legal and extra-legal pressures were used ruthlessly against opponents such as opposition publishers. The Secret Office of the Post Office systematically opened the post of opposition politicians and was not simply an anti-Jacobite precaution, although Jacobites were affected by it, the Earl of Orrery noting in 1724, 'A good while letters cannot be sent without the utmost danger'.[8] Once he had left office, even Townshend referred to the problems of postal interception.[9] On 10 February 1727, the *Craftsman* asked correspondents 'who have anything curious to communicate . . . to send by a special messenger'. Such use of the post encouraged a sense of persecution on the part of Walpole's opponents, and made it difficult for them to take a charitable view of him.

Walpole showed no reluctance to use every means at his disposal. Charles Erskine, a Scottish critic, wrote in 1742 that Walpole's administration should be:

offensive to every true Briton, by his endeavouring by bribery and corruption, and promises and threatenings, to tempt or awe a free people into a slavish dependence upon him, and a sacrificing of their natural right and freedom, of which I had myself a pretty strong proof in the year 1734, when I got a message brought me in the name of a great man assuring me that I should not have nor keep anything of the government if I voted for any person in opposition to the person set up by the Court, to which my answer was, that I was till then undetermined whom I would vote for, but that the message had determined me to vote against any man whom they sent such a message should set up for; and falling also about that time to be a member of Assembly, I got also a message assuring me that if I did not vote for the Moderator proposed by the Court I could not have or keep anything of the government, and as I gave the same answer to this message as I gave to the other, and acted accordingly in both cases, so the threatening which was sent me was soon fulfilled,[10]

. . . and he was dismissed from his official position.

Anger about corruption was linked to widespread concern about the idea of a prime or sole minister. Count Sparre, the Swedish envoy, reported in June 1733 that, although Walpole had 'great capacity and affability', he had 'not been able to escape so great a hatred; but then he has likewise much contributed to it himself by pretending contrary to the genius of this nation, to be absolute in his ministry', which, according to Sparre, was contrary to British history and practices.[11] Samuel Sandys, a prominent opposition Whig, told the Commons in February 1741 that 'sole minister [was] a name and thing unknown to England or any free nations, but taken from a neighbouring nation',[12] presumably France. An opposition pamphlet claimed in 1747 that 'the King, according to the British constitution, is the sole Prime Minister: no subject can execute that power for him without danger to our liberties'.[13]

Nevertheless, given the absence of party discipline, the distribution of places and pensions was the only way of enabling the ministry to gain the co-operation of Parliament. They provided a crucial link between executive and legislative. An appreciation of this helped lead opposition politicians under Carteret and Pulteney, who gained office when Walpole fell in 1742, to discard the reform programme directed against places and pensions that they had advocated whilst in opposition. Furthermore, Walpole's methods were continued throughout the century. 'Junius', the bitter pseudonymous critic of the Grafton ministry, claimed in the *Public Advertiser* of 8 July 1769 that 'in the common arts of domestic corruption, we miss no part of Sir Robert Walpole's system except his abilities'.

Walpole himself made vast gains from his years in office and also flaunted his wealth to a degree that offended many. His son Robert's marriage in 1724 was described as:

'the most splendid wedding there has been in England these many years . . . it makes money circulate for Mr Walpole has been more than ordinarily generous on this occasion and bought all with ready money more like a prince than a commoner'.[14]

Princely magnificence was certainly displayed in his building of a palatial country seat at Houghton.[15] This was more magnificent than the building projects of Harley or Sunderland. Houghton was designed for Walpole by Colen Campbell, an architect working in the newly fashionable neo-Palladian style, and executed by Thomas Ripley, a protégé of Walpole, who was also responsible for building Horatio Walpole's seat at Wolterton. Work began in 1721 and was finished in 1735, although the new house was in use before then. The architect James Gibbs also worked on the house, and was responsible for the domes over the pavilions.

The scale and theme were grandiloquent, as befitted the leading minister of the age. The Stone Hall and the Saloon on the *piano nobile* were grand and magnificent, the former being a cube with 40 foot dimensions. As in a royal palace, the State Rooms were designed to impress. The decoration also was impressive rather than intimate. In the vaulted entrance hall, there was decorative painting by William Kent, and a statute of a gladiator given by the Earl of Pembroke and displayed on a large substructure. The Stone Hall contained a massive fireplace by Rysbrack and there was another impressive chimneypiece in the Dining Room. More generally, the decoration was a riot in gilt and stucco, with an ample use of expensive woods, including much mahogany, for extensive and ornate wood-carving, much of it by James Richards, Master Sculptor and Carver in Wood to the Crown from 1721. Pillars, pilasters, capitals, friezes, marble overmantles, dramatic chimneypieces, brackets, impressive staircases, and lavish tapestries contributed to a heady sense of opulence. The gardens were laid out for Walpole by Charles Bridgeman.

Lady Burlington wrote to her husband, 'I suppose this letter will find you at Houghton . . . I don't know the post town, but I conclude there is no occasion to be very particular in a direction to a place so well known'.[16] No expense had been spared, noted an impressed Hervey in 1727.[17] Five years later, the Duchess of Kent wrote that Walpole's green velvet state bed for Houghton was 'so richly embroidered with gold as to cost some thousand pounds':[18] it was embellished with yards of gold lace.

The cost was the subject of public comment, for example in the ballad *The Norfolk Lanthorn* (1731) and the pamphlet *A Caveat against concluding this Session with an Act of Indemnity* (1742). There was also criticism of the style: 'I think it is neither magnificent nor beautiful, there is very great expense without either judgment or taste'.[19] Alexander Pope had little time for Ripley:

> Heaven visits with a taste the wealthy fool,
> And needs no rod but Ripley with his rule.

Walpole was to be buried there.

The house was filled with some of the finest paintings in Europe to form a collection that surpassed the descriptive power of one visitor in 1756.[20] Letitia Proctor reported in 1764 to her sister Agneta Yorke on a visit to Houghton: 'you may trace the purse of the prime minister throughout the whole . . . the innumerable fine pictures which covered the walls, and hardly allowed a space to show they were hung with crimson damask'. She noted two very fine beds, two very fine bronzes, and a series of excellent paintings including a Rembrandt of Abraham offering Isaac, a Rubens moonlit landscape, a Rubens cartoon and four market pieces by Frans Snyders. The grounds, however wore 'a very ruinous aspect', the absence of a lake was regretted, and, overall, she felt that 'nothing less than Miss Bowes's fortune [based on coal] or another first minister's purse can put it in proper order'.

On her second visit, in 1772, Letitia wrote of 'the outside of the house, or the park, the one in my opinion is too heavy to be pleasing, and the other too flat, to be beautiful'. The 'divine' paintings were another matter and she noted works by, among others, Leonardo, Domenichino and Rubens.[21] The collection was to be sold to Catherine the Great.

The Attorney General, Sir Dudley Ryder, finding Walpole with a new painting when he visited him in 1739, noted in his diary: 'I find pictures are a sort of mistress and his foible. He owns it himself that he cannot see a fine picture and be easy till he has it'.[22] British diplomats were used to help build up the collection. The authenticity of a painting obtained by Waldegrave in

Paris in 1735 was queried, but the envoy defended his action: 'I hear that M. Jervais has discovered that the picture sent you is not a Poussin. It gives a very good idea of his judgment and the connoisseurs here have been very merry about it'.

In 1736, care was taken to get Walpole a catalogue of the paintings of the late Prince Eugene, one of the leading European collections.[23] J.B. Van Loo was among the painters Walpole admired. He also supported British paintings, patronising the young Samuel Scott, a marine painter and drawer of waterfront scenes. Walpole liked the work of John Wootton, a prominent animal and landscape painter known for his hunting scenes. Five of his paintings which belonged to Walpole were engraved for Boydell's *Houghton Gallery*. A critic complained that none of Walpole's paintings showed 'the tragic end of rogues of state'.[24]

The opulence of Houghton is not tangential to Walpole's personality or career. It is difficult to have a good sense of individuals who were in a sense 'pre-biographical' in that they left little that was revelatory about their emotions or private intentions. Indeed, it is no accident that George II, a monarch who wrote little, still lacks an adequate biography. As a consequence, the image of Walpole was largely constructed by outsiders, especially literary critics and hostile caricaturists. However, Walpole's work at Houghton can be seen as in some way indicative of his personality. Much was of course a matter of what was expected of him and of the styles and designs then in vogue.

Yet Walpole's very determination to build Houghton and the pleasure he clearly got there also tell us about his intentions. Despite remaining in the Commons, he wanted his family to arrive and to show that it had arrived. His guests at Houghton included, in November 1731, Duke Francis Stephen of Lorraine, who was to marry Maria Theresa of Austria and to become the Holy Roman Emperor Francis I. In East Anglia, the Duke also visited and went hunting at Euston, the seat of the Duke of Grafton. Walpole's status was thus demonstrated by Houghton's profile: in this case he was equal to a duke. The Houghton party in 1731 also included the Dukes of Devonshire, Grafton, Newcastle and Richmond, the Earls of Albemarle, Burlington, Essex and Scarborough, and Lords Baltimore, Delawar, Herbert, Lovell and Malpas, Sir William Yonge, Sir Henry Bedingfield, Sir Charles Turner, General Churchill, Walpole's eldest son, Lord Walpole, Henry Pelham, and the envoys of Austria and Hessen-Kassel, Count Kinsky and General Diemar. The visit of Lorraine to Houghton featured in the press, both London and provincial, for example the *York Courant* of 9 November and the *London Evening Post* and *Evening Post* of 16 November. At Houghton, the fox-hunting did not go very well, but that for hares made amends.[25]

The extravagant Walpole obviously enjoyed luxury. The family lived mostly on the ground floor at Houghton, which was, according to Hervey, a world of 'hunters, hospitality, noise, dirt and business', but there were also the grand rooms on the *piano nobile* for 'taste, expense, state and parade'. The magnificence of Houghton captured visitors, such as Sir Thomas Robinson in 1731.[26] This sense of display can be variously explained. Whatever the presumed psychological drives, Walpole also enjoyed power and opulence, and this enjoyment did not commend him to his critics.

In London, he socialised at the highest levels. This was necessary once he became the king's leading minister, but Walpole also showed every sign of enjoying the splendour and pomp of opulent magnificence. Thus, for example, in August 1733 Walpole joined Harrington and a number of foreign envoys at dinner at the Duke of Newcastle's,[27] while on 20 January 1735 he joined the Dukes of Newcastle, Portland and Richmond, the Earls of Pembroke and Scarborough, and all the envoys from the states covered by Newcastle as Secretary of State in a grand entertainment held by the Earl of Jersey at his house in Grosvenor Street for the birthday of the Prince of Wales. Such occasions were staged in public, not hidden from view. Thus, the list of guests appeared in the *Universal Spectator* of 25 January. Provincial papers also reported Walpole's socialising. The *Norwich Mercury* of 9 January 1731 reported that Walpole and Newcastle had dined at Cashiobury, the seat of the Earl of Essex.

Entertaining was part of Walpole's political world and method. He regularly dined supporters, seeking by sociability to lessen tensions within the ministry and among his supporters. This helped make the government work. Thus, for example, Walpole wrote to Townshend in June 1723, 'Some of the City gentlemen dined with me on Tuesday, and it was then agreed that Sir Richard Hopkins and Mr Feast should be desired to stand for sheriffs for the ensuing year'. Two months later, 'The Bishop of London dines with me tomorrow, which will enable me to say something of the ecclesiasticks, the next time I have the honour to trouble you'. Gibson indeed suggested changes on the Bench. Hervey dined at Walpole's at the close of 1731 alongside Horatio Walpole, William Clayton, a Lord of the Treasury, Dodington, Wilmington, Winnington and Yonge, a gathering of prominent ministerialists in the Commons on the eve of the session.[28]

Walpole's conspicuous consumption directly contributed to his image as a 'great man', an overly dominant figure, whose grandiose character and pretensions were both cause and consequence of what critics alleged to be an illegitimate political prominence. Thus, the building at Houghton and other forms of opulence became ready symbols of Walpole's political position. This critique moved Walpole away from alternative roles and images, pre-eminently those of Whig stalwart and earthy country gentleman.

The means by which Walpole accumulated his wealth were criticised. It was common for the opposition to publicise the places held by his family. Edward Harley, a Tory MP, estimated that 'the annual worth of the places held by the Walpole family when Lord Orford asked and accepted a pension of £4,000 out of the Excise' was £28,000.[29] This wealth sustained both a lavish lifestyle and the development of the Walpole interest in Norfolk. Townshend noted a jealousy of his position in the county: 'Sir Robert and his friends having taken the utmost care to possess everybody that applying to me was the sure way not to succeed. This precaution they thought necessary towards preventing my forming a party against them here'.[30]

Walpole showed great favour to relatives and friends. George Cholmondeley, who married his daughter Mary in 1723, became an MP (1724–33), Governor of Chester (1725–70), Master of the Robes (1726–7), Lord of the Admiralty (1727–8), Master of the Horse to the Prince of Wales (1728–35), Lord Lieutenant and Vice–Admiral of Cheshire (1733–70), Lord Lieutenant of North Wales (1733–61), Lord of the Treasury (1735–6), Privy Councillor (1736), Chancellor of the Duchy of Lancaster (1736–43), and Chamberlain of Cheshire (1736–70). He also became a Knight of the Bath in 1725. Walpole's second son, Edward, became Master of Pleas in the Exchequer in 1727, and Joint Secretary of the Treasury as well as an MP in 1730, becoming, in addition, Secretary to the Lord Lieutenant of Ireland in 1737. Edward resigned both secretaryships in 1739 on being appointed Clerk of the Pells for life, an Exchequer sinecure worth £3,000 a year. Edward's elder brother, Robert, Lord Walpole, had been Clerk of the Pells, as well as being one of the Gentlemen of the King's Bedchamber and, in 1733, was appointed Lord Lieutenant of Devon. In 1738, his younger brother, Horace, gained the Exchequer life sinecures of Usher of the Exchequer, Clerk of the Entreats, and Comptroller of the Pipe, worth about £2,000 a year. In 1741, Sir Robert Walpole's brother, Horatio, gained the Tellership of the Exchequer, a life sinecure worth £3,000 a year: Walpole's former brother-in-law, friend and fellow King's Lynn MP, Charles Turner, had held the Tellership from 1729 until his death in 1738. Walpole's brother Galfridus was made Treasurer of Greenwich Hospital in 1715 and Joint Postmaster General in 1721; the Deputy Treasurership of Greenwich was given to Robert Mann, Walpole's unofficial banker. Mann subsequently became a Collector of the Port of London. A close friend, Charles Churchill rose from Colonel to Lieutenant General and became Governor of Plymouth and Deputy Ranger of St James's Park, which together gave him an annual income of £4,800.

Patronage was not only about family profit. Walpole appreciated, as Pelham was to do in 1746–54, that the utilisation of the patronage resources of the Crown, in order to create a corps of close supporters, combined with the avoidance of contentious legislation, could help to ensure ministerial stability. There was little to fear from the electorate, for even if the ministry was generally unsuccessful in the larger 'open' constituencies – the counties and the large cities – they could still rely on a large number of the 'pocket boroughs', seats that were controlled or heavily influenced by patrons. Some, such as Amersham, Marlborough and Newton, were controlled by Tory families, while Hedon was dominated by Pulteney, but most were at the disposal of the ministerial Whigs or heavily influenced by the government. In the 1741 general election, it was to be the defection from the ministry of a number of patrons – Frederick, Prince of Wales, the Duke of Argyll, Lords Falmouth and Dodington – that led to a result that reduced Walpole's majority to an unacceptably low level. Walpole was well aware of the direct parliamentary benefit of patronage.

Patronage was ubiquitous in eighteenth-century Britain. Patronage networks were a social feature of the age, often controlled by private citizens for socio-economic as well as political purposes, and not merely the aberrant creation of Crown and ministers. Apart from the clientage systems of landed magnates and borough-mongers, patronage relationships of one kind or another were also involved in the gentry's control of parochial appointments in the Church; their bestowing land tenures based on favourable leases, or with the suspension of onerous terms; the commercial relationships between wealthier members of the community and the merchants and artisans whose products and services they consumed; the distribution of commissions and contracts to architects, builders and civil engineers by city corporations as well as by aristocratic patrons; the control exercised by bishops, deans and chapters over both property and benefices; and even the appointment of parish pump officials (constables, church wardens, overseers of the poor) by the influence of social superiors.

Patronage gave currency to personal relations, linking Walpole to a large number of individuals. The resulting relationship exposed Walpole to the pressures of continual flattery and self-seeking attention. In the published dedication to Walpole of *The History of Saguntum*, Frowde declared:

'while you bring the learning and arts of Greece and Rome into the Cabinet; either that to instruct in the depths of reasoning; or these in the rules of governing; no impression can ever be made to our prejudice, from the intrigues or menaces of a foreign power'.

Nine years later, Everard Fawkener, envoy in Constantinople, wrote to seek Walpole's portrait:

'I shall have an unspeakable pleasure in looking on the image of him I am so much bound to, and surveying in that open frank and friendly countenance the truest representation of the most noble and generous heart. I dare not ask so much of your time as to sit for it, but if you will trust one of my brothers with that picture you think most like you, and give the painter leave to see you once by it, I hope a resemblance may be very well taken'.[31]

However much Walpole's ministerial longevity owed to his policies, it is also necessary to underline the importance of his parliamentary management and his control of government patronage. As the Duke of Portland observed in 1725, 'he never does anything for nothing'.[32] A French memorandum of 1736 claimed that whilst Walpole had control over patronage he would enjoy a secure parliamentary majority, and that whilst he had a majority he would retain his control over patronage. According to the memorandum, this circle would be very difficult for the opposition to break, especially if peace were maintained;[33] a reminder of the need to relate patronage and policy.

The management of patronage was far from easy. Newcastle wrote of the newly-elected Parliament in 1734: 'it will require great care, attention and management to set out right, and keep people in good humour'.[34] Confronted by a veritable onslaught of demands for the benefits of patronage – places (offices) and pensions (cash payments) – Walpole was, as he had to be, very astute at managing the patronage resources at his disposal.

As head of the Treasury, Walpole was at the centre of the network of government patronage. There were spheres where his influence was limited due to the role of other patrons. This was particularly true of the army, the Church of England, and Scotland, owing to the position of George II,[35] Bishop Gibson and the Earl of Ilay respectively. That did not mean that Walpole was without influence in these fields. His account of a discussion with Gibson in 1723 about filling vacant bishoprics was very detailed and senior clerics clearly thought it worth their while to seek his support: 'The Bishop of Hereford has wrote to me most strongly to go to Ely'.[36] With Gibson (Bishop of Lincoln, 1716–23, London, 1723–48), Walpole chose an 'ecclesiastical minister' who closely shared his goals. Walpole and Gibson's Church patronage had perhaps the widest social impact of any exercised by the Whigs and achieved a measure of reconciliation between the Tory parochial clergy and the Hanoverian Succession.

Patronage occupied much of Walpole's time. Most of his meetings with the king concerned patronage and a large portion of his surviving correspondence was devoted to the same issues.[37] The wide-ranging nature of Walpole's influence, the role of aristocratic support and the complicated permutations that patronage decisions gave rise to are illustrated by a letter of 1726 from Richard Arundell to his friend the Earl of Burlington, on whose interest he sat, without a contest, as MP for Knaresborough from 1720 until his death in 1758. In 1726, the post of Surveyor General of Works became vacant:

'upon which Sir Robert Walpole recommended me to the king who has consented to give me the employment. Great endeavours have been used to make Kent Comptroller, though to no effect, and he [Sir Robert] told me yesterday that he was obliged to make Ripley Comptroller to obviate the Duke of Devonshire's recommendation, and remove Howard from the Board, who is to have Dartiquenave's place, and Dartiquenave the Gardens and that he had spoke to the king to put Kent into Ripley's employment which was agreed to'.[38]

Arundell had become a favourite of Walpole, who sought his advice on the works at Houghton. William Kent, a protégé of Burlington, had carried out decorative work at Kensington Palace for George I before beginning work at Houghton for Walpole. Ripley was responsible for executing the work at Houghton. He held the post of Comptroller of the Board of Works from 1726 until 1738, and in 1737 was appointed Keeper of George II's private roads, gates and bridges; Arundell held this post from 1731 to 1737, when he became Master of the Mint. Charles Dartiquenave was a Whig socialite, who, in 1726, exchanged the Paymastership of the Royal Works he had held since 1706 for the Surveyor-Generalship of the King's Gardens. The merry-go-round of posts in such groups struck outsiders as corrupt. It certainly gave a flavour to the Walpole regime. Ripley was given not only work at Houghton and Wolterton, but also lucrative jobs on government buildings, especially the Admiralty in Whitehall in 1724–6.

Walpole also featured most regularly in the correspondence of others by virtue of his role in patronage. In 1737, Viscount Lonsdale, the leading Cumbrian Whig, wrote to Sir George Fleming, the Bishop of Carlisle, to assure him that he was happy to see the latter's nephew obtain a vacant post in the Customs at Whitehaven. He added:

'but for my own part I can't contribute at all towards it, for, as I have no reason to think that any of these employments would be given upon my request, it would be very unfitting for me to ask for them. Might I take the liberty of advising your lordship you should write directly to Sir Robert Walpole, for it is he alone that disposes of all these places, and expects application for them to be made to himself'.[39]

Walpole had constantly to disappoint with care, being mindful of the political implications of his actions. Far from being an isolated figure, Walpole was dependent for his success on his ability to win and retain support. In June 1731, John Drummond and Robert Douglas, both MPs, pressed Walpole to obtain a commission in the army for the latter. Walpole assured Douglas: 'that he should be provided for in course, and that it should be done with all the dispatch that could be, but that he behoved to have patience till his turn came which he hoped would be soon'. The impatient Douglas waited again in September on Walpole 'who has given him fresh assurances of being provided for, the young gentleman looked a little surly. Sir Robert told him that young men always walked faster than old men'. Douglas was promoted to captain the following year. This bound him to Walpole, for in 1735 the minister was able to threaten Douglas with its loss when he was dissatisfied with the captain's vote in the Commons.[40]

Whether he convinced suppliants or not, they generally had to accept what he told them. Charles Cathcart reported of a meeting with Walpole in 1716:

'I pressed him hard for the £500 to my sister in law, he made a merit of his having agreed to the £200, when as he said the king had rejected the thing entirely. I do not believe one word of this, but it was by no means proper to let him into that secret'.[41]

Walpole's ability to use secret service funds and other aspects of government patronage ensured that he was under great pressure to do so. A suppliant observing the pressure Walpole was under reflected in 1738, 'you are not much to be envied'. Two years later, Stephen Poyntz, seeking assistance with clerical preferment, hoped that a connection would speak to Walpole, 'to whom I know by experience it is of no use to write in the multiplicity of his affairs'.[42] Five years later, William Yonge, an office-holder who survived his patron's fall, provided evidence of the pressure for patronage. As Secretary at War, a post he held from 1735 until 1746, he wrote to Carteret:

Though I have always had an inclination to favour the colonels with regard to their recommendations of ensigns and second lieutenants, yet I beg leave to observe on this occasion that the great number of vacancies have occasioned strong solicitations from noblemen and gentlemen of weight and interest in their several counties, and, by the long time they have been indisposed of, they are become very importunate and uneasy. I should therefore hope His Majesty would at this time have a more particular regard to recommendations of this nature . . . among these John Fletcher recommended by Sir James Lowther I must name particularly.[43]

Such comments reveal the importance of regarding patronage as an integral part of the social system, rather than as simply a political mechanism. They suggest that opposition complaints of political manipulation require a measure of qualification in terms of prevailing social norms and pressures. However, there is little doubt of the outrage that lay behind many of these criticisms. *Old England*, a prominent London opposition paper, complained in 1745 that the Walpole and Carteret ministries had had 'no regard for personal merit, or experience in military offices' and had made 'a pecuniary interest the only step by which the bravest, the oldest, and the ablest of our soldiers and seamen could rise to the common justice which was due to their rank and services'.[44]

Many self-styled independent politicians were in fact linked to Walpole's patronage network, frequently seeking favours for relatives, friends, protégés and constituents. Sir James Lowther could not have maintained his electoral interest in Cumbria without help from the ministry. John, Lord Perceval also prided himself on his independence, but he relied on Walpole's help to maintain his political interest in Harwich, for which he was an MP.

Yet, there is little doubt that those who fell foul of the minister were treated in a bullying, indeed brutal, fashion. Thus, for example, Walpole responded to Dodington's move into opposition in 1740 by attacking his allies in Weymouth, the Tuckers, in order to destroy Dodington's electoral interests. John Tucker saw Walpole as a monopoliser of patronage: 'the Great Man seems determined by any means to destroy whatever may be called a natural interest in all boroughs where the government have any influence'.

The outgoing mayor, a Tucker ally, was sacked from his post in the customs service, and his successor, Richard Tucker, dismissed from his position as Surveyor of the Crown Quarries in Portland and made subject to legal charges. The Tuckers were also blocked from working the quarries. A week before the election, Walpole offered the Tuckers his support if they would support the ministerial candidates. They refused. Such conduct on Walpole's part, at once ruthless and pragmatic, helped strengthen his position when strong, but could not preserve it when weak. It also did nothing for his popularity,[45] nor for his subsequent image, but neither was foremost in Walpole's mind.

In addition, Walpole seemed willing to accept or overlook rank abuses, and did nothing to assist parliamentary scrutiny of them. Thus, he did not help the Gaols Committee that in 1729–30 revealed shocking conditions in the Fleet Prison. Instead, he was taken to show 'ill will' to the Committee. Furthermore, in some cases the abuses involved political figures close to Walpole. This was seen in two financial scandals that became parliamentary scandals in 1732, the fraudulent sale of the forfeited Derwentwater estates and the mismanagement of the Charitable Corporation. In each case, Walpole sought to shield guilty allies. Thus, in 1733, Walpole was able to ensure that Sir Robert Sutton, one of those most involved in the Charitable Corporation, was found guilty only of 'neglect of duty', rather than the 'many notorious breaches of trust and many indirect and fraudulent practices' of which he was correctly accused.[46]

At the same time, there was an engaged and open character to Walpole's personality, a directness and absence or rigidity, that was impressive. The critical Sarah Marlborough referred to Walpole valuing 'himself upon his temper'.[47] John Campbell noted in the Commons in 1741:

'Sir R. Walpole ended his short answer to Mr Sandys with this verse Nil conscire sibi, nulla pallescese culpa, but instead of nulla he said nulli. As soon as he sat down, Mr Pulteney, who sat near him, told him his mistake, but Sir Robert would have it that nulli was right, and the guinea upon it, which I saw him pay to Mr Pulteney, for he was soon convinced he had lost.'[48]

Walpole, the Electorate and Public Opinion

It is possible to discuss Walpole's hold on power by concentrating on the Crown, Parliament and ministerial factors. Yet that is not a complete picture, not least because it is necessary to probe his relationship with the electoral process and with public opinion. Walpole faced four general elections as leading minister (1722, 1727, 1734 and 1741), and his success in the first three was important in establishing and sustaining his credentials to be the leading minister for domestic affairs. Furthermore, as a negative factor, the ability of the government to survive a hostile public opinion was a major feature of the politics of the period. The press is worthy of special attention, because the criticism of many newspapers helped condition the contemporary and subsequent reputation of Walpole and his government (see Chapter 6).

The early eighteenth-century interest in the political possibilities of print reflected the concern shown by politicians about public opinion. However much politics might appear to be exclusively an occupation or hobby for the upper orders, exercised at Court, in country houses and in Parliament, it is clear that this was not the case. Historians have drawn attention to the often dynamic and sometimes radical character of popular politics and suggested that it was of considerable importance. Attention has been devoted both to the electorate and to those who, though they did not possess the vote, could seek to influence political decisions.

The nature of the electorate and of electoral politics was the crucial intersection of 'high' and popular politics, although the potential impact of the latter was lessened by the nature of the electoral system. There were many boroughs with small electorates, such as Malmesbury with 13 voters, Gatton with 22, and Whitchurch with 85. In Cornwall, 1400 voters elected 42 borough MPs.

Furthermore, irrespective of the size of the electorate, many seats were not contested. There were only 94 contests at the general election of 1741. The comparable figures for 1715, 1722 and 1727 were 119, 154, 114. Eighteenth-century election campaigns were expensive and generally financed by the candidates themselves, especially on the opposition side. In large counties and boroughs, they were often just too expensive to contest. In addition, in many of the small constituencies there was rarely an election. The Earl of Orrery, a Jacobite, complained in 1721, 'there are so many little venal boroughs that 'tis to be apprehended a majority will hardly be carried by the inclinations of the people only'.[1] At the beginning of the century, when its electorate was about 800, the representation of Flintshire was shared by the heads of its leading Tory families, an agreement renewed in 1731. From 1747 the Mostyn family represented the county in every Parliament until 1837.

However, an absence of a contest did not mean that there was no element of representation. Many of the voters were deferential, but this did not mean that they simply responded to instructions. Borough patrons were expected to tend their constituency, dispensing patronage and defending its interests. A failure to do so could lead to the rejection of the patron's influence. William Stanhope, who had been elected for Derby in 1715, complained when not re-elected in 1722 while envoy in Spain. He wrote that his fate had been: 'when out of sight to have all services forgotten, for certainly I did for that town the greatest they had to wish for, by making their river navigable'.[2] In 1732, Sir Richard Grosvenor nearly lost his family's electoral interest in Chester, because of his opposition to a scheme to widen the River Dee in order to help the town's trade.

Elections were not only about rivers. Francis Whitworth, a ministerial candidate defeated at Minehead in 1722, complained, 'one would imagine there was a law made for bribery, and not against it'. His elder brother, Charles, won an uncontested seat at Newport, Isle of Wight, that year. Despite support from the governor of the Isle and the fact that the electorate numbered 24 only, the members of the corporation, the election cost Whitworth £700, although he was assured that 'as matters go, 'tis reckoned a cheap bargain'.

In the large boroughs and large counties, there was a sizeable electorate, about 6000 in Norfolk, over 15,000 in Yorkshire, and nearly 5000 in Bristol. These electorates were difficult to control, and the bitter contests in these seats were seen often as a comment upon the popular will and the popularity of the government, as in 1734 when MPs who had supported the Excise Bill were rejected by such constituencies as Bristol, Kent, Newcastle and Norfolk. In seats with large electorates, there were often several important patrons and relations between them could be of crucial importance. In Sussex, where there were about 4000 voters in the county electorate, the Dukes of Newcastle, Richmond and Somerset devoted considerable effort to influencing their dependants. In 1719, Newcastle claimed that he controlled 16 Commons' votes, most of which were of Sussex MPs. In 1733, 'the Duke of Somerset at the entertainments this Xmas for the tenants and other freeholders under his Grace's influence has insisted on one vote for Mr Pelham, and to reserve their other till farther orders'. A letter from Thomas Coventry, Viscount Deerhurst, to his father, William, 5th Earl of Coventry, about the Worcestershire election of 1741 provides some flavour of electioneering, including the role of vicars as moulders of opinion. The Earl and another prominent landlord, Sir Thomas Lyttelton, put up their eldest sons, Deerhurst and George Lyttelton, as candidates as opposition Whigs, to challenge a sitting Tory MP and another Tory candidate:

We began canvassing at Stourbridge yesterday, and by all accounts no two candidates ever met with such encouragement; indeed I might say the whole town was unanimous, since we had 8 to 1 on our side. The populace among the rest were extremely well pleased, and showed all imaginable joy on our success. The few gentlemen who were well wishers to the other party made an entertainment at an inn where the landlady waited upon them, but the landlord dined with us. Our interest among the mob was so good that they could not get a common huzza and . . . venison, beef and pudding could not draw above 10 people together . . . the Parson . . . has done us as much mischief as he could; he has cast the odious name of pensioner upon my colleague, and since he could not hurt me with that invidious title, he has objected against my nonage, and preached up the doctrine of this kind. In all parts of the town he has explained the unlawfulness of electing a minor, who was a very improper person to be entrusted with the libertys of a free nation. Many more arguments have been urged against us by this worthy divine, which weighed a great deal with some of his parishioners at first, but a personal application and an easy behaviour to the men, and salutes and compliments to their wives made many converts.

Despite this, in the first Worcestershire contest to reach a poll since 1715, the Tories won, each polling over 2,000 votes.[3]

Had public opinion been restricted in its impact to the years in which elections were fought, then it would have made little impression on the political system. However, there were other methods by which the seemingly exclusive political system could be influenced by opinion 'out-of-doors'. Parliament and the ministry could be affected by organised extra-parliamentary pressure groups, by petitions and by nationwide instruction campaigns. The weak nature of the rather small government bureaucracy, and the widespread reliance of the ministry on outside bodies for advice, and even for assistance in the drafting of legislation, helped to increase the impact of lobbying groups.

Ministerial policy and parliamentary decisions were influenced greatly by mercantile pressure groups. The 1726 Act against importing foreign plate was drawn up by the Goldsmiths Company. The progress of the Anglo-Russian commercial negotiations in 1733–4 was affected by the Russia Company whose advice was sought by the ministry. Some mercantile groups, such as the East India Company, had very close links with the ministry.[4] Walpole's personal links with the directors of the major chartered trading companies and of the Bank of England were close, and helped to explain his sound grasp of financial matters and his ability to manage the government's fiscal interests. They also played a major role in enabling these groups to influence the ministry.

Walpole also sought to influence London politics through his City friends,[5] and to increase their power within the metropolis. The City Elections Act of 1725 defined the freeman franchise as narrowly as possible and imposed an aldermanic veto on the actions of the more popular and Tory-inclined Common Council. Walpole's intention was clearly to limit the volatility and independence of popular London politics, and he sought to achieve his aim by means of legislative action and the definition of a favourable group through patronage and shared interests.[6]

Other mercantile groups, such as the merchants trading to the West Indies, did not enjoy the same links with Walpole. However, their pressure-group tactics, a well-organised petitioning and propaganda campaign, were very successful in persuading Parliament to pass a series of measures in their favour, such as the Molasses Act of 1733 and the Sugar Act of 1739.[7] Nevertheless, it was a mistake to claim that Britain was 'governed by a parcel of merchants', or, as in 1718, that the Spanish trade was so essential that the ministry would not risk war with Spain. Mercantile lobbying was vociferous and left much documentary evidence, but this has led to an exaggeration of its importance. Much of the lobbying anyway was at cross-purposes. The *Evening Journal* in 1727 noted: 'The Turkey merchant writes against the East-India Company, the Woollen Manufacturer against the calicoes'. An examination of diplomatic records reveals that the ministry's commitment to the interests of trade was patchy. Relations with minor states could be greatly influenced by the issue. Complaints from the merchants and sugar refiners of Bristol in 1734 led to British pressure for a reversal of Venetian legislation affecting their interests. Moves in 1732–3 to restrict Hamburg efforts to benefit from the East India trade, and in 1734–5 to protect British trade from Danish attempts to blockade Hamburg, reflected pressure from British commercial interests.

However, with larger states, from whom Britain sought political advantage, the picture was very different. The 1720s and 1730s saw most European states passing protectionist legislation that harmed British trade. British diplomats were instructed to complain, and threats of parliamentary retaliation were made, but these complaints were subordinated to the need for good relations. This was certainly the case with Denmark, Sardinia and Sweden. Trade with Russia was sacrificed to political considerations in the 1710s and 1720s. Thus, the effectiveness of commercial lobbying, the openness of the political system to pressure 'out-of-doors' in this sphere, should not be exaggerated. It would have been unrealistic diplomatically to adopt commerce as a guiding principle. As Horatio Walpole pointed out in 1735:

'if a merchant of London, and of Amsterdam were to be the ministers of the political conduct to be observed between England and Holland, instead of preserving a union between the maritime powers, the two nations would be constantly in a war with one another.'[8]

The political impact of commercial pressure, accompanied by popular discontent, was seen in the War of Jenkins' Ear, which broke out in 1739. Spanish attacks on British merchants in the West Indies, who, the Spaniards claimed, with a great deal of truth, sought illicitly to breach the Spanish commercial monopoly in their empire, had been a major parliamentary issue in the late 1720s. Its successful revival a decade later led to accusations of a supposed ministerial failure to defend vital British interests. Sustained pressure from mercantile groups and an opposition press and parliamentary campaign had a significant impact. Horatio Walpole wrote in November 1737 of 'the clamour of the merchants' waking Newcastle up. Two months later, the Spanish first minister, La Quadra, told the British envoy that the government 'ought not to take the noise and clamours of our [British] subjects for well-founded complaints'. The ministry negotiated a settlement with Spain – the Convention of the Pardo – and defended it successfully against virulent opposition attacks in the session of 1739; but when difficulties arose over the diplomatic settlement, their room for political manoeuvre was restricted drastically by the consequences of the domestic debate over policy.[9]

Most of the attempts to influence parliamentary conduct related to legislation for private and local interests, such as turnpike trusts. This reflected the fact that the bulk of parliamentary legislation and time was devoted to these interests, in contrast to the twenty-first century when Parliament is dominated by the legislative programme of the government. As many local interests were in competition (the towns of Newcastle and Sunderland over river improvements, for example), there was a clear need to influence Parliament and much effort was devoted to this end. Lobbying and the presentation of petitions were frequent, with campaigning for these sectional interests related often to the struggles of national politics.

The same techniques were used in the pursuit of political aims, largely by the opposition. Although the ministry was not averse to arranging for suitable petitions and addresses to be presented, Walpole never developed this in a systematic fashion. Possibly this reflected a feeling that the opposition used these methods more successfully, and that it was, therefore, better to condemn the attempt to dictate to Parliament, as ministerial spokesmen did, than to seek to match the opposition. Opposition spokesmen stressed the need to heed opinion 'out-of-doors'. George Dodington warned the Commons in 1743 that if popular anti-Hanoverianism was ignored the people would turn to Jacobitism:

'If every man in this House were to be silent upon that head, the people without doors would soon find out what tools they were made of: they would soon perceive their being sacrificed to the interests and views of Hanover; and this would render every honest man in the nation not only discontented with our public measures, but disaffected to the illustrious family now upon our throne; the necessary consequence of which would be, that our present constitution must overturn our present establishment, or our present establishment must overturn our present constitution.'

The following month, the Earl of Sandwich called upon the Lords to heed the general voice and oppose a continuation of subsidies to Hanover:

'It may be hoped that these settlements will be adopted, and these resolutions formed by every man who hears, what is echoed through the nation, that the British have been considered as subordinate to their own mercenaries . . . that foreign slaves were exalted above the freemen of Great Britain, even by the King of Great Britain, and that on all occasions, on which one nation could be preferred to the other, the preference was given to the darling Hanoverians.'

In the same debate, the Duke of Marlborough declared:

'It is not possible to mention Hanover, or its inhabitants, in any public place, without putting the whole house into a flame, and hearing on every hand expressions of resentment, threats of revenge or clamours of detestation. Hanover is now become a name which cannot be mentioned without provoking rage and malignity, and interrupting the discourse by a digression of abhorrence.'

Ministerial spokesmen disagreed with the idea of following opinion 'out-of-doors'. James, 13th Earl of Morton, a keen supporter of Walpole, agreed that the continuance of the Hanoverian subsidies was unpopular, but argued that, 'the man who would gain the people's favour by injuring their interest, is not a friend, but a sycophant'.[10]

This attitude, which was seen also in ministerial newspapers, such as the *Daily Gazetteer*, could be said to represent a Whig oligarchical distaste for public opinions.[11] It is equally probable that it reflected a decision to rely on a secure parliamentary majority and not to challenge the opposition in the field of public opinion, upon which opponents were perforce obliged to concentrate. The result was that when the ministry was threatened with serious parliamentary difficulties, in 1730, 1733 and 1741–2, it suffered from its relative neglect of extra-parliamentary lobbying. Had Walpole in 1738–9 been able to orchestrate a campaign of petitions, addresses and instructions from groups or constituencies that feared the loss of their trade with Spain, or in 1733 in praise of the Excise scheme, his political, and in particular his parliamentary, position might have been eased. Such lobbying would not have been easy to achieve. Most of the trade with Old Spain (Spain itself as opposed to the Spanish empire) was controlled by Irish Catholics and Jews, groups of limited political importance in Britain;[12] although Pelham's links with Jewish financiers were to help lead to the Jewish Naturalisation Act of 1753.

However, there are few signs that Walpole made any effort to arrange such lobbying, in contrast with the petitions and Addresses in favour of (as well as against) Lord North's American policy in 1775–6 and of Pitt's legislation in the 1790s. The opposition were far more active. All sorts of opportunities were used in order to disseminate their views. The Addresses from opposition strongholds congratulating George II on his accession in 1727, many of which were printed in the newspapers, criticised ministerial policy, and pressed for the retention of Gibraltar, whose return the government was believed to be considering. Before parliamentary sessions during which they were hopeful of success, the opposition mounted major propaganda campaigns, both to create a sympathetic climate of opinion among the political nation and to influence MPs. The first was done largely by means of the press. MPs were sent petitions for the redress of grievances accompanied by 'instructions' from their constituents, requesting them to vote in a particular way and to bring forward certain resolutions in Parliament.

Particularly vigorous opposition campaigns were mounted in 1733 and 1738–42. Walpole claimed, with some justice, that these campaigns were launched and organised by the opposition, but it is also clear that they reflected a hostility to Walpole's policies that was not confined to the section of the political élite which constituted the opposition. Much of the opposition to the Excise Bill came from the towns and reflected not only the view of many of the merchants, but also of sections of the general population who demonstrated in London, parading wooden shoes, the symbols of supposed French slavery, and mobbing Walpole at the entrance to the Commons.

Opposition politicians and hostile diplomats claimed that Walpole and his government neglected London and were unpopular there. Townshend indeed feared in 1725 that London politics were being neglected because 'Claremont [Newcastle's seat] and Norfolk take up a large share of your Grace's and my brother Walpole's thoughts'. Although Walpole sought to build up support in London, he did not have any particular feel for London politics, still more the ability to woo metropolitan opinion. London took a major role in organising opposition activities in 1733 and 1738–42. The press, both ministerial and opposition, was dominated by London, Scottish and provincial newspapers such as the *York Courant* and the *Newcastle Courant*, being composed largely of items from the London press. The press, therefore, served to spread knowledge of metropolitan developments, and to project the opposition viewpoint throughout the country. London 'instructions' were copied in other constituencies, and in 1732 the *Craftsman*, after reporting the preparation of instructions in London, urged that this practice be emulated elsewhere. Some MPs took note of their constituents' views on political matters. In 1742, Andrew Mitchell, Under-Secretary for Scotland, argued that most of the MPs who voted for the repeal of the Septennial Act 'gave their assent only to please their constituents'. The same year, Thomas Carew, a Tory MP, responded to a public letter from supporters in his Minehead constituency by sending an account of the political situation and his activities that was designed to be communicated to his 'good friends'.[13]

In 1728, Richard Buckner, the estate agent of the Duke of Richmond, wrote from Sussex to his master, then on holiday in Iberia:

'Politics is the only prevailing conversation at present, and there is no company, or set of men of what degree so ever, who does not take upon them to decide matters as peremptorily as if they were at the bottom of the secret . . . They loudly complain of stagnation of trade, the capture of so many merchant ships, the dilatory proceedings of the Congress, and such general topics extracted from the Craftsman and Fog',[14]

. . . the last the titles of the two leading London opposition newspapers. Eleven years later, a medal criticising alleged British cravenness towards Spain circulated in Warwickshire, where it was claimed that 500 were sold. An Edinburgh commentator observed in 1742, 'At present every tailor here is turned politician'.[15]

Work on the 'popular' opposition to Walpole relies primarily on urban evidence. Studies of eighteenth-century towns have revealed that they were of great importance in the creation and definition of political attitudes.[16] However, the extent of their influence over the countryside is difficult to evaluate, particularly as most of the sources for popular political interest and participation, such as newspapers, are of urban origin. Clearly rural, like urban, interest and participation in national politics varied greatly. In 1715, Edward Southwell discerned little interest in the struggle between George I and the Jacobites, and claimed that Somerset and Gloucestershire were, 'like to all Wales perfectly indolent which gets the better the King or the Rebels so as to toss Cross or Pile', presumably a reference to a popular game.[17]

In addition, struggles for local power and patronage, even if expressed in party terms, did not necessarily relate to or have any links with national political struggles. Though numerous urban areas, both large and small, lacked parliamentary representation in the eighteenth century, many of them, however, did have a 'politics' of their own, so that corporation elections, not to mention sundry local building projects, were often fiercely contested. Studies of local politics and of elections do not always reveal the dominance of national concerns. In 1733, John Plumptre, soon to be elected MP for Nottingham, reported from the city to the Duke of Newcastle: 'I do not hear that the Excise Bill has made any great alteration, amongst the freeholders, one way or another; except amongst such of them as are concerned in trade, and such as were wavering from us and grumblers before who now take a handle from it to justify a behaviour which they had been much at a loss to give a reason to.' There was no contest in 1734, the Tories and the Whigs each putting up one candidate only, in order to save expense, an agreement maintained in each general election from 1727 until Nottingham was contested in 1754. In Hull, national politics played little role in local affairs.

On the other hand, Cholmley Turner's 'former actions' as MP, including his support for the Convention of the Pardo, the Septennial Act, the standing army and ministerial fiscal demands, were mentioned or alluded to in public and private attempts to elicit support for the Tory candidate in the Yorkshire by-election in 1741. In 1744, Sir John Cust, pro-government MP for Grantham, was informed by a Lincolnshire protégé: 'In the neighbourhood your voting for the Hanoverians has been . . . represented to ignorant people in very bad colours . . . no pains have been spared to get aright, and it is pretty much so by this time. [18]

There is need for caution in extrapolating from the political culture of print, with its starkly differentiated partisan positions, to that of the localities. It is probable that historians, in concentrating on the fashionable subject of urban studies, have neglected the interests of the bulk of the population, and possible that the stress on urban activities has led to an undervaluation of rural conservatism. There is also the danger that in social and cultural history disproportionate attention has been devoted to urban developments. Most of the obvious manifestations of culture in the early eighteenth century – theatres, subscription concerts, reading rooms, libraries, bookshops, assembly rooms, the growth of the press – were urban, as were many of the schemes for social 'improvement' and/or control: poor relief, welfare provision, crime control and medical improvement. The extent to which rural society shared in their benefits is unclear. The pattern which has emerged from studies of education is suggestive. Towns, especially market towns, advanced in the early eighteenth century while the village poor had few educational resources. By the late eighteenth century, in contrast, country education was generally much better, while the industrialising towns fell sharply back. The countryside was not cut off from the towns; the latter played a major role as markets for the countryside and as centres of, and for, consumption; whilst road links improved with the spread of turnpike trusts by the mid-century. There was less overt competition between urban and rural industry than in many areas of Europe.

It has been argued that the eighteenth century witnessed the development of a consumer society in Britain.[19] Pedlars from towns brought wares to the countryside; rural readers read newspapers, acquiring information about urban opinions, fashions and products. However, it is too easy to assume that rural society responded rapidly or evenly to urban developments, or that rural values and opinions were determined by those of the towns. The *Craftsman* might write of London in 1727 that, 'the eyes of the whole nation are constantly fixed on the conduct and proceedings of this city, as the Primum Mobile of Great Britain', but then the newspaper was printed there.

The electoral system favoured the urban voter disproportionately, particularly if he (the electorate was male) lived in a small borough. The 40 English counties, with an electorate of nearly 160,000, returned only 80 MPs, or one per 2000, whereas the 205 English boroughs, with an electorate of only 101,000, returned 409 MPs, or one for less than 250 voters. Towns with a population of over 10,000 were either under-represented; or, later in the century as more towns grew in size and joined this category, unrepresented, in the sense that their electorate could only vote for county MPs. Political programmes were conceived and debated in London, the largest town, the seat of the Court and the centre of the legislature, executive and judiciary. The public discussion of policy, for example, the contrast between the respective weights in parliamentary and press discussions attached to 'Trade' and the 'Landed Interest' revealed the influence of urban norms, and the political importance of the urban 'cash' economy as opposed to the landed 'wealth' economy. Trade dominated discussion of the economy, and of ministerial policy towards the economy, in an unbalanced fashion, and became a very potent political cause, as Walpole discovered to his cost in 1733 and 1738–9.

The interests of trade and agriculture could not be separated completely, but the latter tended to lack the vocal advocates of the former. Thus, Walpole never received the political credit that he deserved for his pro-agrarian policies of the mid-1730s: the attempt to shift the burden of taxation away from the land tax, and British neutrality in the War of the Polish Succession, which permitted a boom in grain exports to the Mediterranean. The latter was of major benefit for the economy, in terms of specie gained for the nation and aid for the economy of the grain-producing areas. These were depressed as a result of slack domestic demand, caused by the stagnant demographic situation (population) that characterised the age of Walpole, and of low prices caused by good harvests.[20] In comparison, the losses suffered when a few British merchantmen, most of whom had been smuggling, were seized by the

Spaniards in the West Indies were minor, and yet it was these that received attention and became a potent political issue.

It is possible that the urban opposition to Walpole was unrepresentative, first of rural opinion, and, secondly, of feeling in the towns themselves. It is clear that the Excise Bill aroused widespread fears and that Spanish depredations created concern in a few ports, but it is not apparent that this amounted to a sustained, widely-based hostility to the Walpole regime or to the policies of the ministry. In 1733, the Duke of Newcastle found unexpected opposition in Sussex:

'These gentlemen have been in several parts of the county in a body, inflaming the people with the cry of the excise, standing armies, and everything that will serve their turn . . . when I came into the country, I found them universally against the excise, and that the clamours that had been raised upon it, and the supposed consequences of it, had made an impression upon many individuals.'

Nevertheless, he was convinced, with reason, that the ministerial candidates would succeed, while in 1739 he found Sussex 'in very good humour', noting 'hitherto the attempts of the enemy to work them up are unsuccessful'.[21] In 1741, however, supporters of the ministerial candidate in the Yorkshire by-election claimed that the opposition was using the Convention of the Pardo as 'a cant word, adopted without meaning, and echo'd out against the people to inflame and abuse them'.[22]

Many demonstrations of popular concern were episodic, linked to particular grievances that would have caused trouble whoever was in the ministry. This was true of riots based on the economic situation, such as food riots, or the Wiltshire weavers' disturbances, of the riots near Bristol against new turnpike roads in the mid-1730s,[23] and of the Porteous riots in Edinburgh in 1736. The Edinburgh town guard under Captain John Porteous responded to disturbances after Andrew Wilson, a popular smuggler, was executed in 1736. The disturbances were politicized because smuggling was a political (often Jacobite) crime linked to excise and (more generally) 'English' taxes after 1707. Porteous's men fired on the crowd causing fatalities. Porteous was tried, sentenced to death, reprieved and lynched. Walpole was shocked by the riots and angry that the magistrates had done nothing, and he pressed for the reinforcement of the garrison and for firmness.[24] This did not prevent opposition politicians, such as the Tory MP Sir William Wyndham in May 1737, from trying to make political capital out of the riots.[25] Government action against Edinburgh altered its charter, which was against the Act of Union. Claiming that Scotland was being treated like a conquered country, this helped lead the Duke of Argyll into opposition. The Porteous riots were still regarded as sufficiently political for orders against those involved to be reconfirmed in 1746 alongside orders to apprehend Jacobites.

Thomas Hay, writing from Edinburgh in 1742, discerned expressions of discontent at different social levels:

> People here have been of late a little mobbish in different ways the better sort in sowing malicious clamour . . . we have sometimes little poetical satires or comical and satirical pamphlets . . . from London. . . . The lower sort of people sometimes deal in mobbing properly so called. . . . The practice of mobbing ought to be checked. It is not good to accustom the populace to do themselves justice. . . . The abominable practice of raising dead bodies the only cause of the late riots is very provoking which disposes people in general to have some compassion for such a mob as revenged themselves on the persons suspected and therefore upon these occasions matters must be conducted with prudence so as neither to overlook the thing altogether nor to punish the rioters over rigorously. . . . If the inferior magistrates takes good care to punish those villains . . . the populace will discontinue their mobbish practices.[26]

Food riots, such as those in Cornwall in 1727–9 and 1737, North Wales in 1727, and in many areas in 1740, were often against the export of grain from a region where prices were rising and shortages being created in part by the demand from wealthier areas. In 1715, Daniel Dering wrote: 'I have no notion that a crowd of peasants got together can make any resistance against standing regular forces.'[27] However, the attempt to implement the Militia Act of 1757 in Bedfordshire revealed the weakness of the government when faced by a breakdown in law and order. The Lord Lieutenant, John, 4th Duke of Bedford, complained that: '59 men of the Royal Regiment of Horse Guards (which is all the force we have now amongst us) are not sufficient to defend the whole county from the insolence of a riotous rabble.'[28]

Demonstrations of an explicitly political nature were relatively uncommon, except for the semi-ritualised displays of party strength during the elections. The mass of the population may have been concerned about ministerial policy, though there is little evidence on this point, but they did not participate in the political process, either directly by means of voting, or indirectly, by means of extra-parliamentary activity. Some, particularly in the towns, who did not possess the vote, were, nevertheless, willing to attempt to influence the political process. Politics was not the preserve of an oligarchy or a simple matter of patronage. However, to argue that these largely urban elements reflected the whole of extra-parliamentary opinion is mistaken. Were it true it would be difficult to explain how the Whig oligarchy managed to survive, short of postulating some mistaken theory based on coercion. Rather, one could suggest that critical opinion 'out-of-doors' represented the views of a minority; in short, that the Whig oligarchy and its opposition, however widely the latter is defined, were both minorities faced with the apathy, ignorance, poverty and lack of political commitment of the bulk of the population.

Had the Patriot movement or the Tories enjoyed the popular support and emotional dynamic that Methodism was to inspire, they would have presented major threats to the Walpole ministry. That neither did so reflected the strength of religious commitment in a society that was far from secular. Religion was of fundamental importance for ideological, social, political and cultural reasons; norms of conduct and concepts of legitimacy were based on religious ideas. A secular opposition movement therefore stood little chance of gaining widespread popular support for a campaign of political reform and change, unless the government should seek to implement major changes that would have an effect throughout the nation, something the ministry scarcely possessed the machinery to attempt.

In the absence of such moves, opposition political movements were handicapped by their remoteness from the concerns of the bulk of the population and from movements for religious revival, such as the so-called 'Great Awakening' of the eighteenth century which affected Britain, America and Germany. This explains much about the weakness and lack of success of the opposition to Walpole, the Wilkite opposition of the 1760s, the reform movement of the late 1770s and early 1780s, and the opposition to the younger Pitt in the 1790s. However much the opposition might claim to be popular or to reflect the will of the people, neither claim was true. There was no possibility of mobilising a truly radical nationwide popular campaign to bring down the ministry and transform the political system, though the early months of 1780 might be an exception, or of popular resistance to overturn the Whig oligarchy, and the parliamentary opposition did not wish to do either. When, in 1742, Chesterfield reflected on 'popularity which I am convinced will always be against those who are in', he implied that an important distinction existed between dissatisfaction with government and support for a specific alternative.[29]

In the 1732 Commons debate over the ministerial proposal for a revival of the Salt Duty, Edward Vernon, an opposition Whig MP, described the bill as 'only to ease the rich at the expense of the poor', adding that 'ninety nine in a hundred of the people would not put up with the tax, and that he should expect, if he voted for it, to be treated like a polecat and knocked on the head'. Such a method of enforcing the popular will had no influential supporters, although there was concern at the time of the Excise Bill that a small parliamentary majority might lessen chances of popular compliance.[30] Opposition publicists had to be very careful about advocating extra-parliamentary agitation. If, as in November 1742, MPs from constituencies 'whence most violent instructions have been sent' voted in a contrary fashion[31] there was little that could be done to influence their conduct, although on the eve of an election the situation was different, as Walpole discovered to his cost over the Excise scheme.

Royal intervention seemed the sole alternative. The *Craftsman*, in its essay of 6 April 1728, presented the fictional history of the Kingdom of Timbutam in Persia, an allegory of British developments. In this account the rule of the chief minister lasted until royal intervention – 'till the complaints and cries of the people (which were now grown almost universal) reached the Court and pierced the ears of a most indulgent Prince.' Defending Addresses to the monarch, the *Craftsman* of 8 July 1727 claimed: 'The first design of this practice was manifestly to make the Prince regnant acquainted with the genuine sense, and opinions of his People.' In fact neither George I nor George II was willing to heed the 'cries of the people', or of the politicians who argued that Walpole was unpopular. Bolingbroke, although successful in his effort to achieve a personal audience with George I in 1727, failed to persuade him to dismiss Walpole. Stair's attempt in 1733 to influence Queen Caroline against Walpole likewise failed.[32]

The Patriots might claim to represent the people, but they did not wish to increase popular participation in politics and had no real interest in a reform of the electoral system. In part this demonstrated the gap between the 'political nation', centred in London, and the rest of the country. The former was greatly concerned about political questions and prepared to participate in extra-parliamentary action, the latter in general was not. The opposition's failure to bridge this gap was arguably crucial to its fortunes and to the failure of 'Patriotism' as an eighteenth-century movement. However, such an assessment assumes a degree of unity for the opposition that may be misleading. Prominent politicians who wished to manoeuvre themselves into royal and ministerial favour had different objectives from those who had little or no hope of such favour.

STABILITY AND STRIFE

H.T. Dickinson has suggested that: 'political stability did not rest simply on the absence of strife, tension and disputes. It was also the product of a political system that was flexible enough to contain the competing demands of different interests and rival pressure groups'.[33] This is an important point that throws much light on the vexed question of stability. The fact that rival interest groups were willing and able to compete within the system was a source of stability as they did not need to seek to alter the framework. The openness of the parliamentary and government system to lobbying was very significant in this context, as was the fact that most lobbying came from those who possessed power, wealth and status and that these groups were well represented in Parliament and government. However, Dickinson's argument that stability comprehended strife raises the point that standards of tolerable strife could vary.

To appreciate the latter it is necessary to realise that all states in this period possessed a political system that had to cope with disparate and often contrary demands from various pressure groups. In 1773, the French foreign minister told the British envoy: 'that he had an opposition to combat as well as our ministry, and that it should be reciprocally considered that everything could not be done that was desired.' In 1787, the Spanish prime minister, Count Floridablanca, told the British envoy that though Carlos III of Spain: 'had not literally a House of Lords and Commons to satisfy, and a professed opposition to encounter, yet he had also a species of Parliament, a publick, and a discontented party to manage, and that it was not in his power to do in every respect what his inclination might dictate.' In 1733, Cardinal Fleury excused his policies by reference to the force of public opinion.[34]

In this respect, the situation in Britain was similar to that in most of the Continent. The satisfaction of interest groups or the reconciliation of competing groups called for considerable political skills, more so in states, such as Britain, Sweden and the United Provinces, where active representative institutions and a relatively free press enabled the debate over policy to be more public and created additional problems of political management. Walpole possessed these skills and his employment of them played a large role in ensuring political stability during his ministry. He was able to accommodate most of the powerful interest groups in the country, pre-eminently so in the crucial ecclesiastical sphere, where Dissenters and the Church of England were, if not completely contented, at least not placed in a position where they could feel totally defeated. A broadside writer of 1745, allegedly publicising Walpole's will, felt able to suggest that the ex-minister had ordered the engraving on the box that was to contain his embalmed heart of the following lines from Pope's *Essay on Man* (1733):

> For Forms of Government let fools contest,
> Whate'er is best administered, is best:
> For Modes of Faith Act graceless zealots fight;
> His can't be wrong whose life is in the right.[35]

In the political sphere he was less accommodating. Tories did not enjoy many of the fruits of patronage. However, Walpole's policies owed much to Tory ideas, and it was possibly due in part to this, as well as to the unfavourable international situation and the experience of defeat, that Jacobitism was of relatively little importance between the Atterbury Plot and the deterioration of relations with France at the beginning of the 1740s. It was not that support for Jacobitism ceased to exist, but rather that most of the prominent Tories in England proved unwilling to participate actively in Jacobite intrigues in this period. Tories, such as Orrery, sent discouraging reports to the Pretender, informing him that support for the Jacobite cause in England was weak, and that nothing could be done without the assistance of a foreign army.[36] The quiescence of the Jacobites in Britain during the international crisis of 1725–31 and, in particular, on the accession of George II, suggests that the pro-Jacobite Tories did not see any opportunity for action, but also that the Tories were not driven by Walpole's policies to a position of desperation. A master of the art of the politically possible, Walpole understood the position of the Tories and acted accordingly.

Walpole's success raises the general issue of British stability in a period when there was a considerable degree of dissent and occasional unrest. Plumb drew attention to the political changes that helped to create a context for stability, such as the passage of the Septennial Act of 1716 under which it was necessary to have a general election only every seven years.[37] Stair reported from Paris that, 'the passing of this bill for changing the duration of Parliaments gives credit to the King's affairs here and makes them consider the ministry as better established and less precarious'.[38] The Whigs claimed that the previous system, by which, under the Triennial Act of 1694, elections had to be held at least every three years, had led to disorderly elections and the bankruptcy of candidates by frequent expenses. The increasing cost of contesting definitely discouraged some candidates from standing and it appears to have encouraged electoral pacts by which the Whigs and Tories divided the representation to English boroughs and counties, each of which returned two MPs, with the exception of London and Weymouth and Melcombe Regis, each of which returned four. The representation of Knaresborough, for example, was divided between local Whig and Tory interests and the constituency was not contested after the 1715 general election until 1784.

Holmes argued that demographic stagnation and social changes, such as the creation of professional jobs that could help to reduce unemployment among the younger sons of the gentry, helped to create the social stability, without which political stability was not possible. He also drew attention to the demographic and economic conditions that helped to ensure that popular radicalism was limited. Holmes argued that the bulk of the gentry, even when excluded from national power, held back from whipping up popular support against the political system, and were in any case mollified by relative economic prosperity. The same prosperity meant that neither the lower nor the 'middling' orders had grievances serious enough to provoke them into radical political action.[39]

Other historians have questioned the degree of stability. Kenyon drew attention to the violence of public life, and to the weakness of the ministry in the face of public pressure.[40] Colley argued that the proscription of the Tories endangered 'class unity' and produced 'an unprecedented rift in the landed élite – the vital pre-condition of real political instability'.[41] Those scholars who have stressed the importance of Jacobitism have reminded us of a powerful challenge to the Hanoverian system. Cruickshanks drew a distinction between parliamentary stability which, she argued, reflected 'the inability of the Tories to mount an effective and sustained opposition campaign', and the absence of the corresponding political stability outside Parliament.[42] The latter is particularly clear when attention is directed to Jacobitism, Scotland and Ireland. Other scholars drew attention to evidence of popular radicalism and resistance to the policies of the Whig oligarchy.[43]

Clearly an assessment of Walpole's skill in maintaining domestic peace is related to the vexed question of stability. The disorders of the 1740s – the ministerial weakness that led to the fall of Walpole in 1742, the Jacobite rising in 1745, and ministerial divisions and disagreement with the king – would suggest that it is important not to exaggerate the political stability of the period. Under the stress of war, the Walpolean system proved less resilient than it had done hitherto. Equally, the absence of serious radical political pressure from the lower and middling orders in the 1740s, when the political nation was divided and vulnerable, suggests that it would be wrong to regard the preceding Walpolean period as one in which radicalism was suppressed by force or the threat of force. Indeed had there been such a challenge from below in the 1740s it is doubtful whether the non-Jacobite élite could have afforded the luxury of such strong disagreement within itself.

At times, troops were used by Walpole to restore order, particularly in labour disputes when workers had resorted to sometimes quite dramatic violence, such as pulling down houses and mills. The Wiltshire clothworkers of Trowbridge were one group who suffered as a result. The government could also use capital punishment to restore order, one Under-Secretary writing in 1723: "Tis certain the Salisbury Court execution put an end to a great deal of foolish and dangerous rioting; if the Frogs are grown so familiar with the Log, as the fable has it, as to jump upon it again, power must be exerted to let them know their King, and the law that should keep them in awe'.[44] The Log and Stork 'King of the Frogs' fable was frequently used about the Hanoverian Succession.

Nevertheless, continental commentators, such as the Comte de Cambis, French ambassador in 1737–40, were amazed at the extent to which popular disturbances were not punished and law and order were flouted. Given the limited resources for coercion at the disposal of the ministry – there were fewer than 15,000 troops stationed in England – it would have been difficult to suppress widespread popular disturbances. However it was not necessary to do so. Many riots were very specific in their aims, often seeking to fix the price of bread in times of dearth at a level judged acceptable in the popular 'moral economy'. Social inequality was accepted by the bulk of the population, and general attitudes were far more conservative and placid or resigned or apathetic than any concentration on urban radicalism might suggest. British society was predominantly rural; the percentage of the population of England and Wales living in towns of 2,500 inhabitants or more was 18.7 in 1700 and 22.6 in 1750. Until the 1790s there was no need for a coalition of the property-owning classes to defend property and order, if only because the mass of the people saw no way of displacing the existing structures, and did not seek to do so, and even in the 1790s the coalition was far from complete.

The Walpole ministry was not, therefore, placed uneasily upon a seething mass of popular resentment. There were violent popular disturbances, such as those in London in protest against the Gin Act of 1736, an Act that had more effect on the city population than most legislation. However, there were fewer popular disturbances directed against the ministry in England in the 1720s and 1730 than there had been in the 1710s, and violence or the threat of violence played less part in politics than in the late seventeenth century.[45]

Nevertheless, Walpole was concerned about riots, and especially in London. In July 1736, when London workers rioted against the employment of cheaper Irish labour and had to be dispersed by the militia, Walpole wrote to his brother:

I sent several persons both nights to mix with the mob, to learn what their cry and true meaning was, and by all accounts the chief and original grievance is the affair of the Irish, and so understood by the generality of the mob, but in several others, the Gin Act was cried out against, in some few, words of disaffection were thrown out, and one body of men of about eight were led on by a fellow that declared for Liberty and Property. It is said that money was dispersed both nights, but that does not as yet appear to be certain, but although the complaint of the Irish was the first motive, the Jacobites are blending with it all other discontents, endeavouring to stir up the distillers and gin retailers, and to avail themselves of the spirit and fury of the people.

The following month, he reported on the prospects of disorder in London from the Gin Act:

'what seems to me most probable is that the lower sort of brandy-shops, whose poverty secures them from the penalties of the law, may continue to sell in defiance of the law, and in hopes that nobody will think it worth their while to prosecute them, for what they cannot possibly recover'.

In September 1736, troops were deployed in London to prevent planned disturbances over the Act, and Walpole wrote:

'the murmurings and complaints of the common people for want of gin and the great sufferings and losses of the dealers in spiritous liquors in general have created such uneasiness that they will deserve a great deal of attention and consideration, and I am not without my apprehensions that a non-observance of the law, in some, may create great trouble, and a sullen acquiescence and present submission in others, in hopes of gaining redress by Parliament, may lay the foundation of very riotous and mobbish applications when we next meet'.[46]

Walpole's awareness of this public dimension of order and disorder is a necessary counterpoint to any discussion of stability in terms of patronage and parliamentary and electoral management.

6

Walpole and the Press

Much of the battle for public opinion was fought out in the press. The Licensing Act had lapsed in 1695, and, with it, pre-publication controls over newspapers in England and Wales. The consequence had been a major expansion in the press. More newspapers had been founded, new categories – dailies and provincials – had developed, and sales had risen. This had created new issues, opportunities and problems for those involved in public life. Alongside the development of attitudes and strategies that would permit an effective use of the press, there was also the question of how best to respond to the press as an expression of public opinion. Could the latter be defined through the press? How were politicians to respond to press criticism? What was the government to do?

Walpole faced these problems to an unprecedented extent. His was the first ministry that held office for a long period after the lapsing of the Act. There was therefore the question not only of how he would develop a response to the press, but also how newspapers would treat such a novel extent of power. In addition, as a Whig in government, a politician in power, there was the issue of how Walpole would manage the Whig legacy of criticism of authority and help create a new voice of Whiggery. This process was not limited to the press, but newspapers provided a vital register of the shift. Walpole was not the first minister to develop techniques of press management, manipulation and control, but the development of the press and the extent to which both Parliament and the electoral process did not present a regular challenge to the government, made these techniques of particular importance.

'A good Tory will no more dip into a Whig treatise than a Roman Catholic into Tillotson's sermons'. This claim, in the Whig *Flying Post* of 8 January 1713, suggests that had Britain been a bi-partisan society starkly divided by comprehensive party ideologies, then there would have been only a limited role for the press as an agent of persuasion; not that that was its sole role. However, divisions among the Whigs complicated the situation. They forced groups of politicians to support their claims to be the stalwarts of party orthodoxy, and they touched off active quests for support at Westminster and in the political nation. Divisions within party groupings tended to conflate two of the major purposes of the political press, that of persuading non-supporters, not all of whom were opponents, and that of urging supporters to help towards particular goals. The press as an agent of persuasion was particularly important when issues emerged that did not correspond to views already clearly expressed or recently discussed. Such issues required the definition of party views for the benefit of supporters.

The ambiguity of the Whig inheritance was a problem for the Walpole ministry and its defenders. The success of the ministerial Whigs, especially Walpole, in surmounting a series of obstacles – Jacobite conspiracy, the South Sea Bubble, general elections, Whig divisions – and in accommodating various interests – the Hanoverian aspirations of the monarchs, the reversionary interests of George II as Prince of Wales, the ecclesiastical views of the Church of England hierarchy – ensured that these Whigs could consider their political position with less fear of being forced to go into opposition than would otherwise have been the case.

Conversely, those Whigs who went into opposition had to face the problem of attacking a Whig ministry that claimed to represent traditional Whig beliefs, while defining their own position with respect to the Tories. Both ministerial and opposition Whigs sought to assume the identity of Whiggery by claiming its inheritance, a desire that helped to account for the large role played by history in the political essays carried by the press and also the drawing of direct parallels with the situation under Walpole.

Alongside the need of both ministerial and opposition Whigs to assume the mantle of true Whiggery, each group had to defend its particular course and to assume contradictory positions on the definition and role of public opinion in the political system. This process was developed in the press, and encouraged by the intoxicating pressures of newspaper rivalry. The ministerial press, those papers that consistently supported the government, whether subsidised or not, regularly deplored the extent of press comment, claiming that it was seditious in both intent and effect. The opposition press was accused of spreading lies about government policy, and of encouraging faction, an imprecise term by which opposition could be castigated.

Specific accusations directed at opposition newspapers included abetting Jacobitism, and harming foreign policy by revealing secrets and encouraging an image of a divided Britain. The 'Hague Letter' episode of early 1731, when the *Craftsman*, in an item supposedly from The Hague, revealed secret

Anglo-Austrian negotiations, encouraged a particularly marked revival in the ministerial newspapers of the theme of the dangers of press freedom. The success of the *Craftsman*, which was launched by Bolingbroke and Pulteney in 1726, not only in circulation terms but also in becoming a talking point in the political world, helped ensure that, at one level, the struggle between ministerial and opposition press was fought as a debate over press freedom. The *Craftsman* was a non-Jacobite opposition paper that sought to foster co-operation between Tories and opposition Whigs, and to advocate 'Country' policies.

Ministerial newspapers had to reply to the *Craftsman*'s claims that Walpole had abandoned the Whig legacy, but they also found it convenient to defend aspects of government policy, especially foreign policy, by employing the arguments of mysteries of state and royal prerogative. The ministerial press based its constitutional arguments on the sovereignty of Parliament, denying that extra-parliamentary pressures should be heeded and claiming that most of these were manipulated and/or self-interested. The popular appeal of the opposition was not usually denied, but the populace was presented as fickle and foolish.

The nature and value of press criticism was questioned in the ministerial press. The *St James's Journal* of 1 November 1722 claimed that treasonable libels were printed in newspapers in order to increase their sales, while *Applebee's Original Weekly Journal* of 17 November 1722 suggested that the most loyal subjects were those 'that meddle least in public affairs'. The *Whitehall Journal* of 13 November 1722 dealt with liberty of the press by arguing that the liberty to purchase 'sulphur, nitre and arsenic' did not extend to using them for blowing up the Royal Family or mass poisoning. The paper called for 'the silencing of libellers', and condemned not only Tories, but also 'grumbling malcontent scribblers', who sought to gain office. On 26 February 1723, the same paper complained that it could not employ the tone it wished, because the opposition press had given up reason in order to win the people.

These arguments affected the wider perception of the purposes of the Walpole government, although it is unclear how far they should be taken as indicative of his views. Ministerial papers stressed the self-interest of opposition writers,[1] the impossibility of ministerial perfection,[2] the declamatory manner and appeal to the emotions of opposition writing,[3] and their creation of domestic division.[4] A series of papers subsidised by Walpole bitterly attacked the freedom of the opposition press to encourage sedition and/or foreign enemies.[5] Citing Athens and Rome, the *London Journal* of 5 October 1728 claimed that the 'liberty of the press is not essential to a free government'. Some stressed the mercenary nature of opposition writing,[6] others political aspects. The government-subsidised *Free Briton* stated in 1732, 'The writing and publishing of the Hague Letter was an offence against the essential laws of human society'.[7]

The vigour of the opposition press and the government's resort to legal action against it forced the ministerial press to define the reasonable limits of press freedom. Prosecutions led the general debate to become slightly more specific. The *London Journal* distinguished between calumny and accusation. The latter, 'an open, legal charge, to make out which it is necessary to produce witnesses, proofs and evidence', was acceptable, the former, lacking such supports, was not. The *Free Briton* praised 'the sacred rules of public enquiry', but found that 'the spreading of false news is no part of the freedom of the press', adding 'no honest man can defend prosecutions, where opinions offered upon national affairs are proceeded against as criminal; but representations of these affairs are very different points'.[8]

Ministerial papers presented the opposition press as all too effective, both with foreign powers and with a populace 'eager to buy all virulent papers against their superiors'.[9] As a result, they called for restraint on the press,[10] and stressed the absence of any constitutional role for it. The *British Journal* stated in 1727 that it was only reasonable to call a minister, i.e. Walpole, corrupt and evil after he had been condemned by Parliament. The *Daily Gazetteer* stressed the royal prerogative and the position of Parliament as the questioner of policy:

'To suppose that a point of this importance ought to be explained in public prints to every little fellow that asks it, is supposing our government dissolved, and the mob ready to sit in judgment on the legislature'.

At the time of Walpole's fall, the paper suggested 'that there is nothing more useful in a free country than general and moderate discourses on political subjects'.[11] In the view of these pro-Walpole papers, the press had no constitutional role, it was representative only of profit or sedition, and, although the ministry could combat its opinions, it was not necessary to do so. Opposition claims of the corruption of parliamentary representation could be ignored,[12] or matched by questioning the integrity of politicians who sought to stir up the populace. One pamphlet asked, 'Have the authors of a two-penny weekly journal, a right to make a national inquiry?'.[13]

These views were rejected by the opposition press, especially the *Craftsman*. Stressing the liberty of the press as an issue helped to focus interest on the newspaper. This liberty was 'one of the greatest blessings of a free people', 'the chief bulwark and support of liberty in general', 'a point of so essential a nature to the constitution of this kingdom', 'this great bulwark of our constitution'.[14] Walpole could be presented as seeking to suppress the press for sinister motives.[15]

The *Craftsman* presented itself as a defender of 'the public welfare'. There was a need to debate 'the great affairs of peace and war', and the *Craftsman*, 'a pensioner of the people', venal only because it was sold, had the independence to do this.[16] The ministerial press was written off as subsidised, 'a standing army of writers', that included the *British Journal, Daily Courant, Flying Post, Free Briton, Hyp Doctor, London Journal*, and *Weekly Register*.[17] Its political role rendered invalid by corruption, the ministerial press joined Parliament and the Court as an institution unsuited for the expression of free opinion and unable to advise the monarch. Opposition papers claimed that it was a characteristic of arbitrary states to keep the people in ignorance and to prevent them expressing their opinions.[18]

Discussing and contesting the role of the press played a significant part in establishing the views of ministry and opposition on the nature of the political system and the role of public opinion in it. Much was dictated by the exigencies of government and opposition. It was natural for Walpole to try to keep foreign negotiations confidential, and unsurprising that the government should try to censor publications when they were aware of the attempts of Jacobites and foreign powers to disseminate their opinions. Once it was necessary to defend such action, and the bulk of press prosecutions indeed stemmed from these issues, then it is not surprising that the ministerial press developed a general theory hinging on the distinction between liberty and licence. This contrast was a common one in the culture and politics of the period, and central to the wider politics of Walpole and his government.

Arguments for the restriction of press freedom were related to those seeking to limit the role of newspapers and public opinion in the political system, for the more the latter was exalted the less plausible restrictions on press reporting could seem. The relatively high circulation of opposition newspapers fortified their feeling that they represented public opinion, and this encouraged writers sympathetic to Walpole to express doubts about the integrity of a readily manipulated public.

Anti-Walpole writers who urged the importance of public opinion faced the difficulty of explaining the mechanism through which the voice of the public was to be heeded, especially if Parliament was hostile. It was easy for foreign commentators to present Britain as a state ruled by a fickle public opinion, as Chavigny did in the 1730s. In 1738, his Spanish counterpart, Geraldino, claimed that it was difficult to negotiate in Britain, where, he wrote, 'reason and justice could not prevail, unless accommodated to the opinion of the people'.[19]

It was less clear how this opinion was to prevail. The conservative nature of political thought was amply illustrated by the frequency of references to an anticipated royal intervention, either by the Jacobite claimant, or by the reversionary interest, the future George II during the Whig Split, and Frederick Prince of Wales from the late 1730s. The last indeed was a serious threat to Walpole's position. The opposition press was being realistic when it appealed to the monarch, present or future. The two biggest shifts in political fortune in the century, the ushering in of one-party Whig rule in 1714 and its destruction in the early 1760s, were due largely to the personal opinions of Georges I and III. The attack on an evil minister who allegedly misled the monarch could anger the king and even question the royal prerogative of choosing ministers, but a monarch and ministry supported by a loyal Parliament, however corrupt, was difficult to condemn in any other way without rejecting the political system and challenging its social counterpart.

Whatever their limitations, the opposition press was subject to the scrutiny of the Walpole ministry. The resulting action was important in influencing perceptions of Walpole and his methods, and definitely encouraged hostility. Walpole's government concentrated its efforts on the London press, not only because it believed that metropolitan opinion was more significant than that of the provinces, but also as this reflected a correct assessment both of the greater importance and of the greater accessibility to government action of the London over the provincial press. The opposition press indeed boasted of its influence. The first number of the *Universal Spy*, that of 29 April 1732, claimed that 'the great Mr Mist, the patron of journals, has brought us to the democratical state of Athens, to be judges of treaties, and arbitrators of peace and war'.

Ministerial newspapers could scorn these claims, or stress the pernicious strength of opposition papers. The *Flying Post* of 15 December 1730 replied to the *Craftsman*'s boasts of its importance by claiming 'There has nothing happened in the affairs of Europe, but what would have happened if the law had had its effect, and D'Anvers been silenced 3 or 4 years ago . . . The fly upon the chariot wheel!'. The following year, this fly was credited with possessing 'a murmuring trumpet, which blows a political rumour in a few minutes from Berwick to Cornwall'.[20]

Informed repeatedly that the people took their opinions from the press,[21] it was not surprising that politicians, both British and foreign, believed that the newspapers were powerful. Given that historians are uncertain, with reason, as to the influence of the press in Walpole's period, it is understandable that many contemporaries chose to ascribe great influence to this unpredictable, vociferous, constant, politically active, and often politically linked force about which, by modern standards, relatively little was known as to ownership, finances, political linkage and intentions. George Tilson, an Under-Secretary, might feel that opposition propaganda would 'amuse coffee-house politicians, but make little or no impression on people of sense',[22] but others were not so sure, though they tended not to explain how popular attitudes, however defined or quantified, could influence policy.

How far these views influenced Walpole and his colleagues is unclear. By their very nature, the surviving sources tend to stress government intervention in the press. There are memoranda suggesting courses of action, evidence of subsidies paid to particular newspapers, and records of legal action. In State Papers Domestic one does not expect to find preserved letters to ministers saying that newspapers could be ignored. There was no reason to send such letters. Furthermore, as, to a great extent, legal action reflected complaints from domestic informants or foreign envoys,[23] it tends to be evidence of such complaints that survives. There was no systematic reporting by a range of officials on the press that would have permitted accounts that there was nothing to worry about. The same was true of the private correspondence of ministers.

Why then did Walpole subsidise a government and prosecute the opposition press, if newspapers had relatively little direct political impact and a wider effect that was difficult both to assess and to exploit politically? An intuitive answer is that he did so because his predecessors had done so and he might as well do so. The force of habit was very important in eighteenth-century government and once a practice was begun it was rarely discontinued. In addition, Jacobite propaganda encouraged government intervention. Subsidising ministerial papers to counteract the effects of such propaganda could be readily justified. Furthermore, successive ministries were urged to take action by writers keen on subsidies, or by supporters worried about the impact of opposition propaganda.

Ministerial publications were not simply designed to influence the uncommitted, but were also seen as a means of keeping supporters informed. This was seen most clearly in the pamphlets that appeared before each session and set out government policy. Ministerial papers, such as the *Free Briton* in the early 1730s, tended to carry similar items, often extracts from the pamphlets.

Ministerial correspondence suggests that stating the government viewpoint was seen as important, but the anticipated result in terms of persuading readers is obscure. In 1723, Townshend wrote to Walpole concerning:

'the City [of London], where matters appear to be carried with a pretty high hand against the government; and I fear the paper called the *True Briton* is chiefly calculated to animate that ill disposition; however I make no doubt that you will take care to keep the writer within bounds and to have the fallacy of his arguments laid open'.[24]

Whether pieces such as Hoadly's 'Britannicus' essays in the *London Journal* persuaded anyone not hitherto committed of the superior merits of the government case is unclear, but they were also designed to help maintain the cohesion of Walpole's supporters.

Walpole spent far more on the press than the Pelham and Newcastle ministries of the 1750s were to do. William Arnall, author of the *Free Briton*, received £6,000 in 1732–3, and in 1731 the government may have been spending £22,000 annually on subsidising the ministerial press.[25] There was also considerable expenditure on pamphlets, although in 1731 Delafaye wrote that 'never more than 1 or 2 of those pamphlets in a session' that were pro-government 'are ever seen by any person in the administration before they come out in print'.[26] The distribution of pamphlets did not always work out as intended. Henry Goodricke observed in 1732, 'I am thought so much more considerable a person in my own country than I really am, that all the Court pamphlets are sent me from the Post Office gratis, which whets my curiosity to be at the expense of purchasing the answers to them'.[27] A sardonic report in the *York Courant* of 13 March 1739 claimed:

'Within these few days near 20,000 ministerial pamphlets, in defence of the Convention, etc. have been dispersed and given away gratis among the excisemen, custom-house officers, and other officers, civil, ecclesiastical, military etc. which has fallen the price of waste-paper, very considerably'.

Pensions were not only paid to authors to write, but also to dissuade them from so doing: money was spent to neutralise opposition publications. The *London Journal* switched in 1722 from being the platform for John Trenchard and Thomas Gordon's critical 'Cato's Letters' to that for Hoadly's 'Britannicus' essays as a result of government expenditure. Gordon's eventual transfer to the ministerial side was not retarded by appointment as a Commissioner for the Wine Licences. Walpole took a personal interest in the paper when it was run by the government.[28]

Ministerial newspapers could hope to receive advertisements from departments of government (two of the only six advertisements in the *Daily Courant* of 4 September and 9 October 1734), assistance at the Post Office, and benefits to other aspects of their business. Copies of the *Whitehall* and *St James's Evening Post*s were distributed in 1725 from the offices of the Secretaries of State.

Conversely, opposition newspapers had to face the risk of arrest, seizure of papers, detention awaiting trial and legal costs, all potentially as serious as the penalties of a successful prosecution: imprisonment, fines and sureties. Jacobite newspapers were much more severely repressed than their opposition Whig counterparts. The leading newspapers critical of Walpole were able to continue profitable publication despite convictions, but they were much harried. The distribution of a paper could be disrupted. Hawkers did not relish being whipped for crying literature critical of Walpole in the streets. Shopkeepers and others who arranged wholesale and retail sales could not have appreciated imprisonment or other legal action. The sums that printers had to find either as sureties for their appearance in court or fines were often considerable. In addition, the printer could face the arrest of his news gathers, and the arrest and possible suborning of his staff.

Legal action, or the threat of it, certainly had an effect on several papers. A letter in the *Freeholder's Journal* of 31 October 1722 suggested that 'politics are become of late so dangerous a subject to handle', that discussion of them was limited. Charles Delafaye, an Under-Secretary, was congratulated on 'the dulness' of the *True Briton* in 1723. Two years later, Mist announced that he would not print a letter he had received 'as there is a certain person in the world, at present, a little too strong for us'; and the Duke of Wharton, who had exchanged his writing for the *True Briton* for the role of Jacobite diplomat, informed the Austrian government that the cruelty shown so often to British printers had destroyed the freedom of the press. In 1730, Eustace Budgell could not find anyone to handle his anti-Walpole material, while Delafaye 'talked to our Whitehall letter man about his idleness in writing everything he has without better authority for it than towntalk, and he has promised me to be more cautious'. The following year, the *Craftsman* felt unable to print a Spanish declaration critical of Britain and contradicting British ministerial statements 'as we are not yet furnished with sufficient proof to satisfy a court of justice that it was actually delivered'. In 1733, Budgell complained that government intimidation of the booksellers and the printer of his *Bee; or Universal Weekly Pamphlet* was hitting both him and the liberty of the press.[29]

Such restraint might seem to justify claims that Walpole had crushed press freedom. In 1728, the *Craftsman* complained that its circulation was restricted by the Post Office and that the law of libel restrained the press:

> I might add the manner of prosecutions in these cases as a farther restraint on this liberty. The dread of State Messengers, and warrants, which commonly extend not only to the seizure of a man's person, but likewise his papers, even those, which concern his nearest interests and the most secret parts of his life, are sufficient to keep him within the bounds of the law; and, by intimidating booksellers, printers, publishers, etc. frequently derive him of the fruits or design of his labour.

The following year, again on the eve of a parliamentary session, the paper added:

I must however call upon the world to judge whether warrants for seizing persons and papers, without distinction, and even breaking locks, in examinations, commitments and confinement, without liberty of writing, or speaking to any friends in private; whether putting us to the trouble of running about town for bail, upon every taking up, and continuing us, upon divers recognizances (to a very great sum) for almost three years together; whether the expense of several trials, and of preparing for several others, which is near the same; not to say anything of intimidating booksellers, printers and publishers, by these means, and endeavouring to stop the propagation of our papers, by a particular prohibition at the Post-Office. . .

In 1733, a poem dedicated to Pulteney attacked the interpretation of innuendoes in order to establish guilt and condemned jurors for failing 'to stem the tide of oppression'. Seven years later, the Earl of Marchmont thought it worth detailing the treatment of the press in his appeal to the electorate for the forthcoming general election:

If it so happens that a prosecution is resolved on, how is he then proceeded against? Not by a Bill of Indictment brought against him before a Grand Jury; by whom, if it was not found, he would be immediately acquitted without further cost, but by a novel (and I will say a very oppressive) manner of proceeding. An Information is filed against him by the Attorney General, and, if ever so innocent, he must be at the expense of a trial, perhaps destructive to himself and family, as no costs can be given him where the Crown is made a party. Is not the former part of the foregoing instance an unwarrantable strain of power? Is not the latter, though pretended to be not illegal, extremely grievous, and liable to the most dangerous abuse? Will not a treatment of this kind be sufficient to deter a printer from venturing on the publication of any thing, which may thus expose him to the resentment of those in power? And will not the Public by these practices be most effectually deprived of all information which by this means only can be conveyed to them?[30]

Alongside the resilience of the *Craftsman* must be placed the opposition claim that governmental powers restricted their activities. Such powers did not prevent the development of new flourishing opposition papers, such as *Common Sense* and the *Champion*, but they were used with success against a number of Jacobite papers. Mist was forced to flee to France, from where he continued to run his paper. However, all his men tried in 1729 were found guilty 'tho' by a Tory jury'.[31] A lower rate of success attended moves against less clearly seditious papers.

Walpole was careful in his prosecutions. In 1724, Thomas Payne was fined £400 and sentenced to a year in prison for publishing the *True Briton*. However, Walpole had denied Wharton the publicity of a trial, the Sacheverell and Oxford (Harley) trials having induced a degree of caution over trying prominent individuals, and indeed there was little attempt to follow up judicially the identity of authors. This would have been difficult, but printers could have been persuaded to testify. Instead, ministries chose to attack the printers and publishers.[32]

In dealing with less clearly seditious papers, ministries were in a weaker position. It was not so easy to secure widespread support for legal action, and there were more doubts about the likelihood of securing convictions. Widespread support was important not simply from the point of view of juries, but because successive ministries wished to maintain their Whig credentials. The unsuccessful prosecution of Richard Francklin, the publisher of the *Craftsman*, in November 1729 was not an encouraging precedent. An opponent reported Walpole's response: 'The Great One cannot speak with decency, of either trial, judge, or jury'. Though the problem of recalcitrant London jurors, which had played a significant role in the 1729 case, was remedied by the Juries Act of 1730, permitting judges to appoint special juries, the publicity the *Craftsman* had earned in 1729 was a warning against making a *cause célèbre* for a second time.[33] A ministerial pamphlet of 1731 claimed that Walpole had:

'abused his power, in suffering a libel to be published weekly for near five years together, and dispersed with all imaginable diligence and industry, not only in all the counties and towns of England, but in several other parts of Europe, which was continually stuffed with the most gross and groundless invectives, the most daring and impudent falsehoods'.[34]

It is possible that had the *Craftsman* avoided the sensitive area of negotiations in progress and maintained its more generalised criticism of government policy, the ministry would not have brought the paper to court again, as it did successfully over the Hague Letter of 1731.

The threat of prosecution forced newspapers to adopt an allusive style and an allegorical approach, rich in innuendo and coded words and letters. To that extent, it fulfilled one of the principal purposes of censorship, namely ensuring that pre-publication self-regulation avoided the need for costly and embarrassing government action. This, rather than occasional spectacular trials, was the essential element of the censorship system; but it could not prevent a highly abusive opposition press. The Walpole ministry did not attempt to harass papers such as the *London Evening Post* or the *Craftsman* as they had harassed the Jacobite press, and Delafaye admitted in 1732, 'We can not govern authors and printers'.[35]

There were occasional suggestions, probably produced by no more than irritation, that tougher action would be taken unless the press moderated itself. There were accusations in 1737, at the time of the introduction of the Stage Licensing Act, that the ministry intended to extend pre-publication censorship to the press, but these were unfounded. The publicity that several prohibited plays enjoyed and the size of the editions of their scripts that were successfully rushed into print were not a good advertisement for the impact of censorship, but there was a surprising lack of opposition to the principle of censorship of the stage and, by 1745, the theatre had largely withdrawn from politics, its opposition to the Act silenced.[36]

All newspapers were affected by the Second Stamp Act passed in 1725. This closed loopholes left by the First Act of 1712, which had introduced taxation of the press, and, in particular, encouraged papers to restrict their length to four pages. Had Walpole tried to extend censorship to the press he would have found it difficult. Policing a small number of theatres was far easier than supervising the activities of a large number of presses, and the immediacy expected from news would have posed a major problem for any system of pre-publication censorship. In the mid-1720s opposition material had been printed on a press in the London house of the Duke of Bedford.[37] The prospect of raiding such houses would not have appealed to Walpole. It would have violated an implicit principle of press regulation, namely that it entailed punishments for printers, not politicians.

In 1739, the British government intercepted a letter from the Dutch foreign minister, Fagel, to his envoy in London, both experienced commentators on British politics:

'Certainly the manner in which he [Walpole] is abused, exceeds all bounds and is an abuse of the liberty of the press which ought not to be suffered, for many of those writings very much savour of sedition . . . can produce nothing but great hatred and divisions that cannot fail being prejudicial to the public welfare: However the remedy is not easy to be found out, because the evil is in the minds, and it seems passions have got the upper hand'.[38]

At the same time, juries had supported the ministry in prominent trials inspired by *Mist's Weekly Journal* and the *Craftsman* in 1729 and 1731 respectively, and in 1740 a pamphleteer claimed 'I have known many an honest Englishman laugh, and extremely fond to read a paper, who, if he had been upon the jury that was to try the author, would have voted for his losing his ears for his impudence'.[39] Certainly, when, as acting Secretary of State, Walpole was responsible for moves against the *True Briton*, he had met with success. He also survived the great press assault of the late 1720s and early 1730s, which was part of a general failure of opposition. Walpole was not overthrown in, or as a result of, the Excise crisis, and the electoral challenge in 1734 was beaten.

The ideal of a united opposition 'Country' party collapsed, as opposition Whigs and Tories clashed in 1734–6 over foreign policy and ecclesiastical issues, and its progenitor, Bolingbroke, retired to France.

These developments had their echo in the press. Mist returned to London in 1736 and made his peace with the ministry, and an attempt to keep *Fog's Weekly Journal* going as an opposition paper under different ownership ended in failure. The *Craftsman*'s circulation fell and it headed towards internal division. Stair complained to Sarah, Duchess of Marlborough in 1737 that the issues 'have had nothing in them a great while'.[40]

A fresh press assault was to be launched in Walpole's last years as minister, especially in *Common Sense* and the *Champion*,[41] but the Walpole ministry had not given up surveillance of the press. In 1740, John Meres, the printer of the *Daily Post* and the *London Evening Post*, was arrested and then released with a warning about his conduct of the latter.[42] Walpole was not alone in feeling that opposition writings were less impressive (and certainly less original) than those in 1726–33.[43] However, the opposition was better able to exploit the issue of national honour than it had done in the late 1720s. There are many diplomatic and political reasons which help to account for this, but there is no doubt that the opposition campaign of 1738–9 was more sustained, popular and effective than the attack on foreign policy in the late 1720s. The extent of the popularity of the opposition case may be queried, but there was no countervailing popular support for the ministerial policy, a feature reflected in the manner in which government papers, such as the *Daily Gazetteer*, and ministerial politicians attacked the role being claimed for public opinion.

In the 1720s and early 1730s, ministerial speakers and newspapers had condemned the ease with which the opposition could manipulate opinion, but they had been, on the whole, cautious about attacking the role of public opinion. In the late 1730s there was a discernible shift. In particular, the *Daily Gazetteer*, the leading pro-government publicity organ in the latter years of the Walpole ministry, betrayed a deep suspicion of the public's interest in politics. The long-standing power of the Walpole ministry had produced a political ideology that was different in character to the concepts moulded during an alteration of power and opposition.

Furthermore, the ministry was no longer replying to opposition criticisms with the energy, skill and success it had displayed a decade earlier: it found it harder to persuade people that it was defending national honour and interests. It is difficult to say whether this was cause or effect (or both) of Walpole's apparently increasing reliance on his parliamentary majority. To a certain extent, Walpole had lost the propaganda battle. Ministerial apologists were correct in arguing that the opposition did not enjoy the support of the bulk of the population, but the ministerial failure to sway metropolitan opinion was of great importance in enabling the opposition to represent itself as the voice of the political nation. Such a failure cannot be seen as a matter of press regulation. Instead, it makes sense only in the context of Walpole's policies. In turning to them, we are reminding ourselves that issues of image and perception rested on a solid kernel of legislation and administration, policy and its criticism.

7

Policies

Emphasising the means by which power was retained and debated should not detract attention from the role of Walpole's policies. Again, there are problems of prioritisation. Should the emphasis be on finance or religion, diplomacy or the British dimension? Should it be on containment – the response to and survival of challenges – or on attempts to change circumstances? Furthermore, there are problems in attributing policy initiatives and also in distinguishing particular departures amidst the practices of government. This chapter begins with the re-active policies before turning to their pro-active counterparts, although, of course, there was no clear-cut distinction between them. Nevertheless, a focus on the former, some of which have already been covered from one angle in the treatment of patronage, is a reminder that the degree of initiative enjoyed by the ministry was limited.

WALPOLE AND THE TORIES

Policies were shaped by Walpole's response to the challenge of Toryism. Unlike Harley, the leading Tory minister in 1710–14, Walpole condemned the idea of a mixed ministry. When, in 1723, Bolingbroke proposed one to him, Walpole 'answered it was both impossible and unadvisable for me to enter into any such negotiation'. That summer, Townshend wrote to Walpole about another approach for a mixed ministry: 'I think the manner in which you received Lord Kinnoull's overtures was exactly right, since nothing can be more dangerous than to enter into negotiations with the Tories, or even to labour under the suspicion of it at this time'. Walpole argued that the Tories were sympathetic to the Jacobite cause.[1]

This remained Walpole's attitude throughout his ministry. He was convinced that Jacobitism was a serious threat and that the Tories were willing to support the Jacobite cause. The extent to which this was true has been debated by historians without any generally accepted conclusion being reached. It has been argued that Jacobitism was a popular force after 1715, and it is certainly true that the Jacobites continued to conspire and also sought foreign assistance. There was more to Jacobitism than the drinking of 'treasonable healths'.[2]

Jacobitism seemed particularly threatening when Britain was opposed by states able to mount an invasion, as in 1725–7 when relations with Austria and Spain were particularly poor, and in 1731 and 1733–5 when war with France seemed a prospect. Conversely, when international relations were calmer, as in 1723 and 1736–7, then the situation appeared less threatening. Any judgement of the extent of the Jacobite challenge has to be related to the particular conjuncture.

There was considerable anxiety about Jacobitism and it was of political importance. 'The History of the Norfolk Steward', an account of Walpole published in the *Craftsman* on 2 September 1727, claimed that the Steward used Squire Welsh [James III] in order to frighten the people, and this was also a theme of opposition parliamentarians, such as Pulteney in December 1740. Walpole rejected such attempts to minimise the threat. He established a most efficient network to spy on the Jacobites, especially by intercepting their messages, and was aware that they could become a very serious threat, given sufficient foreign assistance.[3] Walpole also used diplomats to help with the 'secret intelligences' he ran. In November 1733, he wrote to Waldegrave, 'I cannot but think in this time of general commotion, all offers are to be entertained, which can possibly tend to any discoveries'.[4] The assumption that politics was essentially a struggle between Jacobites and supporters of the Protestant Succession was criticised by Walpole's opponents, but was not held by the minister alone. Indeed, it was a powerful basis of Whig loyalty that helped to tarnish opposition Whigs, such as Walpole himself in the late 1710s. Walpole's opposition to any idea of a mixed ministry was well known:

'Mr Walpole is against admitting any of the Tories into the ministry or places of public trust. He thinks the first will be spies upon them to their own party, and the last will betray them on the first favourable occasion'.[5]

However, though determined to prevent the Tories from gaining power, Walpole, when in office, followed policies that did not challenge Tory views excessively. Walpole's policies contrasted with the alarmist Tory propaganda concerning Whig intentions that had been produced from 1714 onwards. There was no comparison between Walpole's policies and those attributed to the Whigs in such Tory tracts as Francis Atterbury's *English Advice to the Freeholders of England* (1715). Walpole's policies were convergent, not divergent: there was a Walpolean consensus politics.

His foreign policy, with its stress on minimising foreign commitments and thus ending the need for subsidy treaties with foreign states and enabling the ministry to reduce taxation, corresponded with traditional Tory notions. In 1723, Walpole responded to an apparent Baltic crisis by writing 'my Politics are to keep free from all engagements as long as we possibly can'.[6] Chavigny claimed in 1734 that Walpole and the opposition shared common views on foreign policy. Two years later, he reported a conversation with Walpole in which the latter expressed delight that he was free of the bad system that Stanhope had left him with and that Britain was no longer closely involved in European affairs. These were views that the Tories could accept. In 1718, the ministerial MP, Sir David Dalrymple, claimed that the opposition through their 'enmity to the Government have wrought up this nation to a hatred of war though unavoidable and the country gentlemen . . . cry out against taxes'.[7]

That year, when in opposition, Walpole had joined with the Tories in attacking both the Quadruple Alliance, by which Britain had become closely involved in Italian politics, and the dispatch of a fleet to the Mediterranean to protect the Austrian position in Italy against Spanish attack. In 1732, 1733 and 1734,when the Austrians pressed the Walpole ministry to send a fleet to prevent a similar attack, which materialised in 1733 and was developed in 1734, no ships were sent. Similarly the Walpole ministry resisted pressure to become involved first in the contested election of 1733 for the throne of Poland and then in the subsequent War of the Polish Succession of 1733–5. In this respect Walpole's stance corresponded more closely with that of the Tories than it did either with some of his ministerial colleagues or with the group of opposition Whigs led by Pulteney, both of which sought intervention in the war on the Austrian side. War was seen by Walpole as a threat to the political order.[8]

RELIGIOUS POLITICS

The Tory party tended to see itself as the defender of the Anglican Church, threatened by the Dissenters and their political allies the Whigs. The strength of religious feeling and the continued vitality of religious divisions in early eighteenth-century Europe must not be underestimated, and Britain, as in so much else, was no exception to the usual European situation. Religious divisions played a major role in late seventeenth-century politics and had been largely responsible for the bitterness of the party struggle between the Whigs and Tories.[9] Walpole's refusal to legislate in favour of the Dissenters played a major role in reducing the political consequences of religious differences and in encouraging the strengthening of Whig Anglicanism. In 1718, when in opposition, he spoke vigorously in defence of the position of the Church of England and this became his policy when in office. Walpole pointed out to Tories, such as Edward Harley, that he took 'care of the Church'.[10] After 1719

Sir Robert Walpole, 1st Earl of Orford (1676–1745) *by* Michael Dahl (1656–1743)
(*Wakefield Museums and Galleries/Bridgeman Art Library*)

Rebuilt after 1720, Houghton Hall could accommodate over 100 guests at an hour's notice. From the painting by Jean Marc Winckler, by kind permission of Lord Cholmondely

(Photograph courtesy of Jarrold Publishing, Norwich)

George II (1683–1760, succeeded 1727) *by* Charles Jervas (1675?–1739) *(Guildhall Art Gallery/Bridgeman Art Library)*

Sarah, Duchess of Marlborough, after Maria Verelst, 1823 *by* William Darby (1786–1847) *(Wallace Collection/Bridgeman Art Library)*

'Chairing the Member'. Politics in the Age of Enlightenment could be a rough business, as this satirical painting by Hogarth (1697–1764) shows

(By courtesy of the Trustees of Sir John Soane's Museum)

Secretary of State, Charles, 2nd Viscount Townshend (1674–1738), known as 'Turnip' Townshend, was Walpole's brother-in-law. Artist unknown

(National Portrait Gallery)

Tory clergyman and satirist, Jonathan Swift, 1718 *by* Charles Jervas (1675?–1739)

(National Portrait Gallery)

Spencer Compton, 1710 *by* Sir
Godfrey Kneller (1646–1723).
'Lack of political skills' did not
prevent his ennoblement as Earl
of Wilmington in 1727
        (*National Portrait Gallery*)

'Sir Robert Walpole Addressing his Cabinet'
by Joseph Goupy (*c.* 1680–1768)
        (*British Museum/Bridgeman Art Library*)

John Campbell, 2nd Duke of Argyll and
Duke of Greenwich, 1725 *by* William
Aikman (1682–1731) 'managed Scotland'
for Walpole
        (*National Portrait Gallery*)

the Whigs dropped Church reform and relief for Dissenters from their legislative programme. In 1736, Walpole opposed repeal of the Test Act, although he was careful not to criticise the Dissenters.

The political difficulties that arose in 1736 when Church issues were again widely debated in Parliament confirmed the wisdom of the policy for the intervening years, as did the tension created by earlier attempts by anti-clerical Whigs to pass reform measures.[11] Walpole preferred to manage the Church and universities by means of patronage, rather than by legislation and administrative innovation. Filling vacant bishoprics was a more congenial form of management, and the staunchly Anglican Whig Lord Perceval was able to write in 1722: 'When a few more of the Dignitaries drop off and a little care shall be taken of the Universities, we may hope to see a thorough change in the clergy, and then they will recover the esteem which they have forfeited through the misbehaviour of too many yet remaining among them.' Five years later, a Jacobite complained that the ministry had the support of all the bishops that attended Parliament.[12]

The cry of 'the Church in danger' was heard less frequently in the 1720s and early 1730s, when an effective co-operation between Walpole and the most influential cleric, Bishop Gibson of London, replaced the tension between the Stanhope–Sunderland ministry and Archbishop Wake. In 1751, a Dissenter wrote: 'the generality of the Bench have learnt of Sir Robert Walpole to regard and insist on the Act of Toleration as the Boundary between the Established Church, and the Dissenters . . . no favour is to be expected either from the Government or their Lordships beyond what that Act by a fair construction entitles us to'.[13]

Commercial lobbies were matched by religious pressure groups.[14] The episcopacy enjoyed ready access to the corridors of power, and did not need to resort to extra-parliamentary campaigns.[15] Furthermore the uneasy relationship between the predominantly Whig and pro-ministerial episcopacy, and the largely Tory parochial clergy, a relationship which had led to the prorogation in 1717 of Convocation, the clerical Parliament, could not have encouraged the higher clergy to instigate such campaigns.[16] The Societies for the Reformation of Manners, institutions which indicated the strength and social awareness of Anglican piety, could have been used to exert pressure, but the episcopacy preferred to trust to their more reliable links with the Whig ministry. Such links did not preclude religious campaigns, such as that which Gibson mounted in the 1730s in his diocese of London, but they made them dependent on leadership from the top.

If the Church of England had operated in a different fashion it is possible that the explosion of popular piety associated with John Wesley and the Methodist movement he launched in the late 1730s could have been contained within the Church. John and Charles Wesley remained members of the Church of England all their lives and in 1756 the Methodist conference ended with a strong declaration by the Wesleys of their determination 'to live and die in the communion of the Church of England'. The ferment associated with Methodism, a tiny movement in the 1730s and 1740s but one that was to grow rapidly, indicated the strength of religious feeling among large sections of the community, particularly in the growing industrial communities and among the poor, groups unevenly served by the Church of England. Methodism rose to a certain extent on the ashes of Jacobitism, gaining support from much of the same constituency. The methods used by the Methodists – field preaching, itinerant lay preachers, and a cellular organisation based on the class, a group which met weekly, helped to channel their dynamism into an effective structure.[17] In eighteenth-century France, particularly in Paris, popular piety created major difficulties for the government.[18] Methodism did not present the same problems in Britain. Avoiding the radical implications of his preaching of the equality of all believers, John Wesley preached that the social hierarchy was divinely ordained. Autocratic by temperament, Wesley had no time for democracy.

Possibly Methodism helped to secure the social, if not the religious, stability of eighteenth-century Britain. Methodism can be viewed as a substitute for revolution, promising Salvation and a personal assurance of grace as an escape from an engagement with this-worldly struggles. The major problem with such an analysis is that there is scant evidence, particularly for the first half of the century, that Britain was teetering on the brink of revolution, or that, if it was, Methodism was influential enough to prevent it. Despite, by modern standards, appalling social and economic inequalities and atrocious living conditions for a sizeable percentage of the population, revolutionary ideology was largely absent. The view that Methodism acted as a lightning conductor for the socio-economic strains present in society, and growing as a result of agrarian and industrial change, founders on the absence of indications of a widespread disenchantment with the system, and the absence of such indications can make talk of appalling conditions and inequalities appear anachronistic and heavily value-laden.

Methodism did not operate as a lobby – Wesley having very few links with the Whig establishment and indeed, at one level, having Tory and Jacobite sympathies and being in revolt against it – but the Dissenting denominations sought to exploit their links with the Whigs. The Quakers, their activities co-ordinated by a permanent central committee, succeeded in securing amendments to legislation allowing them to affirm rather than to swear oaths, and in 1736 came close to obtaining a Tithe Act which would have removed the threat of prosecution for the non-payment of tithes. The Dissenters set up in 1727 a joint committee of ministers to concert pressure in favour of Indemnity Acts to allow them to hold office without taking the sacrament in the Church of England. Acts were passed accordingly in 1727–9, 1731 and 1733–43. They also established a lay organisation – the Dissenting Deputies – which sought to secure the repeal of the Test and Corporation Acts, and mounted major lobbying campaigns among parliamentarians in 1736 and 1739. They failed, Walpole warning the Commons that it must 'consider what was the opinion of people without doors, especially the Church'. Allegations that the Deputies were in Walpole's pocket have been refuted.[19] However, to some extent, the Whigs fuelled the expectations of Dissenters. In 1734, Walpole and Queen Caroline asked Hoadly to use his influence with Dissenters to persuade them to withdraw their demands for relief.

The Dissenters' success in achieving a serious parliamentary discussion of their interests reflected the openness of the political system to effective lobbying, as their achievement was disproportionate to their numerical strength. At the same time, Walpole's willingness to secure £1000 per annum in 1723 for the widows of Dissenting ministers, to support Indemnity Acts and to oppose the repeal of the Test and Corporation Acts, was typical of the balancing conciliatory nature of his political art and also revealed much about his ecclesiastical policy. In 1751, his brother Horatio wrote:

> the late Lord Townshend and my Brother laid it down as a fundamental principle in their management of affairs . . . not to suffer any religious dispute to be canvassed in Parliament, or any attempt to be made, if they could prevent it, being sensible that, however reasonable and conciliating any proposition might be to make a stricter union and harmony among all Protestants well affected to the Government, yet the High Church party that is disaffected is so numerous, and warm and ready to lay hold of any occasion to inflame the nation, that any alteration in the form of doctrine of the Church of England would be, although in itself desirable, and right, and perhaps trivial, a dangerous attempt, as productive of greater troubles, than the good expected from it could compensate.[20]

Walpole's ecclesiastical policy helped to lessen political tension, though the Tories remained concerned over the position of the Dissenters, and, against Tory wishes, there was no reintroduction of the Occasional Conformity Act. Furthermore, the Whig monopoly of higher clerical positions and the promotion of clerics judged heterodox by the Tories aroused fury. In the Church, Walpole's policies were hindered because he was too exclusive in his use of patronage for the higher positions. Walpole did not accommodate ambitious moderate Tories such as Thomas Sherlock. Benjamin Hoadly, a low-churchman long dreaded by the high-Church faction as intending to level all barriers between the Church and Dissent, had his party zeal rewarded successively with the bishoprics of Bangor (1715), Hereford (1721), Salisbury (1723) and Winchester (1734). In his dioceses, Hoadly promoted many who seemed overly heterodox to the Tories, and not without success, for, in his Winchester diocese, Hoadly's policy of giving patronage to Low Churchmen and breaking down the barriers with Dissent had the effect of comprehending them in Church. However, it is necessary to be cautious about arguing from Hoadly's promotion to Walpole's policies. In 1723, Townshend wrote to Walpole revealing the attitudes of the two to ecclesiastical politics and the number of interests that had to be reconciled:

> I agree with you in opinion as to the character and inclinations of the present Bishop of Salisbury, but as he is well with the King (of which I had a late instance) and in high reputation with the mob of the Whig party, I think it will be very impolitic, at the same time that so much power is put into his hands, to sour him by refusing him the feather of Closet-Keeper. Let his present inclinations towards us be what they will I am confident his very weaknesses make him easy to be gained. Besides that I take the Deanery of the Chapel to be in reality the more important post of the two, and more proper for the Bishop of London to whose see it more naturally belongs.[21]

Walpole did not strike commentators as especially religious and his attitude offended many. Richard Wilkes, a Staffordshire doctor, noted in his diary: 'There never was . . . in this nation a set of men who laughed so much at religion . . . as Sir Robert Walpole and his hirelings have done'. Walpole's faith was certainly not intellectual. His son Horace recorded in 1750 that the new Bishop of Durham [Joseph Butler] was 'a metaphysical author, much patronised by the late Queen: she never could make my father read his book . . . he told her, his religion was fixed, and that he did not want to change or improve it.'[22] The role of political, especially parliamentary, rather than religious, considerations in church appointments can be seen in a letter written in 1743 by Newcastle to Carteret, then with George II in the Empire (Germany). Newcastle was Recorder of Nottingham:

> I am again to trouble your Lordship with relation to a living which is vacant, and in His Majesty's gift. I mean the Vicarage of Claybrooke in Leicestershire. I send your Lordship inclosed an application from the Mayor and Aldermen of Nottingham on behalf of Mr Hutchinson, a gentleman of one of the first families in that county, and whose brother has an estate there of upwards of £2,000 a year. The Gentleman himself is extremely well qualified in every respect, and most zealous for His Majesty's interest. I

humbly hope His Majesty will be so good, as to confer this living upon him. and that the more, as the town of Nottingham, and the City of Bristol were the only towns in all England, that sent up contrary Instructions to their Members, and this present mark of favour to the Corporation of Nottingham will be extremely well received, and may soon have a good effect: Mr Warren, one of their present members, and a very violent Tory, is so ill, that it is thought he cannot last many weeks: and I am persuaded, that, in case of his death, we shall have a very zealous, and a very good Whig chosen in his room.[23]

In the late 1730s, renewed pressure from the Dissenters, and the breakdown of the alliance with Gibson, due to a clash over religious patronage and differences over the tithe question, created difficulties. However, there was no resumption of the Stanhope–Sunderland programme of repeal and Walpole took care not to support the Dissenters excessively, with the one important exception of the Tithe Bill of 1736, to which he underestimated the likely opposition. Walpole was genuinely shaken by the clergy's attack (unforgivably, in his view, supported and articulated by Gibson), the one time he almost forgot the lesson of Sacheverell and provoked clergy-led popular Toryism. Gibson was passed over in the succession to Wake at Canterbury. However, Walpole was unwilling to support repeal of the Test and Corporation Acts. His policy in the crisis of 1718 prefigured his subsequent policy.

The ministry's decision in 1718–19 to drop the proposed legislation in favour of the Dissenters, particularly that pertaining to the corporations, removed a substantial challenge to the control of the Tory gentry over much of provincial England. Such a challenge, reminiscent in some ways of late Stuart policies (Walpole in 1718 compared government schemes with those of James II, who had created alarm by his pro-Dissenter policy), was not to be repeated. The merest suggestion that the envisaged extension of the Excise legislation in 1733 would lead to the imposition of a new level of central government control provoked strong opposition. The largely undisturbed government of Britain's localities in the age of Walpole was one of the most characteristic features of the period. It was also part of the unstated relationship between Walpole and the political community that helped to produce, and was itself the product of, stability.

TAXATION

Taxation was explicitly part of a government strategy to maintain order and lessen support for opposition. In 1732, Newcastle painted an optimistic prospect and was confident that it would continue, 'considering how great an ease has, in this session, been given to the people with regard to their taxes, and that the produce of the Sinking Fund will, in the compass of a few years, greatly reduce the debt of the nation'.[24] The Excise proposals of 1733, withdrawn in response to a storm of parliamentary and press criticism, were (ironically) part of a fiscal strategy that reflected Walpole's desire to woo rural political opinion, much of which was Tory. He hoped to transfer the bulk of taxation from land – the land tax – to consumption. From 1722 to 1726, in 1730, and again from 1733–9, Walpole was able to keep the land tax down to two shillings (ten pence in today's money) in the pound, and in 1731 and 1732 he managed to cut it to one shilling. In 1737, the government defended its taxation policy on the grounds that it was wrong to over-load the landed interest. When the land tax rose in 1727, in order to finance the military expenditure created by a cold war with Austria and Spain, a Jacobite observed 'the four shillings in the pound does affect the landed men'. In contrast, John Selwyn, an MP close to Walpole, was sceptical about the opposition's chances in 1730: 'two shillings per pound and no more will stop a great deal of clamour. That argument is felt more sensibly than the righteous reasoning of a Patriot'.[25]

Since the assessments for the land tax were largely traditional ones, not reflecting the current value of property, low rates of taxation were a double concession to the landed groups – that is, the politically vital groups – in society. This policy was helped by peace and by Walpole's astute handling of the National Debt, but it depended on an ability to raise indirect taxation. In 1732, Walpole reintroduced the Salt Duty which he had abolished two years earlier. He argued that it was a fair tax as nearly everyone contributed to it: the opposition speakers retorted that the poor had to spend a larger proportion of their income to pay the duty.

The following year, Walpole proposed to extend the Excise to wine and tobacco. His failure to do so reflected the opposition's success in exploiting largely misplaced fears concerning the intention and consequences of the scheme, though Excise was always unpopular. Walpole himself regarded the scheme as simply another technical financial measure similar to many that were passed regularly by the ministry. He was confident that Parliament would support the scheme and was unable to understand the public outcry that it aroused.

A pro-government song, produced for the 1734 general election, explicitly contrasted the rural interest with opposition to the Excise:

> Freeholders and tenants draw near
> . . .
> Next year every man that has ground
> Four shillings must pay in the pound,

All this must be done,
That knaves may cheat on

. . .

We farmers must toil, and must sweat,
All the hard bread of carefulness eat,
That smugglers may thrive,
Nay in luxury live

. . .

No exciseman their shops must come nigh
Least their tricks and abuses he spy

. . .

Brave boys there's but this to be done,
And that's at the next election
We must choose men of land,
Who by farmers will stand.[26]

WALPOLE AND THE LOCALITIES

The willingness of the ministry to allow local landowners to rule their localities contrasted with developments in certain other states in Europe. Although it is now widely accepted that 'absolutism' is a misnomer when used to describe European states in the period 1650–1750 and that the governments of these states did not seek to destroy aristocratic power, it is nevertheless true that some states, particularly Prussia, Russia and Sardinia, and in the later eighteenth century, Austria, witnessed serious attempts to extend central control of the localities, partly by means of enrolling the aristocracy in the service of the state. In late-seventeenth century Britain there had been intimations of a similar policy. However, the eighteenth century witnessed an extraordinary divergence between on the one hand the remarkable growth and increased sophistication of central government agencies, particularly the navy, the state fiscal system (the most sophisticated in Europe) and the Excise,[27] and on the other the manner in which the localities were governed. Essentially this was a matter of self-government by the propertied. The ministry relied upon Justices of the Peace, who were usually prominent local landowners. The Land Tax Commissioners were also local gentry and the tax was notorious for the unfairness of its assessments, with wide disparities between particular counties. Thus Britain, which in the Bank of England and the Treasury had two of the most sophisticated institutions in monarchical Europe, also had a direct tax system that was operated in an inefficient and unfair fashion. There was no attempt in Britain to introduce a land survey that could serve as a rational basis for taxation, as happened in Lombardy and Piedmont.[28]

The Whigs carried out a purge of many of the Tory JPs after they came to power in 1714, and, judging from Lancashire and Cheshire, it was most marked in 1716. This purge had achieved its aim by 1719, ensuring that the Tories had only minority status in the Commissions of the Peace, and Walpole made no effort to complete it. It sufficed that the Tories were not strong enough to dominate the Commissions; there was no attempt to remove them completely from positions of authority. There was, therefore, a difference in character between the proscription of the Tories in the 1710s and that under Walpole.

Whether the Stanhope–Sunderland ministry would have sought to extend their assault on the legal position of the Church of England and their attempt to remodel the House of Lords (the Peerage Bill) and the universities by attempting to alter the nature of local government in Britain is unclear. The purge of other local offices (Lord Lieutenancy, Deputy Lieutenancies, Custos Rotulorum, Duchy offices in Cornwall and Lancaster) was more complete than that of the JPs. Only the shrievalty, which was a financial burden, was left to Tories. It could be suggested that the modelling of borough charters in order to alter local government and parliamentary representation was not practical politics for any party after 1683 because the entire political class was affected by the legacy of James II and caught up in its propaganda on this point. However, this would probably not have dissuaded Sunderland.

What is clear is that Walpole had no such intentions. Purging the JPs to ensure that the existing system operated in favour of the ministry was not the same as seeking to change the fundamental nature of that system. However, many of the new Whig JPs were not of gentry origins, and this was greeted with outrage in what was still an extremely hierarchical society in which social status was held to equate with merit. The Tories pressed for higher landed qualifications for JPs in 1719 and 1722, succeeded in 1732, and tried to take it further in 1745 and 1747. Governmental control over the choice of JPs could greatly offend local views. In 1719, John Clavering noted, 'the alterations in the Commission of the Peace makes a great noise here; two Members of Parliament are left out of the Commission'.[29]

Walpole's policy was to avoid provoking the Tories, but this did not mean that they were satisfied. Their opposition was contained, not conciliated. They remained proscribed, and careers in some of the professions, so valuable for the younger sons of the landed gentry, were effectively closed to the Tories. The armed forces had been purged in 1714–15, and few Tories were appointed thereafter. A new Commission for Army Debts was established in 1715 to replace the Tory one. Promotion to senior positions in the Church, the law, the diplomatic service and at Court was far easier for Whigs, and many of the Tories appointed owed their positions to a willingness to avoid political commitments. The cut in the land tax benefited Whig country gentlemen as well as Tories.

The Whigs purged the JPs, not because they hoped to carry out a revolution in government, but because they were unsure of the loyalties of the Tories and anxious about the security situation. The purge can be seen as a response to the Jacobite rising in 1715 rather than as the first stage in an attempt to create a Whig absolutism. It would be wrong to ascribe to Walpole alone Britain's failure to follow the continental trend and to become an absolutism, an enlightened despotism, or a well-ordered police state, terms that have been used to describe European developments. The situation was far more complex, and, in particular, it is necessary to consider the legacy of late seventeenth-century developments – the 'Glorious' Revolution of 1688, and the limitations on monarchical power devised subsequently in 1689–1701 – and the political culture of Britain, a society where resistance and contractual theories were of great importance, particularly as a result of recent history. However, it is true that under the first two Georges opportunities existed for increasing government authority. The suppression of the Jacobite rising of 1715 helped to discredit the opposition, just as the failures of the Rye House Plot (1683) and of the Argyll and Monmouth risings (1685) helped to strengthen the position of Charles II and James II. James was overthrown by a foreign invasion, while, in contrast, in the 1720s and 1730s the Jacobite position was actually undermined by a peaceful foreign policy offering little prospect of support for a pro-Stuart invasion. Britain was in alliance with France, its most dangerous potential rival, from 1716 until the Anglo-Austrian alliance of 1731–3 that followed the Second Treaty of Vienna. Walpole's foreign policy also ensured that conflict was avoided with France for the rest of the decade.

Walpole's systematic use of the resources of ministerial patronage helped to keep Parliament quiescent. The ministry regularly enjoyed large majorities, and opposition campaigns to bring about its fall were singularly unsuccessful. In 1731–2, the Parlement of Paris, the leading judicial body in France, created more problems than did the Westminster Parliament for their respective ministries, although Louis XV could overrule the Parlement with a *Lit de Justice* in a way that George II could not. Furthermore, the disturbances over the Excise were much more widespread than those in France in the 1730s.

A minister like Sunderland might have sought to exploit the situation in order to increase government power in Britain, or to make opposition more difficult. There could have been a systematic remodelling of borough charters or a reimposition of press censorship. The latter was certainly mentioned on several occasions. That no such steps were taken was partly due to Walpole. He helped to block Sunderland's schemes in the late 1710s by creating a powerful opposition. Bolingbroke and Pulteney sought to create in the late 1720s and 1730s a 'country' opposition that would unite Tories and opposition Whigs.[30] Their attempt failed to bring down Walpole. Instead it was he who was most successful in fusing elements of the Whig and Tory inheritances. The 1710s had seen extreme, partisan government, first by the Tories, and then by the Whig Stanhope–Sunderland ministry. One commentator observed in 1715, 'when great employments are given to great men, it is natural for them to wish their friends, relations and dependents should be under them in the inferior offices rather than strangers and friends to a late ministry'.[31]

Walpole benefited from a disenchantment with this experience, as well as from a growing conservatism in Whig thought,[32] and the end of the War of the Spanish Succession and its attendant political tensions. His ministry was very much a Whig one in its composition, but the policies he followed, particularly in ecclesiastical affairs, and the initiatives he deliberately refrained from taking helped to ensure widespread acquiescence in the continuance of the ministry. Unlike during the Stanhope–Sunderland government, ministerial Whiggery absorbed enough of moderate Toryism under Walpole to make itself generally acceptable to a fundamentally conservative nation.

This was not the sum total of Walpolean policies. As suggested at the outset, re-active and pro-active policies can not be readily distinguished. Nevertheless, having discussed how ecclesiastical, tax and foreign policies were in part a response to domestic challenges, it is also worth approaching the two latter in terms of Walpole's positive contributions.

WALPOLE AS FINANCIAL MANAGER

Finance represented one of the greatest sources of difficulties for eighteenth-century European governments. By European standards Britain was, for a major power, in a singularly fortunate position. The funded National Debt based on the Bank of England, founded in 1694, enabled British ministries to borrow large sums at low rates of interest. Whereas in the early 1690s the government was paying up to 14 per cent for long-term loans, the rate of interest fell to 6–7 per cent in 1702–14, 4 percent in the late 1720s, at or below 3 per cent in the late 1730s; and, after a wartime rise, to 3 per cent in 1750. The system was not, however, without its problems, both political and financial. There was considerable concern about the rise in the National Debt. Due essentially to war expenditure this rose significantly. Over 30 per cent of the total government expenditure during the Nine Years' War and the War of the Spanish Succession was financed by public borrowing, and the National Debt at George I's accession was £40 million, with an annual interest charge of £2 million. The size of the debt worried contemporaries who feared not only the drain of annual interest payments to creditors, but also the possibility of national bankruptcy. Its very size might discourage further loans, or, in the event of a crisis of confidence, cause a run on the Bank as creditors sought the return of their capital.

When Walpole became First Lord of the Treasury for the first time, in October 1715, the bulk of the redeemable National Debt still carried interest at over 6 per cent. After studying the whole area of finance, Walpole was responsible for a plan put forward by the Commons, sitting as a Committee of the Whole House in March 1717. This envisaged a number of changes, including reducing the interest on the redeemable part of the debt to 5 per cent and repaying dissentients. The savings made by the reduction of the interest were to be paid into a Sinking Fund, to be used to help repay the debt. Although Walpole resigned in April, the Stanhope–Sunderland ministry had most of the proposals enacted that summer.

By the late 1720s the Sinking Fund had increased to over £1 million a year. Thanks to this, Walpole was able to cut the debt by nearly £13 million by his fall in 1742 but, because he increased the debt by £6½ million worth of new borrowing, the net decrease was only £6¼ million. This was only a small part of the debt but, due to further reductions in interest payments, Walpole was able to make a bigger percentage cut in the annual charge of the debt. This fell from over £2 million in 1721 to £1,890,000 in 1741.

Such measures increased confidence and in turn made it easier to conduct the government's financial affairs at a reasonable rate of interest. The beneficial political consequences that were anticipated from financial restructuring and restraint were outlined in the *Supplement to the Freeholder's Journal* of 14 December 1722:

> The confining the expense of the year 1723 to the usual malt tax and two shillings in the pound on land, the raising of this supply at an interest not exceeding 3 per cent and the reducing of above one million of the short annuities from 5 to 3% interest . . . must be a very agreeable surprise to all the freeholders of Great Britain, and give them the pleasing hopes, that the National Debt will, for the future, annually decrease; and that the taxes, which are most grievous to the People, and especially those which are discouraging to our trade and manufactures, will gradually lessen. This undoubtedly will, and perhaps nothing else can, effectually support the National Credit; and will also greatly tend to cure those discontents and dissatisfactions which are apprehended to be very general . . . it seems to be the indispensable duty of every gentleman in the House of Commons . . . to contribute their utmost assistance to the effecting so good a work.

Thus, Walpole's influence in the Commons was designed to foster a financial regime of economy and debt reduction, while his success in introducing this regime was held up as a reason for the maintenance of his influence. However, the use to which the Sinking Fund was put was not free from criticism. It was regarded as insufficient on the basis of the failure to pay off most of the debt. This peacetime failure, repeated during subsequent periods of peace, ensured that after each war the debt was at a new high. It rose appreciably during the conflicts of 1739–48 and 1756–63 and in 1775, on the eve of another major war, it stood at £127 million. An anonymous writer, who in 1813 praised the introduction of income tax as an attempt to equalise revenue and expenditure, claimed that:

> From the period of the complete introduction of the Funding System . . . to the close of the American War, the object of our measures of finance during war appeared to be only to provide for the immediate expenses of the year, by borrowing such sums as were necessary for any extraordinary charge incurred, and by imposing such taxes as might meet the interest of the loan leaving to the period of peace the consideration of any provision for the repayment of debt; and this being attempted at irregular periods and on no permanent system, was never carried into effectual execution; the total amount of debt redeemed between the Peace of Utrecht and the close of the American war being no more than £8,330,000.[33]

Part of the reason for this was Walpole's use of the Sinking Fund for other purposes. The Fund had no trustees appointed to regulate it and ministers, following Walpole's example, were to be tempted to use it, with parliamentary consent, to alleviate difficulties that required expenditure.

The Sinking Fund was used by Walpole as security for new loans, to anticipate annual taxes, and to meet specific problems. In 1727, the extra £100,000 Walpole needed to increase George II's Civil List to £800,000 came from the Fund and in 1733–4 the fall in revenues produced by the cut of the land tax to 1 shilling in the pound, and the need to arm in response to the prospect of intervention in the War of the Polish Succession, were met by drawing from the Fund, a policy that was to be followed thereafter by Walpole. In effect the land tax was kept low, with beneficial political consequences, by delaying the repayment of the National Debt. This use of the Sinking Fund aroused considerable criticism and was taken by opposition spokesmen to be further evidence of an undesirable level of financial manipulation on the part of Walpole. Had more of the debt been redeemed then the annual interest charge, which had to be met through taxation or new loans, would have fallen correspondingly. The hope that this annual charge could be cut was one of the reasons for the 1737 proposal from Sir John Barnard, MP for the City of London, that interest rates on government debts should be cut from 4 to 3 per cent. John Drummond MP expressed the hope that the cut would allow the government to 'take off the soap and candle and leather taxes or what should be found most burdensome to the people and manufacturers'. The measure divided politicians along unfamiliar lines, but Walpole helped to defeat it on the grounds that it would harm small investors, limit ministerial flexibility in financial policy and be difficult to implement. The defeat also protected the interest enjoyed by the major city financiers whom Walpole was close to and who were vital lenders to the government.[34] It was to help them that Walpole had defeated an attempt in 1730 by Barnard to end the East India Company's monopoly of trade with India and the Far East.

The details of financial policy were contentious, as the Excise crisis of 1733 and the reduction of interest controversy in 1737 made clear. However, the general thrust of Walpole's financial policy was prudent and popular, or, at least, not unpopular. Walpole wanted to keep taxes low, particularly taxes on an agricultural interest affected by stagnation, and he felt that the maintenance of peace was the best means to achieve this. He sought successfully to bring order and stability to government finances both because he believed that that would make it easier to finance government and because he argued that such stability was essential to the rest of the economy. His success arose from his ability, not least his comprehensive understanding of the interrelated complexities of public finance, as well as his connections and his strong sense of practicality. The numerous financial memoranda in his surviving papers testify to his energy in this field.

Dedication to public finance was accompanied on Walpole's part by measures to aid economic activity. He attempted to develop British industry and trade. Written by Walpole, the royal speech opening Parliament on 19 October 1721 declared:

> . . . we should be extremely wanting to ourselves, if we neglected to improve the favourable opportunity, which this general tranquillity gives us, of extending our commerce, upon which the riches and grandeur of this nation chiefly depend. It is very obvious, that nothing would more conduce to the obtaining so public a good, than to make the exportation of our own manufactures, and the importation of the commodities used in the manufacturing of them, as practicable and easy as may be; by this means the balance of trade may be preserved in our favour, our navigation increased, and greater numbers of our poor employed.
>
> I must, therefore, recommend it to you, gentlemen of the House of Commons, to consider how far the duties upon these branches may be taken off, and replaced, without any violation of public faith, or laying any new burden upon my people.

In 1722, the export duties on most British manufactured products were abolished. Import duties on foreign raw materials required for these products were reduced or abolished. Potential competitors within the British empire, in Ireland and North America, were hindered. Attempts were made to improve the customs service. Walpole was not alone among politicians in his interest in economic and financial affairs but he displayed an impressive aptitude and consistency of purpose. Walpole's interest in measures to help the cloth industry was reported in the *Norwich Mercury* of 10 January 1730: 'Several of the most eminent traders in our manufactures have been sent for by Sir Robert Walpole to give their opinion in this matter, in order to lay the whole before Parliament'. His preparations and drafts for speeches on financial matters, for example against Barnard's 1737 proposal,[35] revealed great knowledge and a mastery of detail. His high reputation as a financial manager was well deserved, even though his role as a minister concerned with money helped to encourage criticism of him on the grounds both of supposed personal corruption and of the use of corrupt practices in order to entice others to provide support.

The strength of Walpole's position as financial manager for the government and country could be linked to other aspects of his political position. Robert Wodrow noted in 1724:

> Mr Walpole at present manages all. He has raised his reputation and interest exceedingly by his dealings with the Dutch. The monied people there have a high value for him, because of his appearances in the end of the Queen's [Anne's] reign in favour of liberty, and are willing to trust their money in his hands at three per cent. This put him in case to deal with the three great Companys in England, the Bank, India, and South Sea, and to bring them to his own terms, as to the National Debt, and being thus in case to guide these three, and consequently the House of Commons, he is got to the head of affairs, and is become absolutely necessary to the King.[36]

A determination to keep taxes low did not win Walpole an active popularity. Instead, the Excise demonstrated his political vulnerability in the financial sphere. The legislation, however, could be abandoned. No such remedy was to be on offer in the political agitation over relations with Spain in 1738–9. Indeed, it was the protracted nature of the crisis that contributed greatly to its severity, helping to lend force, through reiteration, to the opposition charge that Walpole was not defending national interests, and specifically those of the trading interest. *Common Sense* claimed on 17 February 1739 that Walpole had said 'that he hoped to make all the merchants of England as poor as so many German princes'. Indeed, much of the comment reflected a rich strain of paranoia. Once war with Spain had broken out,

Sir James Lowther could write from London: 'The London traders reckon things have been managed worse than they need have been on purpose to distress this city'.[37]

FOREIGN POLICY

Walpole's contribution to foreign policy tends to be underrated, not least because scholars of diplomatic history are apt to concentrate on the details of negotiations rather than the political factors affecting the formation and defence of foreign policy. Graham Gibbs was scathing in his references to Walpole:

'a minister as ill-at-ease in the field of foreign affairs, and as ill-equipped to conduct foreign affairs, as Walpole himself . . . Robert Walpole's ignorance of foreign affairs was a matter for contemporary comment by those who were closest to himself as well as by his enemies and neutral observers . . . a self-confessed ignoramus in foreign affairs, – whose ignorance was a matter of widespread, if at times oblique, contemporary comment'.

Gibbs' view, however, suffers from a reliance upon questionable commentators: Hervey and Frederick the Great. Aside from these two, Gibbs also quoted from the dispatches of Giuseppe Ossorio, the Sardinian envoy in London, but the reference he printed was from a dispatch sent in 1730, soon after Ossorio had arrived, and Gibbs failed to note that Ossorio changed his attitude as he got to know Walpole better.

Sir Richard Lodge was another critic:

'Walpole was not at his best in dealing with foreign affairs, he was no match in subtlety for French diplomatists, he lowered England from the commanding position which it held under Stanhope and Townshend to something not far removed from ignominy, and he might have done better if he had adhered to his earlier attitude, later resumed by Henry Pelham, that a Prime Minister is a critic rather than a dictator of foreign policy, and that the conduct of diplomacy should be left to the secretaries of state'.

This judgement, however, was based on hindsight: 'Many modern scholars would adopt the view advanced by [the Duke of] Newcastle in 1752 that if Walpole had fought the House of Bourbon in 1733 the Austrian Succession War need never have been fought at all, or at any rate not on so large a scale'.[38]

Maybe not, but was Walpole expected to anticipate the Austrian failure in the Austro-Turkish War of 1737–9, or Frederick the Great's attack on Austria in 1740? Sir George Clark's conclusion is a safer one than Lodge's: 'There are times when short views are best, and the treacherous age of Walpole may well have been one of them'.[39] Furthermore, Lodge's view that policy could have been left to the Secretaries of State is erroneous. Policy was given cohesion if there was a dominant Secretary of State, as Townshend was in 1724–9, but when the two Secretaries were divided, as in 1721–4 then this division had political consequences. This helped push Walpole into a more directly active role.

It was widely believed that he took his views on foreign policy from his brother Horatio, and relied greatly upon him and also, in the 1720s, Townshend.[40] Walpole had no diplomatic experience, indeed did not know the Continent, and was bad at languages.[41] Foreign policy was neither his first concern, nor his ministerial responsibility, nor was it his prime interest.

Nevertheless, Walpole was, as his drafts and speeches showed, knowledgeable about foreign affairs,[42] played a role in the drafting of instructions, read despatches,[43] saw foreign intercepts, participated actively in Council discussions of foreign affairs, had frequent discussions with foreign envoys, spoke to at least some British diplomats before their missions,[44] and had a confidential correspondence with two key diplomats, his own brother, and Waldegrave at Paris, as well as with Fawkener, envoy at Constantinople from the close of 1735. The first was the most important. Thus, for example, in August 1730, Walpole wrote to Horatio about pressing Fleury on the true nature of French policy, adding 'It was thought more advisable for me to write to you privately upon the subject than for the Secretary of State to send you any orders upon it'.[45] Fawkener supplied Tokay wine as well as details of Balkan diplomacy, reflections on the international system, and complaints about being out of pocket on his embassy expenses.[46] At a more minor level, Walpole was responsible for paying diplomats' bills.[47] This provided many opportunities for showing favour or otherwise.

In 1723, Walpole acted with success as Secretary of State during the absence of the two Secretaries in Hanover, and his role was such that business was delayed when he went to Houghton in July. In response to pressure from George I for a promise of assistance for Sweden if it was attacked by Peter the Great of Russia, Walpole expressed his concern that competition among the ministers for royal favour 'should transport us into very rash engagements'. He was able to offer cogent reasons, which show his acute awareness of the relationship of foreign and fiscal policy, and his sense that public opinion and Parliament had to be managed:

The £150,000 may certainly be had . . . I cannot but wish from my heart that this money may not be demanded . . . nor do I see how it can be employed at all by way of prevention, for if the Czar's fleet was ready to sail, any agreement for this subsidy will come too late, and the blow be struck before a force can be got ready to repel it . . . I am mightily inclined to be cautious . . . if we enter precipitately into any engagements upon this occasion, we shall not carry the nation, nor perhaps the Parliament along with us, but if we wait and are driven into it, it will be seen and thought to be the interest of Great Britain alone that made us to engage . . . I wish to God we may at least for a little time remain neuters, and look on, if all the rest of Europe do the same thing.

Aside from also warning about the danger of Russian support for the Jacobites, Walpole was concerned that the Russian threat to Sweden would affect credit 'as all our money matters here depend entirely upon credit'.[48] Fortunately, Townshend had George I's offer of help to Sweden worded cautiously and the Russians did not attack.

Walpole also spoke with foreign envoys; in 1723, for example, the Austrian envoy, who pressed him against British measures directed against the Ostend Company, an Austrian company for trade with India. That year, the French envoy pressed Walpole on behalf of British Catholics.[49]

In May 1729, when George II and Townshend went to Hanover, Walpole had a long conference with the Austrian envoy, Count Kinsky, although the Duke of Grafton, the Lord Chamberlain, had to act as an interpreter in order to prevent any misunderstandings. Kinsky was more detailed in his approach to Walpole than he had been with Newcastle.[50]

Walpole's role in foreign policy increased in the 1730s. In 1732, Ossorio claimed that Walpole's views were crucial in any negotiation of importance. He met foreign envoys more frequently, and clearly dominated the two Secretaries for much of the decade. In 1734 and 1735, he was kept informed of Austrian views via the Hessen-Kassel envoy in Britain from 1725 to 1735, General Ernst Diemar, a visitor at Houghton, who also hunted with Walpole in Richmond. However, for most of May 1735, Diemar found Walpole so occupied with the Commons that he could not deliver a letter from Prince Eugene until the eve of his departure.[51]

To offer some examples of Walpole's meetings with envoys in 1735, on 16 January Prince Kantemir, the Russian envoy 'had a long conference' with Walpole and Harrington, at Sir Robert's house in St James's Square, and when, in February, the Spanish envoy, Montijo, requested a conference with 'His Majesty's ministers', he ended up by seeing Walpole and the two Secretaries on the 11th. Chavigny saw Walpole later in the month. In early April, Walpole and Newcastle saw Montijo, while Walpole and the two Secretaries discussed Horatio's dispatches. On 10 June, when Newcastle, Grafton, Scarborough, the Lord Chancellor and Wager had dined at Walpole's, Newcastle produced a letter from the British envoy in Spain for discussion. In Newcastle's account of a secret conference between himself, Ossorio and Walpole that month, it was Walpole who made all the deductions from the movements of the Sardinian couriers.

Also in June, conversations with the Spaniards were handled through a meeting between Newcastle, Montijo and Walpole at the house of the last. The meetings of the Lords of the Cabinet Council on 8, 9 and 10 July, which met till midnight each night, considering Britain's diplomatic position, were all attended by Walpole, delaying his departure for Houghton. Business and pleasure were mixed. Newcastle wrote on the 8th: 'The Lords dined this day at Walpole's, and we did not finish reading the letters till near twelve o'clock this night'. Walpole and Newcastle also saw the Portuguese envoy for conferences in July. Harrington's 'Private and Particular' letters of 21 August were endorsed as to be seen only by the Queen, Newcastle and Walpole.[52] On 12 December 1735, Walpole and Harrington saw Chavigny and on the 13th Sir Thomas Fitzgerald. Walpole saw 'all the letters before they were sent to the king'. The decision to attempt a private correspondence with Chauvelin and to seek to bribe him was taken by Walpole.[53]

Mocking Walpole in the guise of a doctor, the *Craftsman* of 4 May 1728 claimed 'when he found himself absolute master of the profession here, nothing would satisfy his ambition, but the same arbitrary dominion over all the physicians abroad'. Such a view was inaccurate, for Walpole was totally opposed to an interventionist foreign policy. He had been against Stanhope's Baltic and Mediterranean policies,[54] and in 1736 told Chavigny that he was at last free from the system that Stanhope had left him and that he had been obliged to follow until then'.[55]

Walpole displayed an acute sensitivity, born of long parliamentary experience, to the interrelationships of foreign and domestic politics. He was well aware of the political and fiscal costs of interventionist policies, and feared that they would provoke foreign support for Jacobitism. While acting as Secretary of State in 1723, Walpole wrote to Newcastle of his opposition to 'very rash engagements' and, in the context of foreign policy, that 'my politics are in a narrow compass . . . foreign disturbances . . . alone can confound us here'.[56]

In the first two years of his ministry Walpole's concern with foreign affairs was subordinated to the need to reintroduce fiscal and political stability after the South Sea Bubble, but, thereafter, it increased. Aside from his role in 1723, Walpole also played a leading role when the king went to Hanover, and he was left as one of the Lord Justices in London, especially in 1725 and 1729.[57] There was also a link between foreign policy and domestic stability, because a bellicose foreign policy entailed expenditure and borrowing that affected the sound budgeting that was crucial to Walpole's able and assiduous management of the London money market. Foreign policy was pushed to the fore by political struggles, both ministerial (with Carteret in 1723–4, Townshend in 1729–30), and with the opposition, which concentrated on foreign policy in the sessions in the second half of the 1720s, culminating in that of 1730 when the ministry was in danger of falling.

Walpole was not responsible for the alliances of the 1720s: they stemmed, as with so much of that period, from the previous decade. In 1726, the Imperial Resident, Karl Josef von Palm, had defined Walpole's position:

'Who is the primum mobile in the ministry, 'tis very well known to the whole world that it can be but Mylord Townshend. For his brother [in law] Robert Walpole, though his power and credit be far greater, yet he properly does not meddle with foreign affairs, but receives accounts of them in general leaving for the rest the direction of them entirely to Lord Townshend'.[58]

By 1729, Walpole could not afford this attitude, and he moved firmly and decisively to press George II to remove Townshend and to prevent his replacement by Chesterfield. He also played a major role in the diplomatic shift of 1730–1 from France to Austria. Walpole was less keen on the French alliance than Horatio and readier to subordinate diplomatic to parliamentary considerations: in the summer of 1730 he pressed a disagreeing Horatio to be firm over Dunkirk.[59]

It was a blow that Horatio did not replace Townshend as northern Secretary. He was diplomatically experienced, and could be relied upon by his brother, whilst William Stanhope, ennobled as Lord Harrington, was to oppose Walpole in 1733 in the disputes at Court that followed the defeat of the Excise Scheme. On the other hand, Horatio had a knack of irritating people and would probably have fallen foul of George II.

Foreign affairs did not threaten the stability or parliamentary position of the ministry during the sessions of 1731–33, and there is little sign of Walpole interfering then to any purpose in foreign affairs until the second half of 1733. There were signs of tension, including efforts to replace Harrington by Horatio, but Harrington was not a significant political problem, and the royal trip to Hanover in the summer of 1732 did not pose significant difficulties for Walpole.

In 1733, the situation drifted out of control. Whilst Britain's role was confined to negotiations which did not appear to be urgent, such as those for mediating Austro-Sardinian and Austro-Spanish difficulties, then the potential clash between interventionist diplomacy and a desire to avoid commitments was not pressed. However, the poorly coordinated character of British foreign policy collapsed in 1733 under the dual pressure of the Excise crisis and the outbreak of a European war, that of the Polish Succession (1733–5). Thereafter, Walpole's capacity for manoeuvre was greatly restricted by George II's great interest in the struggle, and his concern for an Austrian victory. At the same time, he had to face opposition attacks in Parliament. Walpole did so by arguing that the government was not responsible for the policies of other states.[60] He also claimed that internal divisions affected Britain's position.[61]

Walpole's attitude to foreign policy was certainly not controlled by his brother in these years. While Horatio relied upon negotiations with the French in order to end the conflict, Robert supported moves to end it by encouraging an Austro-Spanish reconciliation. He wanted to keep Britain neutral and was not inclined to sympathise with the Austrians. The latter was different to the attitude of George II and the two Secretaries. Whilst Newcastle and George II had both been unacquainted with the problems of alliance politics in the 1700s, Walpole remembered the difficulties then encountered in co-operating with Austria. Had Britain aided Austria in 1733–5, then she would have seen trade lost to the neutral Dutch, agriculture denied the benefit of grain exports, the Jacobites aided by the Bourbons, and the prospect of an expensive and troublesome conflict. Critics claimed that Walpole was motivated by a desire to hold onto power, specifically to keep difficult business away from Parliament.[62]

Ability in foreign affairs is not synonymous with knowledge about foreign countries. The latter can produce accurate commentary, but is no guarantee of a policy capable of taking into account internal considerations and fiscal constraints. No one has shown that the more knowledgeable Carteret made a better show of things in 1742–4 during the War of the Austrian Succession, whilst there is little doubt that his policy helped to split the ministry. Had Walpole left foreign policy to the Secretaries, it is probable there would have been a recurrence of his disputes over subsidies with Townshend in 1729. A policy of involvement in Europe would not have been readily supported by Parliament, if it was not clear that vital British interests were endangered.

Walpole played a large role in the negotiation of Anglo-Spanish commercial differences in 1737–9, and Geraldino, the Spanish envoy, contrasted his ability favourably with that of other ministers.[63] The government was criticised for failing to defend British trade in the Caribbean from the exacting supervision and depredations of Spanish colonial government in the West Indies. British merchants, in turn, sought to breach Spanish restrictions on trade with their colonies. Walpole was more conciliatory towards Spain than Newcastle.[64] Walpole's policy succeeded with the negotiation of the Convention of the Pardo in January 1739, and its passage through Parliament that March, only to fail as Britain drifted into war with Spain. The compromises necessary to settle outstanding differences and to implement the Convention proved impossible. This was partly because of a lack of effort by Spain, which hoped for French support, and partly because of the impact on British policy of ministerial differences against a background of popular and parliamentary pressure.

Opposed to conflict with Spain, Walpole also did not wish to fight Prussia when Frederick the Great invaded Austrian-ruled Silesia in December 1740, and the Austrians distrusted him. He did not play a large role in foreign policy in 1740–2, and was responsible neither for the attempts in 1741 to settle Austro-Prussian differences, nor for the negotiations for an anti-Bourbon alliance. France had joined in the attack on Austria in 1741. Opposed to war with France,[65] Walpole was attacked hard in Parliament for his failure to block her schemes.[66] The interventionism of these years, which was further stressed by the ministry that followed Walpole, was alien to his views, although there are no signs that he resisted policy developments.

In his three significant involvements, those of 1729–30, 1733–5, and 1738–9, Walpole supported policies that he knew could be carried out. He thus revealed his appreciation of the central need not to embark on a policy that could not be executed. More generally, Walpole correctly gauged the necessary relationship between foreign policy and domestic considerations, a balance that neither Carteret nor Newcastle was to strike successfully. He was cautious. In 1736, Walpole opposed the idea of a league with Denmark, Sweden and the Dutch:

'I cannot think the state of affairs in any part of Europe . . . enough to make us desire to be engaged sooner or more than we shall necessarily be called upon to be so, let us wait, and see how things will turn out, and then determine what part to take. The late treaties with Denmark and Sweden have been burdensome and expensive, and our subsidies will never be unwelcome to them'.

He was similarly cautious about offering mediation in the Balkan conflict:

'in this case too to wait for events and proper applications, and to be well assured of the real sentiments of both the Imperial and Russian courts, before we offer our good offices, and take any steps which may possibly disoblige, without a probability of doing any good. The same spirit of not being too far forward induces me to think our taking any part as yet in the affair of Berg and Juliers is not advisable'.[67]

This emphasis on practicality and political acceptability characterised Walpole's policies. It was not a case of the ends being subservient to the means of power; but rather an understanding that without the sustaining of those means no ends were possible. To critics this policy appeared craven. Maybe so, but the political system required the stability that this offered.

8

Party and Politics under the First Two Georges

It is important to consider Walpole not only in the context of political structures and policies, but also more explicitly with relation to the party alignments of the period. The classification of political groups is far from easy. Eighteenth-century political parties tended to lack an identifiable national leadership, an organised constituent membership and a recognised corpus of policy and principle around which to cohere and which could serve to link local activists to national activity. However, many modern political parties can only be described as coalitions; they are monolithic neither in organisation nor in policy. This test of a political party might be failed by modern parties in France, India, Italy and the United States.

Some scholars are unhappy about the applicability of a two-party system at the constituency level in the eighteenth century, arguing that, although Whig and Tory alignments did exist under those names in many constituencies, these feuds were often traditional and that family interest was paramount.[1] It is indeed difficult to generalise on the relationship between electoral and parliamentary politics. The links between political behaviour in the localities and at Westminster varied widely, both over time and with reference to the type and size of constituency.

Hostility to outsiders was a frequent factor in local politics, and often a reflection of a strong sense of community. In 1737, Viscount Lonsdale wrote to the Bishop of Carlisle about a local seat: 'I am very glad the Cumberland Gentlemen have agreed in uniting their interests. I hope it will prove a means of keeping out a stranger at Cockermouth.' Three years later, their correspondence revealed the importance of local arrangements between prominent aristocrats, Lonsdale writing: 'I received the honour of your Lordship's letter of the 15th wherein you are pleased to acquaint me that you had a message from my Lord Carlisle . . . which was that he would give no opposition to the present representatives for the county of Cumberland, if I gave none to those two who now serve for the City of Carlisle.' Lonsdale had 'no difficulty of saying that I will give no opposition to the present members'. County politics were clearly very important in this period, as Walpole indeed showed in Norfolk.

At the level of the individual constituency, there was great variety in the alignments, contents and dynamics of politics. A Whig–Tory division existed in Glamorgan that bore little relation to the behaviour of the participants in national politics. The representation of the Flint Boroughs was affected by a struggle for control between the Tory county gentry and George Wynne, who gained control of the borough machinery, using it to create non-resident freemen. As Constable of Flint Castle, he was able to nominate the returning officers and in 1734 they disallowed enough of his opponent's votes to give victory to Wynne, whose election was confirmed on petition by the government's majority in the Commons. Partisan Commons' voting on petitions and the disposal of crucial local posts were obvious examples of the importance of parliamentary politics for those involved in local conflicts, and affected the perception of Walpole's position and methods.

In 1741, the returning officers put Wynne at the head of the poll, but he was unseated on petition in March 1742 by the anti-Walpole majority of the Commons. However, that was the last contest for several decades. After the death of the MP in 1753, a meeting of the local gentry unanimously adopted Sir John Glynne who wrote: 'As this county hath enjoyed great peace and tranquility for these many years in regard to the choice of its representatives, it hath been thought nothing could more contribute to a continuance of it than the nomination of some person to represent the borough who is most likely without any party prejudices to be agreeable to the several persons interested in this election'.[2]

Clearly not all constituencies were dominated by two-party politics and, in some, divisions within one of the parties were paramount. However, this is equally true of modern British politics. In many constituencies, the major political battles are not those between Labour and Conservative, but most commentators agree that national politics, parliamentary debates and the struggles in many constituencies are dominated by this division. In general, in the eighteenth century it was easier to resolve divisions within parties, by means, for example, of the pact between two leading Berkshire Tories to divide the future representation of the county,[3] than to settle the more intractable differences between the parties.

Part of the problem for historians in the case of the eighteenth century is that too little work has been done on local politics, with the conspicuous exception of London, certainly compared with the situation in the first half of the seventeenth century. There are a number of important published works on towns, especially Bristol and Norwich, but there is much still to be done, particularly for rural areas.[4] The nature of eighteenth-century local politics is important, not least because it provided the context for national and parliamentary politics. Much work on the latter has neglected the local context, but this approach appears increasingly inappropriate. The role of Parliament as an arbiter of local interests, or rather as a sphere in which they competed, can be perceived, and the extent to which local government and politics were distinct and independent was less than is sometimes suggested.[5] Lionel Glassey drew attention to the manner in which agencies of central government:

'had established a presence in the localities, and helped to maintain and strengthen the links between Whitehall and the localities in their different ways in the early eighteenth century. The concepts of gentry "autonomy" in the government of the counties, and of an oligarchical independence in the government of the towns, are firmly entrenched, but perhaps they need modification in certain respects. Those charged with the duties of local government not infrequently sought advice and direction from the centre. . . . Complete independence from the centre seems not even to have been desired, let alone achieved.'[6]

Struggles in London affected local patronage. Sir James Lowther wrote in August 1743: 'Mr Pelham is now made first Lord Commissioner of the Treasury in opposition to those that wanted to bring in Lord Carlisle to court, so that places in Cumberland will go better than they have of late.'[7] The Howards, Earls of Carlisle, were, like the Lowthers, a significant factor in Cumbrian politics.

Given such links and the importance of Parliament and the government in affecting life in the localities in a wide range of matters, from the rate of taxation to the composition of the Bench, from the position of Dissenters to turnpike legislation, it is scarcely surprising that national politics had a local dimension. Some scholars have sought to distinguish family interests and traditional feuds from party political behaviour, but this is not always a helpful distinction. Eighteenth-century parties lacked the institutional organisation of their modern counterparts. Instead, in many of the localities, they were essentially organised in terms of family interests, a feature that is still the case in some parts of the world today. 'My Lord's Speedy Influence to his Tenants whom to vote for', a request in 1741 from a Yorkshire Tory to an opposition Whig, was a form of political behaviour that in no way destroys the validity of a party description. John Clavering expressed the hope in Yorkshire in 1722 that the foundation of country assemblies for social purposes 'will have a good effect in making all parties live well together in the country and entirely banish politics which (in the country) breaks all good neighbourhood'.[8] However, three years later, in Bath the

140

visitors were divided into a Whig group, led by the Duke of Richmond, and a Tory one, led by the Duke of Norfolk, which had little to do with each other.

At the level of national politics several historians questioned the rationale and rhetoric of Walpolean politics by denying the existence of a Tory party during the reigns of George I and George II.[9] Peter Thomas's unhappiness with Linda Colley's equation of the terms 'country gentlemen', 'the Country Party' and 'independents' with Tory partisanship was reasonable, but he went too far in arguing that contemporary references by individuals to themselves as Tories do not contribute to the view that there was a Tory party. While to call an individual MP a Tory does not necessarily indicate his association with others, the use of 'Tories' as a collective noun clearly does, and such use was ubiquitous. Furthermore, the distinction between opposition Whigs and Tories was made in some division lists. The sole archival reference Thomas cited came from Sir Roger Newdigate's treatises on party. Writing in 1762, Newdigate denied the existence of a Tory party over the previous half-century.[10] Newdigate, however, like other Tories in George III's reign, was trying to live down a Jacobite past and work his passage into favour. Earlier, he was a Tory in the eyes of most contemporaries. The Whig Sir Charles Hanbury-Williams reported in 1747:

'the county of Middlesex has chose two Whigs by a majority of a thousand that never sent a Whig to Parliament before since the Revolution. And the reason they gave was that the two Whigs had subscribed money in the late Rebellion to defend their country while Sir Roger Newdigate (the first Tory candidate) was heading a Grand Jury who wanted but one vote, to find and present all associations and meetings for associations for the Defence of the Government as riotous assemblys and contrary to law.'[11]

Newdigate was writing in a long tradition of Tories who denied the importance of party distinctions. From the 1720s, Bolingbroke, Wyndham and other Tories who did want office had been deploying an anti-party rhetoric in order both to counter Walpole's Jacobite smear tactics and to elicit support at Court and among disaffected Whigs. Theirs was generally a call that party distinctions should and could be obliterated, rather than a declaration that they already had been. One opposition pamphleteer claimed in 1734 that 'Whig and Tory are only mere names'. In 1735, the *Daily Gazetteer*, the government-subsidised newspaper, claimed that, 'The Tories, or Craftsmen, for they are all one, have for some years endeavoured to disguise themselves with the mask of Whigs'.[12] Other commentators, such as Jacobites and foreign diplomats, were quite willing to refer to the existence of a Tory party.[13] Furthermore, the evidence of the poll books, though incomplete, shows that voters voted on party lines.

To argue, as a number of scholars have done, that the crucial parliamentary division was one of administration and opposition, makes little sense in terms of the period beginning in 1714. A crucial division existed between Tories and opposition Whigs. This was made readily apparent after the Whig split of 1717. Walpole failed to use the Tories either to create an effective opposition coalition that would override past differences or to force himself back into office. This prefigured the Bolingbroke–Pulteney 'Country' campaign. The Tories and the opposition Whigs were divided in 1718 over foreign policy and ecclesiastical issues, just as the Tories and the government Whigs were. The Tories pressed George, Prince of Wales, to vote against the Mutiny Act in the Lords, but he refused to do so. Similar divisions between Tories and opposition Whigs pertained in the 1730s. Furthermore, Jacobitism was an issue that divided the opposition. While supporting the Whig opposition in 1717–20, George, Prince of Wales, received Sir Thomas Hanmer and other Hanoverian Tories, but refused to see High Tories. The situation in many of the constituencies matched that in Westminster. It proved very difficult to obtain adequate co-operation either between Tories and opposition Whigs or between Tories and ministerial Whigs.

It was impossible in the late 1710s to devise suitable terms upon which all or most of the Tory party could join the ministry. In late 1717, exploratory conversations took place between members of the ministry and some of the leading Tories, although there are no signs that anything more than an attempt to recruit one or two prominent Tories was seriously envisaged. Trevor appears to have asked for places for more Tories than the ministry was willing to countenance. He demanded that the ministry discard its schemes for alleviating the legal position of the Dissenters. When George I received Trevor he was made to listen to a defence of the Utrecht settlement, hardly the way to endear the Tories to the king.[14] In 1723, Atterbury claimed that: 'he was offered the Bishopric of Winchester . . . by my Lord Sunderland, but that neither he nor Lord Trevor would engage till they saw the Church and army new modelled.' This the ministry was unwilling to do, and its decision was a wise one. The Tories were too divided to negotiate with satisfactorily. Trevor himself could carry few supporters. The Duke of Chandos, who sought a mixed ministry, explained to Harcourt, a Hanoverian Tory, in January 1718 that he had turned down the offer of a post, because it would be foolish to come into office alone: 'whereas were the assurances which were given me, and which I had authority to give your Lordship, punctually performed, viz. of the Act of Grace and of enlarging the bottom by taking in your Lordship etc. we could undertake to carry on the King's service in spite of all opposition, and by joining with the present ministers effectually support them from the rage of their enemies'.[15] However, an alliance with all, or some, of the Tories was incompatible with the aims of the ministry.

In September 1718, Bishop Gibson claimed that the Tories: 'will not come in at all unless they may come in, in a body. Depend upon it . . . that the Tories who call themselves the most moderate, will never break with the most rigid in order to incorporate with the Whigs: much less will any of them either moderate or rigid, be content to act in subordination to the Whigs.'[16] That subordination, however, was the sole basis upon which most Whigs were willing to deal with Tories.

Individual Tories, such as Harcourt and Trevor, were accommodated, but at the price of abandoning their colleagues and principles. This was not a coalition. 'Agreeable to his last discourse with Mr Walpole', Harcourt was added to the Privy Council in 1722, Newcastle noting: 'He has promised to be with us in every thing, and says the Tory party must be conquered. He comes in entirely to support the King and Whig Interest, and if he does not perform his promise he must expect no favour from the King.'[17] Trevor became Lord Privy Seal on a similar basis in 1726.

In 1723, Newcastle observed: 'All sort of negotiations with the Tories is so dangerous as well as so useless.' In the same letter he noted that not all ministerial figures adopted this attitude. Newcastle did this by making a reference to links between the Tories and Carteret, the Secretary of State for the Southern Department, whom he was to succeed the following year. However, Newcastle also observed that Carteret had broken off with the Tories 'thinking to carry his point with the Whigs, which he knows agreeable to the King'.[18]

Newcastle's letter draws attention to George I. Indeed, one of the surprising aspects of much discussion of the party question in the period 1714–60 is the failure to devote sufficient attention to the position of the monarch. Colley closed the second section of her influential study of the Tories with the observation that: 'their proscription was not irreversible. Always available, to distract from and enervate Tory populism, was the prospect of a Tory return to power by high-political or parliamentary manoeuvre, which would preclude a more extensive and possibly subversive assault on the political and social order.' Earlier in the book Colley claimed that George I in 1717, 1721 and 1725, and George II in 1727, 1744 and 1746 were very attracted by the idea of a mixed ministry.[19]

This argument has been criticised. Reed Browning drew attention to what he termed 'the analytical confusion that underlies Colley's thesis' by juxtaposing her argument summarised above with her contention that 'Proscription preserved the Tory party's identity', and distinguished the Tories from 'Country' Whiggery.[20] Thus for Colley proscription explained both separate identity and internal cohesion, while the prospect of its end accounted for loyalty and participation in the established political process.

However, evidence for the argument that George I and his son sought a mixed ministry[21] is scanty and, by concentrating on Tory rumours, insufficient attention is devoted to the high-political situation. It is necessary to examine seriously the views of George I and George II, as Walpole would have done. The scanty nature of the sources makes this far from easy, but material is available. In discussing the proposed admission of a larger number of Tories to the Commissions of the Peace in 1727, Colley cited George II's instruction to the Lord Chancellor, Lord King, to increase the number of Tories, but she ignored his injunction to 'still keep a majority of those who were known to be most firmly in his interest'. George ordered Lord King to keep that part of his instruction secret, which suggests that he was really seeking to curry popularity or to distinguish between Hanoverian and Jacobite Tories. For Walpole, both in George I's last years and in 1727, the principal threat was posed not by Tories but by alternative ministerial figures, in George I's last years opponents within the ministry, and in 1727 young Whig aristocrats favoured by George II as Prince of Wales. Walpole was arguably more afraid of George II appointing Chesterfield Secretary of State than of the possibility of his raising a Tory such as Sir Thomas Hanmer to the peerage. For example, George II stepped up the awarding of honorary degrees at Cambridge, a measure already pursued in 1726. This helped ensure that in 1727 and 1734 the government candidates won the university seats which had hitherto returned Tories.

Tension within the Whig élite has arguably received insufficient attention, because historians have been most concerned with parliamentary politics and especially those of the Commons. Langford's study of the Excise crisis included an important assessment of the crisis at the Court, but far too little is known about Court politics during the reigns of the first two Georges. The nature of the sources again poses a serious problem. As a result, for example, Hatton's important biography of George I was better for his personality and foreign policy than for his attitudes towards, and role in, British politics. One reviewer commented: 'In the political sphere, George I's marked preference for conversations over memoranda and his strong desire to keep deliberations within a tight circle make the assessment of his role difficult. . . . Because of the nature of the evidence, Hatton's argument respecting the King's political role rests largely on inferences.'[22]

Thus the Court context of élite politics is obscure, and the relationship between monarchs and leading politicians uncertain. If one of the principal purposes of organised political activity was to gain and retain office then it is clear that discussion of the nature of this organisation must include consideration of the relationship with the Crown and, in particular, the monarch's perception of the purposes for which aspirants sought office. This perception is the crucial point in any discussion of Tory Jacobitism. Ian Christie proposed the acid test: 'is X a man with whom in a tight corner I should be happy to stand back to back, sure that he will defend my rear to the last and not turn and shoot me from behind?'.[23]

Those who would deny Tory Jacobitism have not provided any satisfactory suggestion as to how George I and George II were convinced or could be convinced that the Tories were loyal. This is especially important for the period 1714–27,the reign of George I and the accession of his son, during which the Whig ascendancy was established. The conduct of many prominent Tories in this period was scarcely conducive to any argument that the Tory party, whose attitude could only be gauged by that of its leaders, should be trusted by the monarchy. It is probable that for George I and George II an indication as to the politician's possible attitude to Jacobitism was his actual record of votes and speeches on Hanoverian matters, though the scanty nature of the rulers' surviving correspondence must induce some caution on this point. On such a basis, certain Whigs were not sound, but the majority of those who were unreliable were Tories; furthermore, there were separate Whig and Tory reasons for anti-Hanoverian opinions.

Although the Tory ministry in the last years of Anne's reign had created a French alliance that could be seen as a prefiguration of the Anglo-French alliance negotiated by Stanhope in 1716, there were substantial differences between Tory foreign policy in 1713–14[24] and Whig policy several years later. Having betrayed Britain's allies, including Austria, Hanover and the United Provinces, at Utrecht, the Tory leaders after 1714, especially Bolingbroke, were adaptable enough to have been willing to support different alliances, but foreign policy divided them from the ministry for two reasons. The legacy of Utrecht was an important factor, exploited by Walpole, for example in the debate on the Address in 1730, and skilfully presented by Whig propaganda, such as John Toland's *State Anatomy of Great Britain*, which described the Tories as 'men that pretend themselves the only Churchmen, and yet sacrifice the Protestant Interest everywhere'. More significant was the fact that, shorn of Bolingbroke's eager diplomacy and of the exigencies of office, many Tories had reverted to the 'Country' policy of opposing an interventionist role in European politics; or what Sunderland called 'the old Tory notion that England can subsist by itself'. However loyal or disloyal the Tories were to the house of Hanover, most were stridently anti-Hanoverian in proclaiming their support for a 'British' as opposed to a 'Hanoverian' foreign policy. In the Lords in 1718, Trevor 'spoke with great vehemence against' the Mutiny Bill and 'brought all the popular arguments against a standing army in time of peace'.[25]

Much of the argument against there being meaningful party divisions hinges on the question of whether the Whig–Tory conflict of Anne's reign, Walpole's apprenticeship, should be seen as an anomaly or as the norm of political life in the first half of the century. Claims that the Hanoverian succession was followed by the eclipse of the Tories as serious contenders for office and the initial split and gradual disintegration of the dominant Whig party exaggerate

Whig cohesion in the 1700s and ignore Walpole's success in the early 1720s in creating an effective political system. Some of those Whigs who were excluded or unhappy with their share of influence tended to oppose the ministry in Parliament, but it is possible to make too much of a basic alignment of administration and opposition. Many Whigs who fell out with the ministry did not oppose it in Parliament.

The politics of the period cannot be understood if attention is devoted to Parliament alone, especially if the importance of the House of Lords is overlooked, as is so often the case. Any such concentration appears misplaced if it distracts attention from Court and ministerial politics. This is especially true of one of the more neglected periods of eighteenth-century British history, the early 1720s and also of the last years of that decade. The parliamentary session of 1730 was difficult for Walpole and has justifiably received much attention. However, the ministerial/Court crisis of that year was also extremely important. In British politics the most important developments in the period 1727–31 were the accession of George II, his decision to retain most of his father's ministers, the development of a working relationship between king and ministers, and the causes and consequences of the resignation of Townshend. Compared with these events, the activities, inside and outside Parliament, of the opposition, however defined and described, were of less importance, although there was of course considerable interaction.

Court politics played a major role in the political crisis in 1733.[26] They also featured in the fall of Walpole. This could be presented in terms of the consequences for an increasingly divided ministry of having a divided Court, the 1741 elections enabling the position of the Prince of Wales and a number of other dissatisfied figures to become more immediately crucial. The Whig reshuffle of 1742 was comparable to that of 1720. Court divisions and realignments were as important for the political disputes of the late 1710s and late 1730s–early 1740s, as for the relative ministerial stability of the 1720s and early 1730s. Had Prince Frederick been older in 1730 and 1733 the political crises of those years might well have been very different.

If it is possible to write a high-political history of early eighteenth-century Britain around the Court, it would be misleading to do so, if this led to the neglect of other spheres and causes of political activity. However, it would be no more misleading than to write the history around Parliament and parliamentary majorities. At one level, Parliament was primarily a sphere for political disputes that originated elsewhere. However, Parliament became a crucial focus for the waging of these disputes and no alternative structure to Parliament developed. Christopher Wyvill's attempt to found one in 1779–80 failed, as did radical projects for 'Conventions' in the 1790s. There was a desire to work within Parliament, rather than an alienation from it. One sure sign of an incipient revolution or transfer of power is rightly held to be the slipping away of authority from the established institutions of state, to new, *ad hoc* unofficial bodies. Not many societies have shown fewer symptoms of that than eighteenth-century England; the Thirteen Colonies in North America prior to the outbreak of conflict in 1775 offer an obvious contrast.

The relative importance of Court politics is linked to the question of how far England can be described as an *ancien régime* state, to employ a term used to describe states such as Louis XIV's France. It is certainly possible to demonstrate differences between England and particular European states in, for example, the size of the capital city and the role of towns and of international trade. Equally it is possible to suggest similarities. England was not alone in having to define relationships with a new dynasty with a German homeland, or with subordinate European territories, such as Scotland and Ireland. Local government in England, self-government by the social élite, and the consequent primary political problem, persuading the élite to govern in the interests of the centre, would have been all too familiar to many continental monarchs. The term *ancien régime* is misleading if it is taken to denote a uniform situation and consistent change. However, if the diversity that characterised continental circumstances and developments is appreciated, then England can be more easily comprehended as a country which, like all others, had both unique and comparable features and developments.[27]

If the role of the monarch and Court provides one element of continuity, what continuity existed in the field of political organisation? The argument that, for the period 1689–1720, 'Court and Country' are less appropriate for any model of political structure than Whig and Tory[28] could certainly be extended chronologically. Nevertheless, an element of discontinuity appears in mid-century. Clark argued that his study of the politics of 1754–7:

'revealed in its necessary detail the crucial part of that tactical process by which the party system of the early eighteenth century disintegrated. In those years, the Tories were drawn into a Whig dogfight and deeply compromised; the Whigs were riven by personally-inspired conflicts for power within a ministry which was still formed on the basis of their party unity.'[29]

Such developments were scarcely peculiar to this period. More significant was the process of seeking to conciliate and comprehend opponents within ministerial ranks, a marked tendency in the period that began with the fall of Walpole in 1742 and, indeed, an inspiration that helped to precipitate his fall. The prime beneficiaries, as in the late 1710s and early 1720s, were dissident Whigs, and Tories prepared to renounce their party, but the instability and realignments of the 1740s prepared the ground for those of the following decade. After the crushing defeat of Bonnie Prince Charlie at Culloden in 1746, Jacobitism was less of an option for the Tories and so had less influence on the perception of them by both the Whigs and George II. In the 1750s Tory cohesion and identity were seriously compromised.[30] If proscription of the Tories and what lay behind it were a key to political activity in this period, then expectations concerning the future behaviour of Prince Frederick and his eldest son, George III, along with the actual behaviour of the latter after he came to the throne in 1760, were clearly important. These helped to give a temporary air to the political arrangements of the late 1740s and late 1750s and to compromise any suggestion that administration and opposition were likely to be fixed.

A theory of political organisation for this period has to comprehend two essentially different political worlds, the fundamentally two-party alignment of the first half of the century, within which Walpole operated, and the loose and shifting situation of the 1760s. Walpole was criticised by his opponents for his power and longevity, but they were also subsequently to be seen as exceptional – in part because of the changing political situation, especially the absence of any government of comparable length. A mid-century discontinuity is indicated, centring on the years 1746–62. Events in the last fifteen years of George II's reign were clearly important, especially the effective demise of Jacobitism as a viable option, the consequent changes in the views of many Tories, the regrouping of opposition politicians around Prince Frederick, and the developments that followed his death in 1751. Newcastle and Pitt the Elder both wooed Tory support, while in certain constituencies in the 1750s a process of compromise was under way, Whig candidates seeking Tory support while Tory counterparts were deemed acceptable if they declared loyalty to the Hanoverians and 'a general adherence to the government'.[31]

The policies of George III (1760–1820) were also important. George was determined to assert his independence from his grandfather's ministers. His views on foreign policy and his advancement of his favourite adviser, John, 3rd Earl of Bute, led to clashes with Newcastle and Pitt the Elder who had co-operated in directing the ministry since 1757. Pitt resigned in 1761, Newcastle the following year, and Bute was appointed a Secretary of State in 1761 and then First Lord of the Treasury in May 1762.

Bute's rise aroused outrage and provided the occasion for much anti-Scottish propaganda. The 4th Duke of Devonshire, one of the leading Old Corps Whigs, who held both a seat in the inner Cabinet and a major post at Court as Lord Chamberlain, claimed in November 1760: 'that a King of England, if he attempted to govern by a Favourite, would be unhappy for his affairs would always go ill, unless he placed his confidence in those whose abilities and situation rendered them the most considerable.' He was prepared to be blunt on the point both to George III and to Bute,[32] and it is clear from Devonshire's memoranda that one of the major bases of Old Corps Whig political activity was a belief in their own indispensability. Bute was disliked as an outsider and a royal favourite without political weight. Accustomed to view themselves as the natural advisers of the monarch, the Old Corps Whigs were unprepared to cope with the change from the elderly and exhausted George II to the more vigorous and unpredictable George III.

Although in 1760–2 George III's freedom of manoeuvre was restricted by war, as his grandfather's had been in 1744 and 1746 (and as George III's was later to be in 1782), he was able to dispense with the Old Corps and turn to his favourite, whereas, in 1744 and 1746, George II had failed to keep Carteret in office against the opposition of the Old Corps led by Newcastle and Pelham. By 1760, the Old Corps were suffering seriously from poor leadership. Pelham was dead, Hardwicke and Newcastle old and tired, and the new generation of leaders weak and unimpressive. George III also benefited from war-weariness, from the natural support for a new monarch, and from the influence and power that the Crown possessed which could be considerable if energetically and capably directed. George III's determination to exert his power disorientated the Old Corps Whigs who were used to a relationship between Crown and ministry in which royal initiatives were limited. The combination of political changes that had been in process for about fifteen years and the actions of George III destroyed the old party system which Walpole had dominated. In December 1761, the newly-elected Bamber Gascoyne told the Commons that there was 'faction in the ministry': Whig and Tory had been destroyed, but 'personal parties substituted in their stead'.[33] The Tories atomised, joining a variety of political groups, including the government establishment in the Commons.

For at least the early decades of George III's reign, Commons' support for the government rested not on a party but on a coalition of first, the 'party of the crown, comprising Members of the Commons whose primary interest lay in public or court service, and whose overriding loyalties were to the sovereign and to the principle that the King's government must be carried on'; secondly, groups of active politicians seeking power each with their own followers; and thirdly, independent MPs essentially concerned with local interests but willing to offer loyal, though not uncritical, support. Opposition was comprised of critical independents and of groups of excluded politicians. There was also a 'party of the Crown' in the Lords. This analysis is accurate for the 1760s, 1770s and 1780s: 'The apparent solidarity of the political line-up in the 1770s for or against the policy of maintaining the integrity of Britain's North American empire by force, merely cloaked, it did not supersede, the presence of personal groups'.[34]

The role of competing personal groups, operating without the semi-imperatives of fear and loyalty created by the Jacobite challenge and the response to it, helped to produce ministerial and parliamentary insecurity in the 1760s, as George III struggled to find a ministry that he could trust and co-operate with and that could wield an effective majority in the Commons. The situation was aggravated by some disquiet as to how the constitution must now be viewed and by fears of rapid constitutional change towards royal tyranny or aristocratic oligarchy. The decade also witnessed an increase in extra-parliamentary political activity associated, in particular, with the favourable response in London to the maverick and charismatic John Wilkes in his challenges to the authority of George III's ministers and to Parliament.[35]

However, there was no comparison between the actual and potential extra-parliamentary action that George I and George II's ministries had to confront and that which was faced in the period 1760–90. It was not until indigenous support for the cause of radicalism and for the example of the French Revolution developed in the early 1790s that a challenge similar to that posed by Jacobitism had to be confronted. The British supporters of the American rebels in the 1770s sought to alter the purpose of George III's government, rather than the identity of the ruling dynasty.[36] Most extra-parliamentary action was really a matter of peaceful lobbying. In 1762, William Mure, a Scottish MP and adviser of Bute, who supported the agitation for Scotland to have a militia, as England did, wrote from Edinburgh to his friend Gilbert Elliot:

'. . . our Militia Meeting here. I joined them, both as a well wisher to the cause, and to endeavour to prevent any unbecoming violence in their proceedings; or their improperly taking upon them to prescribe to their representatives by directing them the particular clauses of the Bill that should be passed. In both these I have succeeded. The whole that has been done is . . . sending a circular letter, very temperate, to every county and borough recommending to them to apply in general to their Members, for such a Militia as to the Wisdom of the Legislature might seem expedient.'[37]

The political reconfiguration of the 1750s and 1760s can be related to Walpolean policies. In essence they were the two halves of the ending of a long-standing divide in English and, to a certain extent, British politics that had developed in the seventeenth century. The reintegration of the Tories (and of Scottish elements formerly known for Jacobitism) can be discussed and explained in terms of the 1750s and 1760s, but the crucial prelude was the moderate Whiggism of the Walpole years. This was not the moderation of a mixed or 'broad bottom' ministry, but, instead, a tempering of Whig policies and the abandonment of schemes for radical religious and political change.

Much of Walpole's importance derives from a consideration of what would have happened had he followed different policies. The consequences of any continuation of those of the Stanhope–Sunderland years is a matter of speculation, but another protracted war like that of the Spanish Succession fought, for example, against Austria and Spain in 1725 or 1727, Austria in

1730, or France and Spain in 1733 would have placed heavy burdens on the country, as well as, more specifically, exacerbating the Jacobite threat. Pro-Dissenter policies would have been hazardous, and the prospect of losing general elections might have led to a degree of constitutional and political manipulation that might have undermined any prospect of stability. By avoiding such courses and helping to lower the political temperature, Walpole powerfully contributed both to political stability and to the reconfiguration of the 1750s and 1760s.

The period 1760–90 was essentially politically stable, although this was sorely tested in 1782–4. This may help to explain the ministerial instability of the 1760s: an essential stability enabled the political nation to view ministerial volatility without excessive alarm. A series of short-lived ministries, those of Bute (1762–3), George Grenville (1763–5), the Marquis of Rockingham (1765–6), William Pitt as Earl of Chatham (1766–8), and the Duke of Grafton (1768–70), succeeded one another, until, with Lord North, First Lord of the Treasury (1770–82), George III found a minister whom he could trust and who could manage Parliament, government and elections successfully. As in the case of Walpole and Pelham before him and Pitt the Younger subsequently, North both chose to lead the ministry from the Commons and was an expert on government finances. Like Walpole, North's eventual fall was linked to the prosecution of an unsuccessful war. However, North's achievement in managing the Commons easily in sessions such as that of 1773, and his success in the 1774 general election, reveal that the basis for ministerial and parliamentary stability had not been lost since the fall of Walpole and the death of Pelham. Parliamentary monarchy was still an effective system. It was to be proved so again during the ministry of Pitt the Younger, both during the stable period of 1784–91 and during the subsequent years when Britain and its propertied élite faced domestic radicalism and a powerful France.

The British Dimension

I am so sorry your description of the state of Scotland is so true; I wish we don't come to wish again as King William did, that it were a thousand miles off, and any one were king of it.

George Tilson, Under Secretary, 1723[1]

Walpole's world was still affected by the aftershock of earlier events. The 'Glorious' Revolution of 1688 and the consequent Jacobite challenge influenced English politics and government greatly, not least because of the effects of the two expensive and lengthy wars with France (1689–97, 1702–13) that were due substantially to William III's determination to limit French influence in western Europe. The effect of 1688 on Scotland and Ireland was more direct. It touched off a British civil war, as supporters of William and James struggled for control both of Ireland and Scotland. By 1691 this had resulted in a Williamite triumph in both areas, although neither could be regarded as completely pacified, and the Scottish Highlands remained tense, as episodes such as the massacre of Glencoe of 1692 revealed.

A new order was created in each kingdom. The Episcopal order of the Church of Scotland was overturned in favour of a Presbyterian government. The Scots universities and schools were purged, as again after 1715. As a result of procedural changes in the 1690s, the ability of the Edinburgh Parliament to take initiatives was enhanced and it took a number that revealed its independence of the executive. In Ireland, the Catholic aspirations that had been encouraged during the reign of James II were crushed in the Protestant victory of the battle of the Boyne in 1690. English politicians did not doubt that Jacobite aspirations remained strong in both kingdoms, particularly after 1707 in Scotland. These were made more threatening by the possibility of French and Spanish assistance for the Jacobites. French support had played a major role in the Irish resistance to Williamite conquest, and in 1708 a French invasion force, including 'James III' ('VIII' of Scotland) nearly effected a landing on the east coast of Scotland.[2]

SCOTLAND

Jacobitism and the strategic threat posed by Scotland and Ireland both engendered English concern and pushed together those politicians and groups in the three kingdoms who were opposed to Jacobitism. The Union of 1707 arose essentially from English concern about the possible hazards posed by an autonomous, if not independent, Scotland. There was little support for the measure in Scotland, and its passage through the Scottish Parliament ultimately depended on corruption and self-interest. There was less need for a Union with Ireland: a shared anti-Catholicism helped keep the English government and the Parliament of Ireland in Dublin in rough harmony.

Union with England ensured that Scottish parliamentary politics would be waged in a Parliament (Westminster) where Scotland's representation was limited: 45 MPs and 16 representative peers out of 558 MPs and about 200 peers. As a result, Court and ministerial politics in London became more important for Scotland. Equally, it became necessary for English ministers seeking a secure parliamentary majority to control the votes of Scottish representatives and, therefore, the management of Scotland in a parliamentary sense became important. After 1707 Scotland was clearly a political as well as a security problem. This was exploited by Scottish politicians who sought to play the English party game in order to gain governmental patronage that would improve their position in London and Scotland.

Contemporary commentators were in no doubt of the importance of Scottish parliamentarians in Westminster. Vernon alleged in 1732 that the Salt Duty passed in the Commons 'merely by the weight of the Scots members'. Henry Fox MP regarded their role as crucial in the fall of his patron Walpole: 'The Scotch are 24 against us and but 16 for us and there has been the Treachery.'[3]

The comment of one Scottish MP, Gilbert Elliot, on an important division in 1755, 'Of the Scotch, few only were in the minority',[4] could have been repeated on many occasions. However, this role led to attention being given to their management and therefore to allegations of corruption. Lord Perceval wrote in 1715:

'I saw a warrant today signed by the king wherein were pensions granted to 19 Scotch Lords and 3 commoners, the highest was but £300 the lowest £100. Mr Baron Scroop said that 6 of the 16 Scots peers chosen to sit in the present Parliament are included in another warrant, but their pensions are each £800. The rest have good employments. It may be truly said that nation is bought. £4000 used to buy their Parliament.'[5]

The Scottish Presbyterian cleric Robert Wodrow complained in 1726 that the Scottish MPs had neglected Scotland's interests during the parliamentary debates over the Malt tax: 'we now see under what influence our Members of Parliament are, and that they must be reimbursed in the charges they are at in their elections and attendance in Parliament; and it is much to be feared, the most part are influenced by pensions or hopes.'[6]

The corruption of those elected, however injurious to Scottish confidence in their representatives, could not suffice for English politicians confronted by the willingness of their Scottish counterparts to align with English groups. Instead, this willingness was utilised in order to secure the management of Scotland. In 1716, General Cadogan observed, 'the Scotch affairs have now so very near a connexion with the English ones'.[7] In 1708, the chief executive organ of government in Scotland, the Scottish Privy Council, had been abolished. Although the surviving Scottish officers of state sat in the British Privy Council, government policy was not formulated there, but rather in the Inner Cabinet, in which there was no Scottish member during the first half of the century. For much of the period, namely 1708–11, 1713–14, 1714–15, 1716–25 and 1742–6 there was a third Secretary of State responsible for Scotland. However, this post, held by major Scottish aristocrats, the last three being the Duke of Montrose (1714–15), the Duke of Roxburgh (1716–25) and the Marquis of Tweeddale (1742–6), did not confer control over all aspects of government in Scotland. The officers of the revenue and of the armed forces were outside the Secretary's control, and the relevant ministers in London, therefore, wielded considerable power.

Walpole had no confidence in Roxburgh, who had backed Stanhope and Sunderland, and he blamed him for the disturbances in 1725 over the Malt tax. Roxburgh was dismissed and the Secretaryship abolished, although the blow was softened by an annual pension of £3,000.[8] The Scottish political crisis of 1725 obliged Walpole to take a more active role in Scottish politics,[9] and led him to seek an alliance with John, 2nd Duke of Argyll, and his brother, Archibald Campbell, Earl of Ilay, later, from 1743 until 1761, 3rd Duke of Argyll. Though neither was made Scottish Secretary of State, they managed Scotland for Walpole and, in turn, wielded most government patronage in Scotland. Ilay was responsible for most of the work of patronage. Charles Delafaye, an Under-Secretary of State, wrote of him in 1725, 'he seems singly to support His Majesty's authority and that of the laws'.[10] A number of other aristocrats were, also, of some importance. The 3rd Earl of Loudoun was Commissioner to the General Assembly of the Church of Scotland and, as such, was instructed by George II in 1730 and 1731 'to suffer nothing to be done in the assembly to the prejudice of our authority or prerogative'. Similarly, opposition leaders turned to Scottish allies to manage the opposition cause. In

1740, Carteret wrote to the Marquis of Tweeddale, 'I don't doubt but your Lordship will desire all your friends of the House of Commons to be here at the opening of the Parliament'.[11]

Ilay remained loyal to Walpole after Argyll broke with him in 1740. However, Scottish management thereafter was disturbed for a number of years. The division in the Campbell family affected the general election results in 1741 and Carteret, when he gained office in 1742, supported the remains of the *Squadrone*, the Scottish Whig faction that had backed Stanhope and Sunderland, making Tweeddale Secretary of State for Scotland. However, the alliance between the Old Corps Whigs and the Campbells, created by Walpole, survived the challenge both of the *Squadrone* and of Jacobitism, and Ilay, now Duke of Argyll and the wealthiest Scottish peer, managed Scotland from 1746 until his death in 1761.[12]

In one important respect, Scottish management was a failure. In 1745, most of Scotland easily fell to Bonnie Prince Charlie, Charles Edward Stuart, the son of the Pretender, despite his coming with only a tiny following. Stephen Poyntz, one-time governor of the Duke of Cumberland, reacted with concern to what he saw as a moral challenge:

'That a nation like Scotland which makes the strictest profession of the Protestant Religion and values itself on respecting the sanctity of an oath should suffer the Pretender's son with a handful of rabble to walk the Protestant Succession out of that Kingdom, without lifting up a single weapon or hand against him, is astonishing to the last degree, and fills one with dreadful apprehensions for the behaviour of England, where a dissolute indifference for everything sacred and serious, and a luxurious impatience of dangers and hardships more generally prevails.'[13]

A 'Memorial concerning the state of the Highlands and Islands of Scotland' published in a London Whig newspaper, the *Flying Post*, on 7 March 1723 had claimed that they were the greatest threat to Britain: 'as these people will never fail to join with foreign Popish powers, to advance the interests they have espoused; so they always have been, and infallibly will be instruments and tools in the hands of those who have a design to enslave or embroil the British nation.'

The article continued by casting a sceptical eye on government attempts to disarm the Highlands and by claiming that naval blockade would never be completely successful, both views that were to be vindicated in 1745. George I himself had in 1725 felt it necessary to recommend 'the careful execution of his orders by Major General Wade with respect to the disarming the Highlands'. Wade was instructed to continue the construction of fortifications and barracks in northern Scotland, Townshend writing: 'The King looks upon the securing that weak part as extremely necessary to discourage the Jacobites'.[14]

Nevertheless, the failure of Jacobite risings and conspiracies between 1708 and 1722 and the settlement of the Malt tax disturbances of 1725, which Walpole had followed closely, helping to draft instructions, diminished fears about Scotland.[15] Violence, such as the brawl at the public dinner held to celebrate the Roxburghshire election of 1726, when the newly elected MP killed a local gentleman who had not voted for him, was generally of a habitual kind, rather than aimed against the government. The Lord Advocate, Duncan Forbes, informed Newcastle in 1728 that disaffection 'was wearing out apace'.[16]

In fact, Jacobitism was to revive from the late 1730s, in part because the monopolisation of patronage by the Campbell interest left little practical recourse for loyal opposition. In 1726, Wodrow had queried: 'how far it be for the general interest of Scotland that we have a Scots secretary, since he must be of one of our sides, and so those of the other side [will] find much difficulty in their applications.'[17] The harsh response to the Porteous riots in 1736 also undermined government popularity. Nevertheless, it is probable that there would have been no Jacobite rising but for British involvement in the War of the Austrian Succession. It was this which led Louis XV to plan an invasion in 1744 and to invite the Stuarts to France. Bonnie Prince Charlie's march to Derby in 1745, the greatest crisis faced by the eighteenth-century British state, would have been even more serious had French forces invaded southern England as they planned to do and as the British ministry feared they would.

The suppression of the '45 was followed by a determined attempt to alter the political, social and strategic structure of the Highlands in order to make another rebellion impossible. The clans were disarmed and the clan system broken up, while roads to open up the Highlands and forts to awe them were constructed, a continuation of a policy that had led to regular expenditure during the Walpole years. Regalities and hereditable jurisdictions were abolished in pursuit of a policy explained in the title of an anonymous pamphlet, published in Edinburgh in 1746, *Superiorities displayed; or Scotland's grievance, by reason of the slavish dependence of the people . . . and of the many hereditary jurisdictions over them. Wherein is shown, that these have been the handles of rebellion in preceding ages . . . and that, upon their removal, and putting the People of Scotland on the footing of those in England, the seeds of rebellion will be plucked up for ever.* The rebellion and its suppression gave cause and opportunity for the sort of radical state-directed action against inherited privilege, especially regional and aristocratic privilege, that was so unusual in early eighteenth-century Europe and so rare in Britain.

Thereafter, the ministry in London devoted little attention to Scotland. Indeed, under Argyll's management, Scottish politics were less contentious in the 1750s than their London counterparts. Scotland made a major contribution to the British war effort in the Seven Years' War (1756–63). To the five specifically Scottish foot regiments in existence in 1756, at least another five were added. Charles Townshend, visiting Scotland at the end of the 1750s, was rhapsodical when he reported: 'it is a very rising country: industry is general: the improvements are rapid: the lowest rank of subjects is emancipated from traditional slavery: commerce driven from England by high taxes, luxury and abuse, seeks the simplicity, frugality and exemptions of Scotland, and this part of Britain must in time, from these causes, succeed to the plenty, prosperity, cultivation, wealth, luxury, abuses and decline of England.'[18]

Townshend was correct to note signs of economic development, while the Scottish poor law was regularly lauded also. Links between the two kingdoms, ranging from postal services to aristocratic intermarriage, improved.

The process was not always harmonious. Carteret had told the House of Lords in 1743 that: 'the people of this nation in particular have always been jealous of foreigners, nay, even of their fellow-subjects; for it is hardly possible to do justice to the Scottish or Irish, without raising a clamour among the English'.[19] The rise under George III of first Bute and later Lord Chief Justice Mansfield was accompanied by bitter denunciations of Scots who came south to make their fortune. 'They send us whole cargoes of their staple commodity, half-bred doctors and surgeons to poison and destroy our health' was one of the complaints of a correspondent of a London newspaper in 1771.

However, these indications of tension were trivial compared to the fears of Scottish attack in 1745. Sir David Dalrymple observed in 1763:

'It has been often a matter of astonishment to me why a minister in England should think a minister here necessary; we are so well broke, so thoroughly paced that we can be managed by a whipcord as well as by a double bridle, and yet the no-significancy of such tools serves in this country for talents and influence, and were that necessary, would supply the place of integrity likewise.'

Scotland was no longer a security risk nor particularly difficult to govern. If, in 1761, a customs collector at Dumfries could report that gangs of smugglers numbering up to fifty were travelling inland with their goods in defiance of the outnumbered customs officers,[20] the position was no different along much of the eastern and southern coasts of England. Mentioning Scotland, *Common Sense* reflected on 7 May 1737 that 'smaller dominions united to greater, no matter upon what terms [they] become dependent upon them'.

This issue was essentially settled militarily in 1689, 1715–16, 1719 and 1745–6, not that the Jacobite cause simply opposed Scotland to England. Many Scots were firm opponents of the Stuarts and supporters of the Protestant Succession. To bolster this position, the half-century after the Union witnessed the development of a system of management in which patronage and shared interests replaced coercion. Force was replaced by necessary accommodation with leading Scots. The rewards for London included the need to keep few troops in Scotland and the overwhelming reliability of Scottish MPs. For Scotland the management of the 3rd Duke of Argyll brought a partisan patronage system, but one directed by a Scot who was sensitive to Scottish interests and represented them in London; in many respects he was similar to Walpole. When Argyll died in 1761, Scotland was not waiting to rebel, and disaffection was limited.

IRELAND

Whereas the number of Catholics in Scotland was small, they formed the majority of the population of Ireland. The seventeenth-century legacy of Catholic risings in Ireland and of Irish panics in England was such that sensitivity to events in Ireland, whether real or rumoured, was strong on the other side of the Irish Sea. There had been considerable concern when in 1689 the Dublin Parliament, composed almost wholly of Catholics and under the protection of James II, had repealed the Acts giving expression to the Restoration land settlements. The London press frequently referred to Catholic activity, proselytisation and acts of violence in Ireland, the *General Evening Post* of 12 February 1734, for example, reporting that in Meath, 'information of many Polish priests, friars and monasteries, not heard of till this enquiry', had been discovered. The recruiting of Irishmen for the Irish regiments in French service caused particular concern in the 1730s, and was a tricky issue in 1730 when the two powers were allies. Newcastle confided to his brother his conviction that 'we shall have it in Parliament, and when it comes there, I believe it will be more universally blamed, even by our own friends, than anything we have done'.[21]

The Jacobites were optimistic about their support in Ireland, and in 1731 the French *chargé d'affaires* in London reported that Ireland, treated tyrannically as it was, was in despair.[22] However, Delafaye was to be proved correct in his view, expressed in 1725: 'I can have no notion of a scheme of our enemies upon Ireland where there is an army, and where all the Protestants (in whose hands is the wealth and power), bad as they are, are so nearly concerned in point of private interest to resist such an attempt.'[23] The Protestant Ascendancy was strongly established. Under the Banishment Act of 1697, hundreds of Catholic clerics had been banished under pain of execution if they returned. The castration of Catholic clerics was subsequently considered. Under the penal statutes passed in the first half of the eighteenth century Catholics were prevented from freely acquiring or bequeathing land or property, and were disfranchised and debarred from all political, military and legal offices. In 1691, Catholics were disqualified from sitting in the Dublin Parliament; in 1727, from voting in elections to it. Acts forbade mixed marriages,

Catholic schools and the bearing of arms by Catholics. It has been estimated that the percentage of land in Catholic hands fell from 59 in 1641 to 22 in 1688, 14 in 1703 and 5 in 1778, though some of the Protestant ownership was only token.

The Penal Code was designed essentially to destroy the political and economic power of Catholicism rather than the faith itself. The ability of the Anglican establishment to proselytise was limited by its general failure to communicate with a still largely Gaelic-speaking population. In contrast, the Catholic colleges stipulated a knowledge of that language as a requirement for the mission. The Catholic percentage of the population did not diminish, because the Catholic clergy, wearing secular dress and secretly celebrating mass, continued their work, sustained by a strong oral culture, the emotional link with a sense of national identity, by hedge-school teaching and by a fair amount of tacit government acceptance. Serious repression was episodic. If it had been possible to implement the religious clauses of the Penal Code and if a persistent attempt had been made to do so, then Catholicism might have been seriously challenged, though the military forces in the island were not large, and the result in 1715 and 1745 might have been Jacobite insurrections. Instead, a crucial feature of both years was that there was no Irish rising despite the continued tradition of Jacobitism among the majority of the population. 'The numbers of Roman Catholics in Ireland' was one reason why James Craggs, one of the Secretaries of State, feared that a Spanish pro-Jacobite invasion force would be directed there in 1719.[24] Catholic clerics in Ireland still prayed for 'James III' in the 1730s, as did Scottish Episcopalians (formally until 1788), and the draconian Irish wartime legislation of 1697, 1703–4 and 1709 was inspired by fears of Catholic disloyalty and links with France, though persecution usually slackened in peacetime. However, long-standing religious grievances helped to exacerbate political disaffection in the 1790s.

Though the Protestant Ascendancy in Ireland, centred on the Parliament in Dublin, had a shared interest with England in keeping Ireland quiet, this did not prevent problems from developing in the relationship between London and Dublin. Viewed from Westminster, management was not free of difficulties, even though London was firmly in control. The executive in Dublin Castle, headed by the Lord Lieutenant, was appointed from London and responsible to British officers of state. The crown enjoyed a large 'hereditary revenue' in Ireland. The Irish Parliament had no right to prepare legislation, that being the task of the Irish Privy Council, whose bills had to be approved by the Privy Council in London. The Westminster Parliament itself also possessed the power to legislate for Ireland. Its Declaratory Act of 1720 declared its 'full power and authority to make Laws and Statutes . . . to bind the Kingdom and People of Ireland', and denied to the Irish House of Lords any appellate jurisdiction from the Irish courts.[25]

England's constitutional and political dominance led to measures that aroused anger in Ireland. The granting of Irish lands and pensions to favoured courtiers in London exacerbated the problem of absentee landowners and revenue-holders with the consequent drain of money out of the country.[26] Legislation in Westminster, the result of persistent protectionist lobbying by the English woollen interest, hindered Irish wool exports, one pamphlet complaining in 1731 'it is as well to be hanged as starved'.[27] In 1722, a Wolverhampton ironmaster, William Wood, purchased a patent to mint copper coins for Ireland, a measure that aroused a storm of complaint in Ireland where it was seen as a threat to the economy and a consequence of Ireland's vulnerable constitutional position. The controversy created serious difficulties for the officials and politicians in Dublin. In 1724, Townshend noted that he had received from William Conolly, Speaker of the Irish House of Commons from 1715 to 1729, his:

'answer to the orders that have been lately sent him in relation to the new coinage. He says that as Commissioner of the Revenue he is bound to follow any directions he receives from His Majesty, but as his acting immediately in consequence of those orders, may lay him under some difficulties as Speaker of the House of Commons, he desires a little time to consider of some expedient to reconcile those two characters.'[28]

On 24 November 1722, the *British Journal*, had called for a reform in the way that Ireland was governed 'when our superiors are at leisure from greater affairs'. Pressing the need to preserve the dependence of the colonies, this London paper argued that Ireland was:

'too powerful to be treated only as a colony; and that if we design to continue them friends, the best way to do it, is to imitate the example of merchants and shopkeepers; that is, when their apprentices are acquainted with their trade and their customers, and are out of their time, to take them into partnership, rather than to set them up for themselves in their neighbourhood.'

There was to be no partnership, at least for the bulk of the Irish population, but the relationship between London and Ireland was not as one-sided as the constitutional arrangements might suggest. The Irish Parliament had to be managed, not least because of the need to finance the military budget, and Lord Lieutenants, such as the Duke of Bolton in 1717,[29] were very concerned about the difficulties that this posed. The solution was to use Irish political managers who were known as undertakers and this introduced a further element of compromise. Furthermore, Irish politicians could seek to influence policy in London by lobbying[30] and by their links with British politicians. The latter played a role in the divisions in Irish politics in the reigns of Anne and George I, with a Whig–Tory divide being followed by a Whig triumph in the general election of 1715 and a subsequent Whig split in which a struggle for office was central. This division persisted into the early 1720s, Lord Chancellor Midleton looking to Carteret for support against the Duke of Grafton, Lord Lieutenant from 1720 to 1724, and Walpole.

In combination with the storm over Wood's Halfpence, this produced a difficult situation that was solved by the replacement of Grafton by Carteret, a move that Walpole hoped would wreck him,[31] the fall of Midleton in 1725 (with his rival Conolly confirmed as chief undertaker), and the recall of Wood's patent, also in 1725. Although intended primarily to ease Walpole's position at Court, by removing Carteret from a position, a Secretaryship of State, in which he could develop royal favour, the changes of 1724–5 helped to quieten Irish politics.

Divisions and disputes did not cease but there was to be no political crisis compelling the attention of London comparable to that of 1722–5 for the rest of the Walpole ministry, though Walpole continued to keep an eye on Irish politics, and appointed reliable English supporters to key posts.[32] Carteret's successors, the Dukes of Dorset (1730–7) and Devonshire (1737–45), lacked his ability and political skills, but an essential harmony of interest, combined with the deployment of government patronage by Irish undertakers, helped to keep Ireland and the Anglo-Irish relationship fundamentally stable, although recent scholars have found Walpole's political management wanting. He subordinated the management of Ireland to considerations of English patronage, and his attempt to limit the independence of Irish undertakers helped create needless difficulties.[33] Nevertheless, an official in Dublin, was able to write in 1742 to a counterpart in London: 'Our Parliament have acted with great unanimity and gave the supply with great cheerfulness. I am glad I can tell you that his Grace [the Duke of Devonshire] has had as easy a session of Parliament as ever was known, I wish your Parliament when they meet would act after the same manner'. The situation was just as peaceful in 1744.[34]

This stability was to dissolve slowly after the '45 with the growth of Protestant Irish patriotism and constitutional sensitivity. In 1753–6, the 'Money Bill Dispute', a quarrel over whether the Crown or the Dublin Parliament had the right to dispose of a surplus in the Irish Treasury arising from Irish taxation, led to a bitter and wide-ranging controversy in which the Lord Lieutenant was defied by the undertakers and forced to back down. The removal of the external and internal threat of Jacobitism led to a change in the Anglo–Irish relationship and a reassessment of attitudes that was to provide the context for a series of political and constitutional disputes. In a similar fashion, the crushing of the French threat to Britain's North American colonies during the Seven Years' War helped to prepare the ground for post-war constitutional disputes between these colonies and London. No constitution was so watertight as to preclude the possibility of disputes, and the ambiguous processes of compromise that constituted such a large part of government and patronage were subject in periods of tension to comparable difficulties.

THE STABILITY OF THE BRITISH ISLES

One of the major problems confronting the rulers and governments of many European states was their relationship with regions where their authority and power were especially circumscribed. The nature of the problem varied greatly and was understandably less serious for minor states. In all large states, however, the problem existed, particularly with respect to regions gained through conquest and dynastic succession in which local privileges and a sense of separate identity had been preserved. This was not invariably the case. For example, the Swedish region of Ingria was conquered by Peter the Great of Russia during the Great Northern War (1700–21), later becoming the province of St Petersburg. During the war most of the landowners left or were expelled and Peter, acknowledging no prior right of ownership, began settlement and development policies accordingly. Such policies were, however, common only in eastern Europe, in cases of colonial expansion, and, in western Europe, in the wake of rebellions which had been suppressed without negotiation.

Local privileges and a sense of separate identity were of scant value to the Irish Catholics, or to Scottish Jacobites. The substantial emigration of Irish Catholic gentry under the terms of the Treaty of Limerick (1691) reflected their recognition that they had little future in Ireland, as did the subsequent emigration of Irish Catholics to seek their fortune abroad, not least by service in foreign armies. About 19,000 Irish left the country soon after the treaty. By 1749, only 8 out of 114 Irish peers were Catholics.

However, for the politically involved groups, at least, a sense of separate identity and national privileges played a significant role in the relationship between on the one hand England and on the other Scotland and Ireland, though not Wales. Ireland retained its Parliament, Scotland had a different national church and legal system, and both Ireland and Scotland required specialised management. Hostility to Jacobitism linked the Irish and Scottish political establishments, as remodelled after 1714, to London, producing a pressure for co-operation distinct from the customary aspirations that eased the path of management. In addition, the sense of separate identity was attenuated, especially at the level of the social and political élite, by the decline of the Celtic languages and the growing appeal of English cultural norms and customs. Welsh, Irish and Scots sought to benefit from links with England, a process facilitated by the spread of English. The decline of a separate cultural identity, for example among the Welsh gentry of Glamorgan after about 1740, played an important, though intangible, role in the increasing hegemony of English ideas, although in Scotland this was qualified by the influence of the Scottish Enlightenment. Although the Irish Protestant élite became more conscious of a possible national role, they continued to identify culturally with England, rather than with the bulk of the Irish population.

The Welsh and Scottish landed élite became increasingly Anglocentric, a process that had long been at work in Wales.[35] This played a major role in the growing British stability which was such a notable feature of the century until the 1770s, when developments in Ireland made the relationship between England and Ireland more contentious and difficult. Had the '45 succeeded, then it would have been foolish to write of growing stability, but the increased acceptance and exploitation of England's cultural hegemony helped to ensure that there were no more '45s.

10

Walpole's Fall and Thereafter

Will nothing ever drive ye to despair,
Ye hungry swarms of Grubstreet, and Rag-fair?
. . .
See Walpole brighter from your venom rise,
See him disdain your unavailing lies,
And all your empty menaces despise.
In conscious justice cloathed, your arts he views,
Yet calmly great his candid course pursues:
All rancour, party, pique, expunged his mind;
Regardless of himself – to serve Mankind.

Anon., They are Not (1740), p. 7

THE LIMITS OF MANAGEMENT: WALPOLE'S FALL

Walpole's position deteriorated markedly in 1739. Spanish depredations struck a powerful chord and offered the opposition a new platform in place of the somewhat tired, and certainly much repeated, charges about corrupt and autocratic government. In early 1739, government majorities in both the Commons and the Lords fell[1] and there were rumours that ministers and courtiers, for example Wilmington, would defect to the enemy. Foreign envoys reported that Walpole's position was vulnerable.[2] Such reports were intercepted by the government, while British diplomats emphasised their concern about foreign perceptions.[3] Walpole, however, did not collapse under the pressure, and the decision by the opposition to withdraw from the Commons in protest against the passage of the Convention of the Pardo with Spain through the Commons on 8 March helped reduce the parliamentary pressure on him. The Lords also passed the Convention by 95 votes to 74. The Commons division was 260 to 232, the fullest House known for many years.

News of the attacks on Walpole were widely circulated through the press, so that parliamentary exchanges helped condition national perceptions. Thus, for example, Richard Wilkes, a Staffordshire doctor, recorded in March 1739:

'Never was more uneasiness about any affair than the Convention, nor was ever more said both within the House and out of it against a minister. Mr Pitt told Sir Robert he did not think himself inferior to him in anything and clapping his hand upon his breast said he was much superior to him in honesty, and Mr Pulteney said he was ready to prove 30 members of that House bribed, yet no particular notice was taken of them'.[4]

However, war broke out because of disputes over the implementation of the Convention of the Pardo. The South Sea Company was unwilling to pay money it owed the Spanish crown, and Newcastle decided to countermand orders for the British fleet to leave the Mediterranean. Taken in response to public unease, this measure proved unacceptable to the Spanish government and led it to abandon the path of conciliation and to refuse to fulfil its obligations under the Convention.

The War of Jenkins' Ear was begun despite Walpole's prediction that it would lead to major difficulties.[5] Having been criticised in 1738 and early 1739 for not being willing to fight, the ministry benefited in the short term from the outbreak of war, which was officially declared on 19 October. In the debate on the Address on 15 November 1739, Pulteney spoke 'for vigorously and unanimously supporting the King in the war, and letting every thing give way to the common national cause and the support of this government'. Herbert Mackworth, newly-elected Tory MP for Cardiff Boroughs, was in no great hurry to attend a quiet House: 'I don't find there is likely to be any very important question this session . . . it is much doubted whether the Place Bill will be attempted'.[6] When it was, on 29 January 1740, the government majority was 222 to 206. On 21 February, Walpole defeated Pulteney's motion for an address to George II to lay before the Commons all the papers relating to the Convention, by a majority of 247 to 196. On 10 December 1740, the government was able to get its demand for funds for more soldiers through the Commons by 252 to 197.

However, the government also soon found itself facing sustained criticism both within and outside Parliament, over the unsuccessful and insufficiently glorious conduct of the war. Admiral Vernon's early triumph in capturing Porto Bello on the isthmus of Panama in November 1739 led to a wave of jingoism that encouraged the political commitment of military resources to empire,[7] although opposition newspapers, such as *Common Sense* on 10 May 1740 claimed that Walpole was angry at Vernon's success. In the volatile political atmosphere of the closing years of the Walpole ministry, the government felt it necessary to respond to expectations about the prospects from action in the

Caribbean. The proponents of the so-called 'Blue Water' strategy argued that war could be profitably conducted against Spain by mounting attacks on her colonial empire.

The situation was far less promising than was generally believed in Britain. The difficulty of organising trans-oceanic operations, as well as concern that France would come to the assistance of her ally, Spain, limited British activity, while local defences and diseases proved sufficient to protect Spanish possessions. Vernon had destroyed the fortifications of Porto Bello, for he was in no position to retain them. In 1740, he achieved little bar an ineffective bombardment of Cartagena and the capture of Chagres. Vernon was affected by a serious shortage of sailors, a lack of naval stores, and concern about the movement of the Brest squadron, the main French fleet. Oglethorpe's attack on St Augustine in Florida failed in the face of effective Spanish resistance. Walpole suffered from the absence of any spectacular success with which he could be associated and through which he could gain the prestige and respect that were so important to government. He was accused of delaying the dispatch of forces to the West Indies.[8] The anniversary of the capture of Porto Bello provided an opportunity for extensive opposition celebrations designed to throw critical light on Walpole.

In 1741, the situation appeared to change with the arrival of a substantial force under Rear-Admiral Sir Chaloner Ogle and Brigadier General Thomas Wentworth. This force was launched against Cartagena on the coast of modern Colombia. Supporting fortresses were captured in March and the fall of the city appeared imminent, but an assault on the hill fort which dominated it failed and, after disagreements about the best way to launch another attack in the face of heavy losses through disease, the troops re-embarked in April.

The unexpected failure led to bitter recriminations, with Vernon blaming Wentworth for moving too slowly to attack. The most recent study exonerates Wentworth from much of the criticism and directs attention to Vernon's volatile nature and to the problems this created for combined operations. In addition, Vernon, totally misjudging the strength of the Spanish position and the determination and ability of its defenders, refused to land his sailors in support, and this helped ensure defeat.[9]

The Cartagena expedition was carefully planned but, in part, failed due to a dispatch of insufficient resources. Later success during the Seven Years' War, in which Havana fell in 1762, was due not to an innovative strategy, but rather to the deployment of greater resources and to better co-operation between army and navy commanders.

The fate of the attack on Cartagena seemingly demonstrated the truth of opposition claims that the war was being conducted badly, and it was followed by unsuccessful attempts on Santiago de Cuba and Panama, the failure of which owed much to poor command decisions by Vernon.[10] Nevertheless, the opposition failed in the attempts of 1739, 1740 and 1741 to bring down the ministry, attempts which culminated on 13 February 1741 in motions in both Houses for the removal of Walpole from office. The tone and content of the opposition attacks were strident and bitter. On 13 February 1741, Pitt criticised the minister's 'satiety of power' and claimed that 'he who had lost the confidence of all mankind should not be permitted to continue at the head of the king's government'. However, the Tories had not been consulted about the motions and the suspicion that most of them felt of the opposition Whigs led many of them to vote against the motion or to abstain. Pulteney blamed their action on Jacobitism, specifically the hope that Walpole's unpopularity would 'bring matters to the point', while claiming that some of their leaders had promised support, but it was clear to informed contemporaries that the Tories were being made use of, and were not likely to gain much from an opposition victory. Edward Harley was unimpressed by the motion, not least by what he perceived as the brute reliance on a parliamentary vote which reminded him of the attack on the Tory ministers after the accession of George I:

The charge was general being an account of his administration as to our affairs at home and abroad, no particular facts were stated nor any evidence produced either viva voce or written to support the charge, or to bring it home particularly to Sir Robert Walpole so as to distinguish him from any of the rest of the administration or Privy Council. As the accusation was founded on common fame and every member was to judge by his own private opinion, many of the Tories whose principles abhor even the shadow of Bills of Pains and Penalties, or to censure anyone without evidence refused to vote in the question and withdrew. Some few of them divided against it. Several of the Tories for it as thinking it matter of advice only to the king to remove a minister whom all were satisfied was a very ill one.

The motion was defeated in the Commons by 290 to 106 and also failed in the Lords.[11]

The debates and divisions on 13 February 1741 undermined opposition cohesion, and this was accentuated on 9 April when the opposition Whigs supported the government on a vote of credit of £300,000 designed to enable the government to support Maria Theresa of Austria in the developing crisis over the Austrian Succession that had begun when Frederick II (the Great) of Prussia invaded Silesia in December 1740: 'for preventing the subversion of the House of Austria . . . and supporting the liberties and balance of power in Europe'. The Tories were unhappy about the undertaking to defend Hanover if it was attacked on that account.[12] Walpole made it clear that aid to Austria was part of a strategy of constructing an anti-Bourbon coalition: 'the only power that can sensibly injure us by obstructing our commerce, or invading our dominions, is France, against which no confederacy can be formed, except with the House of Austria, that can afford us any efficacious support'.[13]

Walpole was able to maintain his position in the Commons until after the 1741 elections. However, he was placed under increasing difficulties as a result of divisions within the government, Newcastle challenging his foreign policy and patronage decisions. Ossorio suggested that Queen Caroline's death in 1737 had removed a crucial moderator of ministerial divisions. In 1739, there was division over negotiations with Spain and subsequent strategy, and over Walpole's support for Hervey's appointment as Lord Privy Seal. Newcastle opposed this,[14] but Hervey gained the post in May 1740. In 1740, although relations were not always poor,[15] Newcastle kept Walpole in the dark about his correspondence with Harrington, who had accompanied George II to Hanover.

Furthermore, the Tories and opposition Whigs combined effectively in the new Parliament at the end of 1741, some of the former acting partly in response to instructions from the Pretender, the latter encouraged by the active opposition of Frederick, Prince of Wales. In many constituencies, the Tories and the opposition Whigs had already co-operated in the general election held in May 1741; 286 ministerial supporters, 131 opposition Whigs and 136 Tories were elected, Walpole's majority falling from 42 at the end of the last Parliament to 19 owing to defeats in Cornwall and Scotland, in the first of which Prince Frederick was very influential. The loss of the Duke of Argyll's support was important in Scotland. Although the respective weight of opinion and patronage are difficult to weigh, it was also the case that there was a groundswell of opinion against the government. This had not prevented Walpole from winning in 1734, but in 1741 it can be seen as of importance in encouraging an important measure of opposition co-operation, however temporary, during the elections and in the crucial divisions of the following winter. To give but two examples from October 1740, John Tucker wrote from Weymouth:

'the violence and oppression which is offered here and in other places to those who have most zealously exerted themselves for the present establishment has made the gentlemen of this country lay aside party distinctions and resolve to unite for the common good. There was a very considerable number of them met on this occasion at Shaftesbury the 25th past, where they unanimously determined to continue their assemblies in different parts of the county in order to support and promote the elections of any gentlemen who stand on an independent interest'.

Sir James Lowther claimed that:

'the cry against officers and pensions increases to such a degree it can hardly be resisted, and the barbarous behaviour of a Scotch Lieutenant Colonel in murdering people for not choosing his friends for magistrates makes a prodigious clamour against having so many soldiers in the House. People are so enraged all over the kingdom at this governing by pensions and giving every place in the nation and favouring some and oppressing others to influence elections, there never was the like'.[16]

Lowther noted a continuation of Walpole's patronage methods in the midst of the developing crisis:

'Sir Robert has promised me faithfully that George Fletcher shall be made an ensign in an old regiment with the first that are signed by the King which will be soon. They promise fair just at the opening of the session but care for none but those that will go through thick and thin. There is a most desperate clamour against his measures, and especially that he has neglected to furnish Admiral Vernon with orders and stores'.[17]

Walpole made major efforts to mobilise his support in the new Commons, which first met on 1 December 1741. Placemen, such as the Scottish MP Sir James Grant, received personal letters asking them to attend the first day of the session as 'it is very probable that matters of the greatest importance will come under immediate consideration'.[18] However, his inability to retain his majority reflected the refusal of a few ministerial MPs to attend debates on election petitions. As in 1733, at the time of the Excise crisis, the ministry was damaged by the abstention, rather than the outright desertion, of some of its supporters. Explaining bad parliamentary news, Newcastle informed his wife, 'it was occasioned by the absence of friends', a view shared by the Earl of Morton and by Lord Hartington who noted of one crucial division, 'we lost it entirely by our own people's deserting us'.[19]

Walpole was not without several advantages. The opposition was divided, several of its leaders seeking an accommodation with the ministry. Co-operation between Tories and opposition Whigs could be sustained on election petitions, but it is not clear that the Tories would have maintained their support of a united opposition for very long. They had not done so in 1718, nor in February 1741, although the situation was very different in December 1741 as there was a programme of reforms agreed between opposition Whigs and Tories. Furthermore, the tide of European conflict turned against Austria in late 1741, a bad development for a ministry that had been accused by the opposition of failing to support Austria, and thus endangering the European balance of power.

Walpole appears to have been not entirely unwilling to resign and retire to the House of Lords, provided that the opposition leaders would promise not to persecute him after his departure. He was old and unwell, and the strain of managing the Commons was beginning to tell, but he had not forgotten his time in the Tower 30 years before. Benjamin Keene, envoy in Spain and a protégé of Walpole, wrote to a fellow envoy in March 1739:

'The last public papers are full of storms and petitions, and the not to be satisfied part of the nation seems to be cutting out work for a long and irksome session. I find by experience that he who cannot despise noise is not fit for a public employment. But let him despise it as much as he pleases it must disgust him at the long run and make him weary of public business'.[20]

Walpole gave no public sign that that was his attitude, but in February 1740 he told Dudley Ryder that:

'he would certainly be glad to quit, but the violent opposition made it necessary for him not to turn his back, which if he did his enemies might take advantage of it and attack him with more advantage. That he had the only confidence with the King, with whom he often talked freely. That the King often showed him letters and complaints which he had received privately against him . . . the King always then flew into passions against Sir Robert's enemies . . . he said that he would now quit if he could put the administration of affairs into any other hand that was fit.'[21]

Walpole's health was less resilient than in the past: he was affected by gout and the stone. His death was falsely reported in September 1738. In May 1739, John Couraud, an Under-Secretary, noted, 'such sudden and violent attacks as his last was, are not so soon got over by a person of his age'.[22] Furthermore, his illnesses were no secret.[23] The jaundiced, yet ever hopeful, Sarah Marlborough wrote in May 1740: 'Some people say that Sir Robert has a dropsy in his stomach, that he can't possibly live long'.[24] Two months later, however, Newcastle was able to reassure his brother: 'Sir Robert is gone this day to Houghton, in as good health, and as good spirits, as I ever saw him'.[25]

Once the parliamentary majority of a ministry began to fall and rumours circulated of government changes, it proved very difficult to retain the loyalty of MPs keen to make bargains with those they believed were about to take power. This was a major problem for the ministry in 1733, and again in the winter of 1741–2. In February 1735, when the ministerial majority fell to 53, in a division over increasing the size of the army, Lord Perceval, by then Earl of Egmont, had noted in his diary:

'I hear the Court is not pleased at seeing so small a majority, and on this occasion Mons. Chavigny, the French Ambassador, told my son what the late Lord Sunderland once told him, namely, that whenever an English Minister had but 60 majority in the House of Commons he was undone.'[26]

Various statements were attributed to Walpole. In 1769, one newspaper claimed: 'Sir Robert Walpole used to say, that whenever the Opposition came so near as within forty, he should look on his power as lost'.[27] The following year, it was stated that Walpole had been in the habit of saying that if his majority fell below 100 he would be very concerned, but that if it fell to 50 or lower it would be time to resign.[28]

After the 1741 general election, Walpole enjoyed no such margins. His majority fell to 16 prior to the hearing of election petitions and double returns which became a trial of strength. In divisions on the Bossiney election petition on 9 and 11 December 1741 his majorities were only 7 and 6. Newcastle observed 'it was occasioned by the absence of friends'.[29] Walpole was defeated by 202 to 193 on 14 December on an opposition motion for hearing a petition against the Denbighshire election, and then on 16 December on the chairmanship of the Commons' elections committee, which 'dispirited the friends of that gentleman to a great degree'.[30] J.B. Owen's explanation of the defeats in terms of the deliberate absence of government supporters may hold true for the most part, but on at least one occasion the 'human factor' came into the equation: at 'the Committee of Elections last night, the other party were a great majority for a great number of them dined together in a tavern just by, but our friends were gone all the town over, and many did not come down'.[32] Having lost the Chairmanship, the government lost three divisions on the Westminster election petition, by majorities of 4, 2, and 6. The inability of the king to have sympathetic MPs for where he lived was noted by foreign diplomats.[33]

In a political world without reliable sources of information, it was essential to create the impression of being successful. Walpole was no longer able to do so by the beginning of 1742. He needed a brilliant coup, such as the reconciliation with the Prince of Wales which he indeed sought in the Christmas recess, in order to prevent a leakage of support and remain in power. The prince, however, refused to come to terms until his father dismissed Walpole.[34] The prince's attitude encouraged politicians such as Dorset and Wilmington to believe that Walpole would fall and that it would be better to bargain with the leaders of the opposition than with the minister, especially when the king was nearly 60. Egmont noted that the attempted reconciliation:

'has effectually undone [Walpole], it having fixed such members among the anti-courtiers who were wavering in their conduct, upon suspicion that the Prince might be prevailed on to reconcile himself to his Majesty, whereby his servants by going over to the Court would cast the majority of the House of Commons on the Court side, whereas this full declaration of his Royal Highness against Sir Robert, assures them he will not give them up.'[35]

In addition, the international situation had seriously deteriorated. The vote of credit of April 1741 had been followed by efforts to create a powerful anti-Bourbon alliance. These were wrecked by the consequences of the French advance across the Rhine in August. Henry Fox thought Europe 'undone', while Newcastle thought 'it is impossible for things to look worse than they do at present. God knows what we shall or can do'. Newcastle also offered an example of a tendency that was all too common especially with him but, also, more generally with other political managers, namely a wish that Continental issues could be managed as readily as British politics. Writing of two French generals, he added 'I heartily wish, Belleisle and Maillebois were as easily subdued as the Duke of Somerset and Sergison',[36] a reference to a rival Sussex electoral patron and to Thomas Sergison who had unsuccessfully stood for Lewes against Newcastle's candidates. Walpole was not one to draw such parallels, because he fully grasped the difference.

One French force moved towards Hanover, leading George II, as Elector, to agree a Convention with France on 25 September (ns), by which he promised neutrality and his vote for the French candidate as Emperor, which he duly gave in January 1742. This Convention undermined British policy. Distinctions between George as King and as Elector convinced few. Discussion about foreign policy in Walpole's last session was embittered by the Convention, and the bleak situation abroad contributed to a general sense of matters slipping out of control.

Walpole decided to battle on, but the situation in the Commons continued to deteriorate. On 21 January 1742, Pulteney's motion for a secret committee to inquire into Walpole's administration was only narrowly defeated in the Commons. John Campbell, a Walpole supporter, captured the air of mounting drama in a letter to his wife:

I could not write to anybody by the last post, an unexpected debate of the highest consequence having lasted till between 11 and 12 last night, and the House sat I think ½ a hour after 12. Mr Pulteney moved to refer some papers to a committee which he declared he should if that question was carried move to consist of 21 chose by ballot and to be a committee of secrecy, and that many other papers should afterward be refer'd to them. Such a committee would have been a sovereign council and an inquisition. This you will say was a struggle for the whole and we carried it only 253 against 250. I believe no man alive remembers so great a number present at any debate . . . On the other side Sir William Gordon, though almost a dying himself [he died on 9 June 1742] and one of his sons drowned that day sevenight, came to the house out of mourning. He has the longest, the blackest, and the most emaciated face you ever saw, and he entered the House after night, with a dirty flannel hood under a black old wig, and with a very long red cloak. The imagination cannot paint I believe anything equal to his figure. One could not but expect a prophecy, All Hail, indeed one could easily believe that the prince of the air who greeted Macbeth by his ambassadors, was come in person to declare the approaching power of some greater favourite . . . I cannot think this ministry can stand with so small and uncertain a majority . . . If we can carry no elections we must soon lose everything. His enemies own Sir Robert Walpole behaves greatly. He looks easy, preserves great temper and presence of mind, and reasons strongly.[37]

A week later, having in the meanwhile lost on a number of petitions and double returns without dividing, Walpole lost the Chippenham election petition by one vote. Campbell wrote to his son on the 30th:

'On Thursday we sat till 12 at night and divided upon a question relating to the right of election at Chippenham. To my apprehension our friends were most clearly in the right, yet we lost it, 236 against 235 . . . Sir Robert Walpole is far from hiding himself, and indeed never appeared so great to me as in his present behaviour. He looks cheerful and composed, and speaks with spirit, ease, and modest dignity. Yet I think he must know that he cannot carry on the public business against so strong a tide, and I confess I see no probability of its turning more in his favour'.[38]

Walpole felt betrayed by Hardwicke and Newcastle, who had advised George II that government business required Walpole's resignation, although the abstention of ministerial MPs such as two of Dorset's sons, was far more important to the parliamentary arithmetic. The government clearly had to be reconstituted for control of Parliament to be regained and that obviously involved the resignation of Walpole.[39] On 2 February, he decided to resign and, on the following day, Parliament was adjourned. Writing on 4 February, Dodington, now an opposition stalwart, saw Providence at work in his fall:

Our laborious attendance in Parliament. . . . I never saw such an attendance either in length, continuance, numbers and spirit on our side. The Union of Parties has been more than the work of Man, such steadiness, mutual affection, and cordiality must have been the Stand of Providence. Those that were called Tories, (for I thank God, we are losing all party Distinctions) have behaved in a manner so noble, so just that it must do them everlasting honour. Their country owes its safety (if it is to he saved) to their behaviour, and I doubt not but they will meet with the honour they deserve. We have overturned our adversary, he is out of all employment, and Earl of Orford, but I think not out of danger.[40]

Campbell's response was very different. On 4 February, he saw Walpole at his levee:

he took me by the hand to the window, desired me and all friends to attend the House for else, said he, they will break the army and ruin the government. I thought his looks showed great concern, and I confess I felt a good deal of concern myself. I pray God this fortnight may be so well employed as to bring the Whigs to agree so far as to support the government and disappoint the Tories . . . What times we live in. Sir Robert Walpole must resign to make way for Sandys's bright parts, Dodington's prudence,

Chesterfield's and Carteret's integrity and Argyll's humility and moderation. Who would have believed two years ago that Sir Robert Walpole or indeed any ministry should be overturned by the members from Scotland and Cornwall.[41]

AFTER THE FALL

Created Earl of Orford on 9 February 1742, and resigning all his posts, Walpole survived the attempts of a secret committee of 21 MPs set up to investigate him and discredit his ministry. Campbell claimed on 27 February, 'There is a very angry spirit in some part of the House, which I fear will produce mischief. I am sure when we were the Majority, we used the then Minority with much more decency and good manners, than we now receive from them'. On 24 March, he added about the events of the previous day:

Mr Pulteney in his speech declared that for his own part he could have wished that the person being removed from power might be allowed to retire in peace, but said the enquiry was necessary to satisfy the people; that is, he must sacrifice his principles, his inclinations and his good faith to popular clamour, a devil of his own raising. . . . He strongly professed himself a Whig and desired to unite us all, in the cause of liberty, and support of the present royal family; but surely it is a new way of uniting the friends of liberty, for some of them to join with the Tories, in calling the rest, and major part, mercenary rascals; for if Lord Orford's administration was so iniquitous, what must we be, who supported and approved it. You see into what difficulties and contradictions a man is brought by his passions and ambition, and affecting popularity, that is in other words preferring the false flattery and giddy noisy applause of knaves and fools, to the sober and sincere approbation of men of sense and virtue and of his own conscience.

In this response to public opinion, Campbell linked the opinion of those 'out-of-doors' whom it was unworthy to heed, to a lack of self-control in the individual politician, Pulteney, who had inspired them.[42]

Walpole took the matter so seriously that he had many of his papers burnt, thus creating a great obstacle to understanding how he worked. In addition, many Cornish borough records vanished at the time of Walpole's fall; probably destroyed because of the pending enquiry. Under attack, Walpole was forced to respond to the moves of others. On 26 March, he wrote from Houghton to Mary, his surviving daughter by Maria Skerret:

'nothing but complaints of the most dismal weather that has not suffered me to ride out once since I came hither; my inclinations are entirely to be with you, but I find I shall not be at liberty to fix my day till I hear on Monday by this night's post what is thought proper for me to do'.[43]

Walpole had obtained for Mary a patent of precedence for an Earl's daughter, an unpopular step that offended many as she was illegitimate.

Sarah Marlborough was not alone in arguing that Walpole should receive a severe punishment, 'because I really think the Constitution cannot be recovered without some example being made'.[44] An investigation of the distribution of the secret service funds was thwarted, however, when Nicholas Paxton, the Solicitor to the Treasury, and John Scrope, the Secretary to the Treasury, refused to testify against Walpole. They argued that they were accountable only to George II as the money had been paid by the king's special warrant. The opposition passed a bill through the Commons to indemnify those who would testify, only to see the Court majority in the Lords reject it on 25 May 'by a majority of 52 which was near two to one'.[45] A leading opposition newspaper, the *London Evening Post*, in its issue of 10 July 1742, juxtaposed the collapse of the inquiry into Walpole with an item on the death sentence for some petty thieves, adding the comment 'such is the difference of stealing a shilling or £20,000'. A new motion for a secret committee on Walpole's conduct was defeated on 1 December 1742. In January 1744, the Earl of Westmorland complained in the Lords that Walpole had been allowed to retire from posts he had 'wickedly and unskilfully discharged with all the rewards of wisdom and integrity'.[46]

Indeed, when George II had offered Pulteney office, he made the condition that Walpole should be 'screened from all future resentments'. Pulteney rejected the condition, but assured the king via Newcastle that he was 'by no means a man of blood'.[47] This was a measure of the stability secured by Walpole: he gave up power without the consequences suffered by Bolingbroke, Harley and Ormonde because he had stabilised parliamentary politics.

The opposition alliance disintegrated speedily, with Carteret, Pulteney and others who were together termed 'New Whigs' taking office in a ministry that included most of the Old Corps Whigs, the former supporters of the Walpole ministry. The Tories and certain of the opposition Whigs complained bitterly of their abandonment by their former allies, who also neglected most of their programme for legislation against corruption. The programme of reforms agreed between opposition Whigs and Tories was abandoned by Pulteney and Sandys. One Tory MP, Edward Digby, reflected that the Tories had been successful in pulling down the old regime, but not in constructing a new system.[48] A Tory motion for the repeal of the Septennial Act was defeated on 31 March. The differing response of Whigs to developments reflected the degree to which Walpole's fall had not sealed their divisions. John Tucker argued that 'nothing but annual Parliaments will ever stop the torrent of corruption . . . this you may rely on as a fundamental and . . . that no administration will ever come into it for very obvious reasons therefore corruption and a standing army'.

Campbell wrote:

Mr Pulteney spoke and strongly showed septennial parliaments were better than triennial. He said indeed that he preferred annual to either . . . confessing that it was not proper to reduce it to annual in the present conjuncture of affairs; and truly I am apt to believe he will never find a time when he will think it proper; but I suppose he had a mind to say something to soothe the populace, and I think he voted for the repeal of this act a few years ago, so we must suppose he would then have made it annual; but could not venture to do so, in the present dangerous and uncertain state; and that way we must reconcile the two votes and make this great man consistent with himself but is it not as plain as the light at noon, that those patriots who voted against it now, were for it a few years ago, only to raise a popular cry against the then Prime Minister.[49]

The Tory MP Edward Harley noted when the Place Bill was rejected in the Lords in April 1742, 'Lord Carteret voted against the Bill though he had always spoke for it when he was out of place'. Later that month, Harley wrote: 'Mr Pulteney presented a bill to exclude certain officers from being members of the House of Commons. A sham bill of no use'.[50] Thomas Hay wrote from Edinburgh to the Marquis of Tweeddale, an ally of Carteret's who had been made Secretary of State for Scotland:

'in general the use that is made of such incidents here is to represent the present ministry as differing only in name from the former but really the same and pursuing the same measures in every respect and what affords a great handle for such suggestions is the keeping in place or taking the assistance of those formerly employed or in the Earl of Orford's interest though it is visible the rash and ill advised measures of some of the old opposition party who yet stand out made what has been done absolutely necessary.'[51]

Tucker saw 'the Walpolian system of government' as continuing, the quest for places leading MPs to forget patriotism.[52] General disenchantment with the ratting of the New Whigs led to a revival of Walpole's popularity. The possibility of his return was mentioned by several commentators. In December 1742, the London banker, Sir Matthew Decker, noted that it was generally thought that: 'my Lord Orford gets ground daily. I had last Sunday a visit of a Tory Member who was so dissatisfied with the new folks, that he protested he was sorry he had ever given a vote against him, and went further by saying that if an address was proposed in the House, to the King, for reestablishing the said Lord he would give his vote for it, and he was sure many of his stamp would do the same, and if this should happen I shall be one of the number that shall not be surprised at it, as I am at nothing that happens in this country.'[53] Others were less sure about Walpole's acceptability. Tucker blamed the loss of an appeal to the Lords in December 1742 over the Weymouth charter on Orford's direct intervention.[54]

Walpole's youngest son, Horace, reflected in 1745 when his father died, 'he had lived . . . to see . . . his enemies brought to infamy for their ignorance or villainy, and the world allowing him to be the only man in England fit to be what he had been'. Horace added in 1748: 'what ample revenge every year gives my father against his Patriot enemies! Had he never deserved well himself, posterity must still have the greatest opinion of him, when they see on what rascal foundations were built all the pretences to virtue, which was set up in opposition to him.'[55]

After his fall, Walpole was believed to retain considerable influence with George II, a position similar to that which Lord Bute was believed to hold with George III after his resignation in 1763. It was always simpler to castigate royal views by blaming them on a supposedly evil adviser. In the case of Walpole, it was true that he exercised considerable influence on George from his retirement until his death on 18 March 1745. George sought and valued his advice, and Walpole played a major role in ensuring that in the ministerial rivalry of the period his former protégé, Pelham, triumphed over his former rivals, Pulteney and Carteret. Wilmington had succeeded Walpole at the Treasury. When he died in July 1743, Pelham beat Pulteney, now Earl of Bath, for the post.

The absence in 1742–4 of a minister wielding power comparable to that of Walpole helped to exacerbate tension within the government. Carteret enjoyed royal favour, but did not have the ability or interest to manage Parliament. Newcastle, who sought to do the latter, was determined not to yield to Carteret and was prepared to thwart George II on this point. In September 1743, Newcastle stated that he, Pelham and Hardwicke wished:

> to act with Lord Carteret, with confidence and friendship, provided he really acts in the same manner towards us; but it must be upon the foot of equality and not superiority, of mutual confidence and communication, in all things, as well foreign, as domestic. This is the only way for the King's business to be carried on with ease and success to ourselves and the public. A contrary behaviour must create coolness and diffidence amongst us, tend to division, and the forming separate parties, the consequence of which, must prove the ruin of the one or the other, and be the destruction of the King's affairs.[56]

Walpole had little time for Carteret, but was unimpressed by Newcastle's methods. He told Ryder that 'the Pelhams and Chancellor treat the King in an imprudent manner, not submissive enough, though the King piques himself on not having anybody to dictate to him'.[57]

Walpole was very opposed to the new idea of a broadly based ministry that would include Tories. On 2 February 1742, he wrote to the Duke of Devonshire: 'I am of opinion that the Whig party must be kept together, which may be done with this parliament, if a Whig administration be formed.'[58] Pelham continued Walpole's policy, rejecting, in the autumn of 1743, Chesterfield's pressure for a mixed ministry: 'he will not take in the few Torys proposed, upon the Coalition, but only upon a personal foot, and that even he would rather have them without their followers, than with, for fear of offending the old Whig corps.'[59]

Walpole gave Pelham advice on parliamentary management and on patronage, stressing the importance of the Treasury. In 1744, he played a major role in rallying the Whigs in support of the payment of subsidies for the Hanoverian forces, an object dear to George II's heart although politically contentious. Philip Yorke MP noted, 'Lord Orford certainly took great pains to bring all his friends into the measure', while Edward Harley claimed that: 'the question for the Hanover troops was carried in both Houses by the influence and management of Sir Robert Walpole now Earl of Orford.'[60] For the first time since becoming a peer, Walpole spoke in Parliament on this subject on 24 February 1744. He revealed over the issue his continuing belief that stability depended on a strong Whig party acting in Parliament in support of the Protestant succession.

Facing a troublesome session later that year, George II pressed Walpole via the Earl of Cholmondely, his son-in-law, to come again to London. He referred to Walpole's 'consummate judgment in the interior and domestic affairs of this kingdom', and to his recent service 'in particular in relation to the question of the continuation of the Hanover troops'.

Walpole agreed to attend, but claimed that political difficulties stemmed from the ministerial reconstitution in 1742:

'It has been a long time easy to foresee the unavoidable, and almost insurmountable difficulties that would attend the present system of politics, I wish to God it was as easy to show the way out of them, but be assured that I will in everything to the utmost of my power consult and contribute to the support of the honour, interest, and safety of the King and Kingdom'.

Walpole, however, had to explain the problems he was encountering from his health: 'I have often been out of order this summer with making bloody urine, which has frequently returned upon me from the motion in a coach'.[61] His final political act was to advise George to yield to the Pelhams and abandon Carteret, a minister who could not lead the Commons. Walpole's health deteriorated and the cures attempted exacerbated the situation. He died from a remedy for the stone.

Pelham's policies during his ministry, which lasted, with a brief interruption in 1746, until his death in 1754, represented a continuation of those of Walpole: fiscal restraint, pacific foreign policy, unenterprising legislation, not disturbing the status quo in the Church, a Whig monopoly of power. Helped by a peaceful international situation and by the longevity of George II, Pelham was able to enjoy substantial parliamentary majorities and govern successfully.[62] Walpole's policies neither fell nor failed with the man.

11

Conclusions

Commenting on Walpole's position in the Commons, Sarah Marlborough snapped: 'I really think that they might pass an act there, if they pleased, to take away Magna Carta'.[1] On the other hand, 'Medium', a character in a London play of 1737, reflected: 'He out of office shall often oppose to be employed; and the man in post shall be restive to rise higher! – Well! of all men living, I think a primier [*sic*] Minister the most wretched'.[2]

Though both Walpole's ministerial position and longevity, and the Whig ascendancy in general, were ascribed by many contemporary critics to corruption, both on the part of those who offered bribes and of those who took them, it is clear that political management involved far more than that. The policies that were followed and the abilities of those who wielded power must be considered. Partly because Walpole's abilities were primarily financial and parliamentary, it was natural to suspect and emphasise the role of money in bolstering his position. Chavigny bluntly reported in 1731:

'Mr Walpole is absolute. He wields the royal authority and controls the money and has the one by the other. Never has any English minister lasted for so long but, because of that, he has more to fear. His adherents are not all his supporters and his friends.'[3]

It was easy for critics, both contemporary and later, to underrate the value of stability, to forget the fragility of government, the precariousness of civil peace and the danger of international failure. In contrast, ministerial spokesmen stressed the inevitable fallibility of all government. Lord Chancellor Hardwicke told the Lords in December 1740 that 'every human establishment has its advantages and its inconveniences'. He also argued that political disputes were an integral part of a free government and not, therefore, a proof of crisis, telling the Lords in February 1741, 'in every country where a free government is established, every time must be a time of political altercation'.[4]

This argument is worthy of attention. A political system without dispute was hardly to be expected. Indeed, the problems facing the government, ranging from the Jacobite challenge and the difficult international situation to the primitive economy which kept much of the population in a precarious state exposed, as in 1740, to the consequences of poor harvests, were such that any assumption about an inevitable growth in stability must appear facile. Walpole was well aware of the many and varied dangers posed by instability and conflict. By stressing the fragility and precariousness of the Hanoverian position, recent historical work is only now opening up a perspective in which more emphasis has to be placed on the political skills of those who maintained domestic peace, and more value can be attached to the simple task of keeping the show going, of providing a peaceful structure for political activity and government action.

Walpole successfully furthered the ends for which he sought power: Whig government, commitment to a conservative Whig interpretation of the 'Glorious' Revolution, the survival of the Hanoverian dynasty, and the preservation of peace. In defending these, Walpole believed he was governing for country, crown and party, and he clearly thought bringing these into harmony a major political task. Thus, the increase in the power of the executive under Walpole was designed to serve more than the ends of patronage.

Naturally, peace and stability were not simply due to political leadership. Social and economic developments were also important, although the first half of the century was not a period of marked economic growth and it was arguably the political achievement of peace and, therefore, lower taxes that helped to increase the disposable wealth of the community rather than growth. The political achievement of the Walpole ministry should not be underrated. It can be measured in large part by the difficulties of the period 1714–20 and 1742–8. There was nothing inevitable in the transition that occurred from conspiracy and battlefield to elections and parliamentary government, so that in 1762 the blue-stocking, Elizabeth Montagu, could reflect: 'a virtuoso or a dilletante may stand as secure in these times behind his Chinese rail as the knight on his battlements in former days'.[5] This political achievement owed much in England to Walpole, while in Britain as a whole it was based both on shared interests among landowners and on the threat and use of force against Jacobites.

Walpole's contribution was not only that of skilful management and appropriate policies. In addition, he recognised and responded to the complex range of the Whig tradition, not least its interaction with the problems and pressures of government. There was a continuity, a variety, and a porosity to outside pressures in Whig thought and behaviour and Walpole grasped, and profited from, these.

Although he benefited from wider developments and from ministerial colleagues, there was also a personal importance and achievement which opponents recognised with their attacks on Walpole, baiting him daily like a bull, in the words of Lady Irwin. Edward Weston, an Under Secretary, noted in 1729:

'the new method in which the attacks upon the government are now carried on, and that our enemies are, contrary to what is practised in all modern engagements, levying all their artillery at the commanding officer'.[6]

It would be tempting (and safe) to conclude here, but history is valuable not only in its own right but also as a means to approach the present and future; for the present is simply a stage on the cusp between past and future. The modern parallel that appears to demand consideration is the government of Tony Blair from 1997 and the changes he has brought to the Labour party. Clearly, there are numerous contrasts, ranging from the impact of public politics in an age of mass democracy to Blair's determination to change, or, as he sees it, reform and revitalise, both constitution and country. Equally, instability appears less present a threat than it did to Walpole; although modern governments have to face unprecedented expectations and obligations in terms of economic management, social welfare and law and order.

A full-blooded comparison is thus inappropriate. Instead, it is necessary to focus on the particular issue of how the inchoate and often internally contradictory set of beliefs and practices that pass for party ideologies are reshaped and, at the same time, put under great pressure by the exigencies and compromises of government. Both Walpole and Blair are examples of this, and it is interesting to note the criticism they faced from within their parties, not least over allegations that they borrowed policies and practices from elsewhere (from Stuart and Continental authoritarianism in the case of Walpole and the Conservatives for Blair). Furthermore, an inability to rely on all elements of their party led to charges of cronyism and government by patronage and manipulation.

Walpole would have appreciated the grant of peerages to donors to the prime ministerial 'blind trust' and the acceptance of £1 million from a lobbyist trying to influence government policy, but he was more impressive in a number of respects. He was far better able to handle the Commons and understood its importance. He was also Finance as well as Prime Minister and Commons manager. His ability to discharge all these tasks in part reflected the simpler nature of government, but also was a testimony to his wide-ranging ability and energy. Walpole also lacked Blair's brittleness, and was better able to cope with criticism. Furthermore, Walpole faced a greater task in governing Britain against a recent background of civil war (Jacobite rising, 1715–16), invasion (Spanish in Scotland, 1718), and attempted insurrection (Atterbury Plot, 1722). The comparison is left open for the consideration of readers. History is not a closed book, but a source of constant interest, insights and importance for us, today.

Notes

Preface

1. BL. Egerton Mss. 1711 f. 184.
2. Hervey, I, 3–4.
3. BL. Add. 73770–74088B.
4. BL. Add. 63749A.
5. BL. Add. 74245.
6. W. Coxe, *Memoirs of the Life and Administration of Sir Robert Walpole, Earl of Orford* (3 vols., 1798).

Chapter 1

1. S. Wood, 'Walpole's Constituency: King's Lynn', *History Today*, 30 (Ap. 1980), pp. 40–4.
2. Eg. Walpole to Marlborough, 22 June 1708, 25 Oct. 1709, BL. Add. 74063.
3. BL. Add. 64928 f. 53. See, more generally, D.W. Jones, *War and Economy in the Age of William III and Marlborough* (Oxford, 1988).
4. General Stanhope to Walpole, 4 July (ns), 31 Aug (ns), 1 Sept. (ns), 9 Nov. (ns), 26 Dec. (ns) 1708, 20 Feb. (ns), 21 Ap. (ns), 16 June (ns) 1709, James Craggs to Walpole, 28 Jan. (ns) 1709, BL. Add. 74063.
5. Stanhope to Walpole, 1 May (ns) 1708, General Carpenter to Walpole, 20 Aug. (ns) 1710, BL. Add. 74067, 74063.
6. BL. Add. 9131 f. 8–9. See, more generally, G. Holmes, *The Trial of Dr. Sacheverell* (1973).
7. Horatio to Robert Walpole, 24 June (ns), 4 July (ns), 9 Sept. (ns) 1710, BL. Add. 74063.
8. Bolingbroke to Strafford, 15 Dec. 1711, BL. Add. 73508.
9. F. Harris, 'Robert Walpole, Arthur Maynwaring, and the Letter to a Friend Concerning the Public Debts', *Factotum*, no. 11 (Ap. 1981), pp. 22–3.
10. H. Davis (ed.), *The Prose Writings of Jonathan Swift* (14 vols., Oxford, 1939–68), X, 84.
11. *Reader*, 3 May 1714.

12. Anon., *A Letter to the Right Honourable Robert Walpole* (1716), p. 6; Anon., *The Woeful Treaty* (1716), p. 4.
13. Anon., *The Character and Principles of the Present Set of Whigs* (1711), p. 15.
14. Edward Wortley Montagu, 'Account of the court of George I', in *Letters of Lady Mary Wortley Montagu* (1887), I, 18–19.
15. Relevant papers can be found in BL. Add. 74066.
16. Daniel Dering to Lord Egmont, 27 Aug. 1715, BL. Add. 47028 f. 65.
17. BL. Add. 47028 f. 133; Surrey CRO. 1248/3 fol. 307.
18. Edmund Gibson to Bishop Nicolson, 27 Nov. 1714, 15 Jan., 1 Mar., 6 Oct. 1715, 4 Sept., 16 Oct 1716, Bod. MS. Add. A. 269, pp. 37–9, 41, 61–2; Charles Cathcart to Stair, 21 Sept. 1716, NAS. GD. 135/141/6; S. Cowper (ed.), *Diary of Mary Countess Cowper* (1865) pp. 48, 58.
19. Robert to Horatio Walpole, 6 Mar. 1716, BL. Add. 74063.
20. Cathcart to Loudoun, 28 Aug. 1716, HL. Lo. 7908.
21. The extensive literature includes, B. Williams, *Stanhope: A Study in Eighteenth-Century War and Diplomacy* (Oxford, 1932), pp. 230–52; R. Hatton, *Diplomatic Relations between Great Britain and the Dutch Republic 1714–21* (1950), pp. 133–4, *George I: Elector and King* (1978), pp. 193–202, and 'New Light on George I' in S. Baxter (ed.), *England's Rise to Greatness 1660–1763* (1983), pp. 230–2; J.M. Beattie, *The English Court in the Reign of George I* (Cambridge, 1967), pp. 225–40; J.H. Plumb, *Sir Robert Walpole: The Making of a Statesman* (1956), pp. 222–42; J.J. Murray, *George I, the Baltic and the Whig Split of 1717* (1969); W.A. Speck, 'The Whig Schism under George I', *Huntington Library Quarterly*, 40 (1977), pp. 171–9; C. Jones, 'The Impeachment of the Earl of Oxford and the Whig Schism of 1717: Four New Lists', *Bulletin of the Institute of Historical Research*, 55 (1982), pp. 66–87.
22. Hatton, *George I*, p. 200.
23. P.G.M. Dickson, *The Financial Revolution in England: a Study in the Development of Public Credit, 1688–1756* (1967), p. 87; Anon., *The Defection Considered and the Designs of Those Who Divided the Friends of the Government Set in a True Light* (1717), p. 32.
24. Schulenburg to Görtz, 25 May (ns) 1717, Darmstadt, Staatsarchiv, Gräflich Görtzisches Archiv F23 13/6 f. 44; Robert Arbuthnot to Stair, 30 May 1717, NAS. GD. 135/141/11.
25. BL. Add. 61573 f. 143–4, 150.
26. A. Boyer, *The Political State of Great Britain* (60 vols., 1711–40), XV, 99; Bonet, Prussian envoy, to Frederick William I of Prussia, 8 Feb. (ns) 1718, Merseburg, Deutsches Zentralarchiv, Rep. XI (England), vol. 41.
27. BL. Add. 47028 f. 223.
28. BL. Add. 47028 f. 226, 228.
29. Plumb, *Walpole: Making of a Statesman*, p. 264; Hatton, *George I*, p. 209; L. Colley, *In Defiance of Oligarchy: The Tory Party 1714–60* (Cambridge, 1982), p. 194.
30. Schulenburg to Görtz, 31 Mar. (ns) 1718, Darmstadt F23, 153/6.
31. BL. Add. 37366 f. 95.
32. *Defection Considered . . .*, p. 28.
33. BL. Add. 37367 f. 178; Colley, *Oligarchy*, p. 194.
34. Bonet to Frederick William, 4, 8 Mar. (ns) 1718, Merseburg 41; J.M. Graham (ed.), *Annals and Correspondence of the Viscount and the First and Second Earls of Stair* (2 vols., 1875), II, 87–8.
35. J.P. Kenyon, *Revolution Principles: The Politics of Party 1689–1720* (Cambridge, 1977).

36. N. Sykes, *William Wake* (2 vols., Cambridge, 1957), II, 109, 115, 133; Schulenburg to Görtz, 2 Mar. (ns), 25 May (ns) 1717, Darmstadt F23 153/6.
37. BL. Stowe 242 fols. 187–9; Earl of Hardwicke, *Miscellaneous State Papers from 1501 to 1726* (2 vols. 1778), II, 559–60; Craggs to Stair, 5 Sept. 1717, NAS. GD. 135/141/9.
38. BL. Add. 47028 fols. 220–6; Sykes, *Wake* II, 117; W. Nicolson, *Letters*, (ed.), J. Nichols (2 vols., 1809), II, 471–3; Edmund Gibson to Bishop Nicolson, 13 Sept., 19, 24 Dec. 1718, Bod. Add. MS. A. 269.
39. Plumb, *Walpole: Making of a Statesman*, pp. 208–85.
40. J.F. Naylor (ed.), *The British Aristocracy and the Peerage Bill of 1719* (New York, 1968); C. Jones, 'Venice Preserv'd; or A Plot Discovered': The Political and Social Context of the Peerage Bill of 1719', in Jones (ed.), *A Pillar of the Constitution. The House of Lords in British Politics, 1640–1784* (1989), pp. 79–112.
41. Black, 'Regulating Oxford: Ministerial Intentions in 1719', *Oxoniensia*, 50 (1985), pp. 282–5.
42. Anon., *The Doctrine of Innuendos Discussed* (1731), pp. 16–17; *Craftsman*, 10 Feb. 1727.
43. BL. Add. 37367 f. 303.
44. BL. Add. 47028 f. 257; G.H. Townend, 'Religious Radicalism and Conservatism in the Whig Party under George I: The Repeal of the Occasional Conformity and Schism Acts', *Parliamentary History*, 7 (1988), pp. 24–44.
45. NAS. GD. 220/5268; William Bell to Thomas Clutterbuck, 10 Jan. 1719, Gloucester CRO. D149 F18; *An Epistle to R- W-* (1718), p. 21.
46. BL. Add. 32686 f. 153.
47. Plumb, *Walpole: Making of a Statesman*, pp. 208–85; Hatton, *George I*, pp. 245–6.
48. Cowper to Mrs Clayton, 20 Oct. 1720, Beinecke, Osborn Shelves f c 110 2 f. 12–13.
49. Thomas to Alan Brodrick, 22 Dec. 1720, Guildford, Surrey CRO. Brodrick Mss. 1248/4 f. 377.
50. Dickson, *Financial Revolution*, pp. 90–156; J. Carswell, *The South Sea Bubble* (2nd edn., 1993); *Fog's Weekly Journal*, 19 Ap. 1729.
51. Robert to Horatio, 11 May 1716, BL. Add. 63749A f.1.
52. Destouches to Dubois, French foreign minister, 8 Dec. (ns) 1721, AE. CP. Ang. 338 f. 211.
53. Walpole to Townshend, 18 Oct., Townshend to Walpole, 6 Nov. (ns), Walpole to Townshend, 15 Nov. 1723, PRO. SP. 43/68, 43/5.
54. Broglie, French envoy, to Morville, French foreign minister, 20 July (ns) 1724, AE. CP. Ang. 348 f. 128.
55. *Corn Cutter's Journal*, 28 Jan., *General Evening Post*, 28 Jan., *Daily Post Boy*, 3 Feb. 1735; Diemar, Hessen-Kassel envoy, to Prince Eugene, Austrian minister, 4, 18 Feb. (ns) 1735, HHStA. Grosse Korrespondenz 85a.
56. Hardwicke, *Walpoliana* (1783), p. 10.
57. Robert to Horatio, 29 May 1722, BL. Add. 63749A f. 11.
58. Hervey, II, 211; Walpole to Newcastle, 24 Oct. 1723, BL. Add. 32686 f. 362.
50. HMC. *Carlisle*, p. 85; Ossorio to Charles Emmanuel III, 10, 24 Nov. (ns) 1738, AST. LM. Ing. 45.
60. Poyntz to Thomas Townshend, 29 May 1724, Beinecke, Osborn Shelves C. 201 no. 3.
61. Diemar to Eugene, 1 Mar. (ns) 1735, HHStA. GK. 85a.
62. Walpole to Newcastle, 21 Aug. 1725, PRO. SP. 35/57 f. 255.
63. Account book, BL. Add. 74062.
64. Walpole to Waldegrave, 30 Aug. 1733, Chewton.

65. Account book, BL. Add. 74062.
66. *The Norfolk Congress* (1728); *Fog's Weekly Journal*, 19 Ap. 1729; 'The Progress of Patriotism. A Tale', in *Collection of Poems published in the Craftsman* (1731), p. 49.
67. T. McGeary, 'The Opera Accounts of Sir Robert Walpole', *Restoration and Eighteenth Century Theatre Research*, 2nd series, 11, no. 1 (summer 1996), p. 4.
68. Account book, BL. Add. 74062.
69. Michael Broughton to Charles, 2nd Duke of Richmond, 6 June 1724, Earl of March, *A Duke and his Friends* (2 vols., 1911) I, 90.

Chapter 2

1. Sir Luke Schaub, envoy in Paris, to Carteret, – June (ns) 1722, New York, Public Library, Hardwicke Papers vol. 67.
2 Robert to Horatio, 19 May 1722, BL. Add. 63749A f. 10.
3. G.V. Bennett, *The Tory Crisis in Church and State 1688–1730: The Career of Francis Atterbury, Bishop of Rochester* (Oxford, 1975) and E. Cruickshanks, 'Lord North, Christopher Layer and the Atterbury Plot: 1720–23', in Cruickshanks and Black (eds.), *The Jacobite Challenge* (Edinburgh, 1988), pp. 92–106. The latter corrects the account in Plumb and Bennett.
4. Guildford, Surrey CRO. Brodrick Mss. 1248/5 f. 378.
5. Destouches, French envoy, to Dubois, French foreign minister, 4 Dec. (ns) 1721, AE. CP. Ang. 338 f. 205–6.
6. R. Freebairne to John Hay, 8 Jan. 1722, RA. 57/18.
7. Walpole to Newcastle, 1 Sept. 1724, BL. Add. 32687 f. 54.
8. Dillon to James III, 17 Ap. (ns) 1723, RA. 73/130, cf. 24 Ap. (ns), 73/136.
9. Stair to Loudoun, 2 Jan. 1724, HL. Lo. 7628.
10. Horatio Walpole to Newcastle, 12 Nov. (ns) 1723, BL. Add. 32686 f. 379; Horatio to Robert, 29, 31 Jan. (ns), 26 Feb. (ns) 1724, BL. Add. 63749, CUL. C(H) corresp. 1101; Duke of Bourbon to George I, 24 Jan (ns) 1724, AE. CP. Ang. supplement 7 f. 138; Hatton, *George I*, pp. 137–8, 275.
11. Poyntz to Thomas Townshend, 27 Oct. 1722, Beinecke, Osborn Shelves C 201 no. 1.
12. Walpole to Townshend, 30 Aug. 1723, PRO. SP. 43/4 f. 292.
13. Townshend to Walpole, 17 Sept. (ns) 1723, PRO. SP. 43/5 f. 17.
14. Stair to Loudoun, 9 Jan. 1724, HL. Lo 7667, cf. 18, 28 Jan., 7664, 7625.
15. Hatton, George I, p. 276.
16. Sedgwick, I, 35, 95, 501; HMC. *Onslow*, p. 465; E. Fitzmaurice, *Life of William Earl of Shelburne* (1875) I, 44.
17. Coxe, *Orford*, I, 49–50.
18. Plumb, *Walpole: Making of a Statesman*, pp. 132–3, 151, 171; Hervey, pp. 80–5.
19. Coxe, *Orford*, I, 264–5, II, 340; Hervey, pp. 13–16; A. Foord, *His Majesty's Opposition 1714–1830* (Oxford, 1964), p. 115; H.T. Dickinson, *Bolingbroke* (1970), p. 219.
20. Broglie, 24 July (ns) 1724, AE. CP. Ang. 348 f. 139.
21. Coxe, *Orford*, I, 176–81; Hervey, pp. 39–44; L. Melville, *Lady Suffolk and her Circle* (1824).
22. Newcastle to Townshend, 15 June 1727, BL. Add. 32687.
23. HMC. *Onslow*, pp. 516–17.
24. Peter, Lord King, 'Notes on Domestic and Foreign Affairs during the last years of the reign of George I and the early part of the reign of George II', in appendix to P. King,

Notes

Life of John Locke (2 vols., 1830); P. Vaucher, *Robert Walpole et la Politique de Fleury, 1731–42* (Paris, 1924), p. 35; Instructions for Broglie, 9 Mar. (ns) 1726, AE. CP.Ang. 354; D'Aix to Victor Amadeus II of Sardinia, 30 June (ns) 1727, AST. LM. Ing. 35; Le Coq to Augustus II of Saxony-Poland, 12 Dec. (ns) 1727, Dresden 2676, 18a.

25. *Diary of Mary Countess Cowper*, pp. 163–4; Sarah, Duchess of Marlborough to Captain Fish, 31 July 1727, BL.Add. 61444.
26. King, *Locke* II, p. 46.
27. Newcastle to Townshend, 15 Oct. 1727, BL.Add. 32687; Le Coq to Augustus II, 22 July (ns) 1727, Dresden 2676, 18a.
28. Le Coq to Augustus, 22 July (ns) 1727, Dresden, 2676, 18a; Sedgwick, I, 34, 37.
29. Le Coq to Augustus, 22 July (ns) 1727, Dresden 2676, 18a; Fleury to George II, 2, 11 July (ns) 1727, PRO. SP. 100/7; James Hamilton to 'James III', 14 July, Atterbury to James, 20 Aug. (ns) 1727, RA. 108/73.
30. Earl of Ilchester (ed.), *Lord Hervey and his Friends* (1950), p. 21.
31. Townshend to Wych, 20 Feb. 1728, PRO. SP. 82/45.
32. HMC. *Carlisle*, p. 59.
33. Stephen Poyntz to Horatio Walpole, 16 Jan. (ns) 1729, BL. Add. 63750.
34. HMC. *Egmont*, III, 347.
35. Thomas Pelham MP to Poyntz, 3 Feb. 1729, BL. Althorp Mss. E4.
36. Delafaye to Poyntz, 21, 24, 27 Feb., 10, 13, 17 Mar., 3 Ap., John Selwyn MP. to Poyntz, 10, 17, 31 Mar., Newcastle to Poyntz, 1 Ap., 1729, BL. Althorp Mss. E3.
37. Coxe, *Orford*, I, 335; HMC. *Egmont*, I, 50.
38. HMC. *Egmont*, I, 10, 31, 93–4.
39. Reichenbach to Grumbkow, 24, 28 Mar. (ns), 9, 19 May (ns) 1730, Hull UL. DDHO 3/3.
40. Delafaye to Poyntz, 13 Ap. (os) 1730, BL. Althorp E4.
41. Sydney to Hardwicke, undated, Beinecke, Osborn Files, Sydney.
42. Delafaye to Waldegrave, 13 Jan. 1732, Chewton; Ossorio to Charles Emmanuel, 4 Feb. (ns) 1732, AST. LM. Ing. 39.
43. Walpole's notes of speech on Excise, BL. Add. 74065.
44. BL. Add. 64929 f. 77.
45. Delafaye to Waldegrave, 22, 25 Jan., 1, 15 Feb. 1733, Chewton; Newcastle to Earl of Essex, 4 Mar. 1733, BL. Add. 32781.
46. Goodricke to Edward Hopkins, 6 Feb. 1733, BL. Add. 64939 f. 81.
47. 25 May (ns) 1733, Genoa, Archivio di Stato, Lettere Ministri Inghilterra, 11; P. Langford, *The Excise Crisis: Society and Politics in the Age of Walpole* (Oxford, 1975).
48. George Harbin to –, 11 Ap. 1733, Taunton, Somerset CRO. DD/SAS FA41 C/795.
49. *Wye's Letter*, 21 Aug. 1733; Maidstone, Kent Archive Office U269 C148/12, 23.
50. Mrs Caesar diary, BL. Add. 62558 f. 49; B. Williams, 'The Duke of Newcastle and the Election of 1734', *EHR*, 12 (1897), pp. 448–88.
51. Couraud to Waldegrave, 20 Ap., 30 May 1734, Chewton.
52. Norwich City Library, Assembly Book for 1733, f. 183.
53. Anon., *An Historical Account of the Proceedings of the Last House of Commons . . . Addressed to the New Elected Members* (no date [1734 or 1735]), pp. 45–6.
54. Newcastle to Keene, 12 Feb. 1735, BL. Add. 32787 f. 14; Count Philip Kinsky, Austrian envoy, to Wasner, Austrian diplomat, 22 Feb. (ns) 1735, Vienna, Palais Kinsky, correspondence of Philip Kinsky, 3d; Couraud to Waldegrave, 24 Feb., 1, 6, 13, 17 Mar. 1735, Chewton; De Loss, Saxon envoy, to Augustus III, 5 Ap. (ns) 1735, Dresden 638 IIIa f. 200.
55. Ossorio to Charles Emmanuel, 12 Dec. (ns) 1735, 26 Jan. (ns) 1736, AST. LM. Ing. 42–3.

56. S. Taylor, 'Sir Robert Walpole, the Church of England and the Quakers Tithe Bill of 1736', *HJ*, 28 (1985), pp. 51–77.
57. Horace Walpole, *Book of Materials*, p. 42, Farmington, Connecticut.
58. Anon., *Tell-tale Cupids* (1735), pp. 33, 51; Hervey, I, 86; Plumb, Walpole. *The King's Minister*, pp. 79–81, 113–14; I. Grundy, *Lady Mary Wortley Montagu. Comet of the Enlightenment* (Oxford, 1999), pp. 225, 248–50, 382–3.
59. Harbin to Thomas Carew, 24 Feb. 1737, Taunton, Somerset CRO. Trollop-Bellew papers DD/TB Box 16 FT18; Cobbett, XI, 467.
60. *Common Sense*, 7 May 1737. The most useful discussion is P.L. Woodfine, '"Suspicious Latitudes": Commerce, Colonies, and Patriotism in the 1730s', *Studies in Eighteenth-Century Culture*, 27 (1998), pp. 25–52.

Chapter 3

1. George Harbin to Mrs Bamfyld, Taunton, Somerset CRO. DD/SAS FA41 C/795.
2. C. Roberts, *The Growth of Responsible Government in Stuart England* (Cambridge, 1966); Taylor, 'Robert Walpole, First Earl of Orford', in R. Eccleshall and G. Walker (eds.), *Biographical Dictionary of British Prime Ministers* (1998), pp. 1–14.
3. AE. CP. Ang. 364 f. 395–6, see Black, 'Schöpflin in Britain', in B. Vogler and J. Voss (eds.), *Strasbourg, Schoepflin et l'Europe au XVIIIe siècle* (Bonn, 1996), pp. 243–52.
4. Cobbett, XI, 224.
5. W. Mure (ed.), *Selections from the Family Papers Preserved at Caldwell* (Glasgow, 1854), p. 233; Guildford, Surrey CRO. Brodrick Mss. 1248/4 f. 222, 377.
6. Beinecke, Osborn Shelves C201 No.1; Philip Stanhope, 4th Earl of Chesterfield, *Characters* (1778), p. 31; Delafaye to Poyntz, 26, 30 Jan. 1730, BL. Althorp Mss. E4.
7. Hardwicke, *Walpoliana* (1783), p. 17.
8. Hervey, I, 177–8.
9. Newcastle to Horatio Walpole, 26 Sept. 1724, BL. Add. 32740 f. 461; NAS. GD. 150/3476/101.
10. BL. Add. 62558 f. 4–5; John to Pryse Campbell, 5 Mar., 13 Nov. 1739, 27 Jan. 1743, Carmarthen, Dyfed Archive Service, Cawdor Muniments, box 138.
11. Anon., *A Defence of the People* (1744), p. 80.
12. Frederick William I to Andrié, 24 May (ns) 1739, PRO. SP. 107/24.
13. BL. Add. 47033 f. 59; RA. 103/80.
14. Sandon vol. 432 doc. 30B.
15. Walpole to Sir Thomas Lowther, 2 Jan. 1731, Walpole to Sir John Ramsden, 5 Nov. 1741, Sir James Lowther to Spedding, 9 Dec. 1740, Carlisle, Cumbria CRO. DD Ca 22/1/3, D/Pen/234, D/Lons./W.
16. Guildford, Surrey CRO. Brodrick Mss. 1248/7 f. 19.
17. Walpole to Townshend, 26 June 1723, PRO. SP. 43/66; PRO. SP. 43/4 f. 98; Walpole to Horatio Walpole, – Sept. 1736, BL. Add. 63749 A f. 264–5; Walpole to Lord Malton, 6 Nov. 1739, Sheffield, Archives, Wentworth Woodhouse Mss. M3; C. Jones, 'The House of Lords and the Growth of Parliamentary Stability, 1701–1742', in Jones (ed.), *Britain in the First Age of Party* (1987), pp. 100–1; Black, 'The House of Lords and British Foreign Policy, 1720–48', in Jones (ed.), *A Pillar of the Constitution. The House of Lords in British Politics, 1640–1784* (1989), pp. 113–36.
18. Countess Cowper to Mrs Clayton, no d., Beinecke, Osborn Shelves f c 110 2 f. 16. On Radnor, Walpole to Townshend, 6 Aug. 1723, PRO. SP. 43/4 f. 203.
19. Walpole to Newcastle, 10 Aug. 1723, BL. Add. 32686 f. 301.

20. Guildford, Surrey CRO. Brodrick Mss. 1248/7 f. 19; Edward Harley, diary, 12 Feb. 1741, CUL. Add. 6851 II, f. 29. For the strength of the government position in the Lords, Gibson to Nicolson, 11 Ap. 1721, Bod. Add. MS. A. 269, p. 97; Sarah Marlborough to Duke of Somerset, – Feb. 1734, BL. Add. 61457 f. 125, and to Stair, 3 Mar. 1737, BL. Microfilm 687.
21. J.C. Collins, *Voltaire, Montesquieu and Rousseau in England* (1908); G. Bonno, 'La Culture and la civilisation Britanniques devant l'opinion française de la Paix d'Utrecht aux "Lettres Philosophiques" 1713–34', *Transactions of the American Philosophical Society* (1948).
22. BL. Add. 37388 f. 193, 35363 f. 26–7.
23. *Whitehall Journal*, 4 Dec. 1722; Anon., *Liberty and the Craftsman* (1730), p. 5; *Daily Courant*, 5 Oct. 1734.
24. *London Journal*, 1 Aug. 1724; *Weekly Register*, 4 Sept. 1731.
25. *London Journal*, 9 Feb. 1723.
26. BL. Add. 74065 no. 1.
27. Newcastle to Poyntz, 14 Jan. 1729, BL. Althorp E3.
28. Black, *British Foreign Policy in the Age of Walpole* (Edinburgh, 1985), pp. 27–48.
29. J.B. Owen, 'George II Reconsidered', in J.S. Bromley, P.G.M. Dickson and A. Whiteman (eds.), *Statesmen, Scholars and Merchants* (Oxford, 1973), pp. 113–34.
30. HL. STG. Box 191 (12).
31. Churchill College, Cambridge, Erle-Drax Mss. 2/12; E. Gregg, *Queen Anne* (1980); Hatton, *George I* (2nd edn., New Haven, 2001).
32. Roberts, 'Party and Patronage in Later Stuart England', in Baxter (ed.), *England's Rise to Greatness*, p. 205.
33. AE. CP. Ang. 259 f. 39.
34. BL. Add. 32686 f. 175.
35. NAS. GD. 150/3474/21.
36. Black, 'Parliament and Foreign Policy in the Age of Walpole: the case of the Hessians', in Black (ed.), *Knights Errant and True Englishmen: British Foreign Policy, 1660–1800* (Edinburgh, 1989), pp. 41–54.
37. Townshend to Walpole, 15 Nov. (ns), 10 Dec. (ns) 1723, PRO. SP. 43/5 f. 253, 337.
38. Horatio Walpole to Malton, 10 Oct. 1738, Sheffield, Archives, Wentworth Woodhouse Mss. M3.
39. M. Peters, 'Pitt as a foil to Bute: the public debate over ministerial responsibility and the powers of the Crown', in K. Schweizer (ed.), *Lord Bute: Essays in Re-interpretation* (Leicester, 1988), p. 111.
40. Owen, *The Rise of the Pelhams* (1957), pp. 159–297.
41. Hervey, particularly pp. 261, 750–2.
42. Owen, 'George II Reconsidered'.
43. Hervey to Stephen Fox, 30 Dec. 1731, Ilchester (ed.), *Hervey*, p. 129; Frederick William to Count Degenfeld, 17 Jan. 1733, PRO. SP. 107/8; HMC. *Egmont*, III, 28.
44. Robert to Horatio Walpole, 19 June 1736, BL. Add. 63749A f. 214.
45. Holmes, *British Politics in the Age of Anne* (1967), pp. 440–2; B.W. Hill, *Robert Harley* (1988), p. 239.
46. BL. Add. 32686 f. 193.
47. PRO. SP. 43/4 f. 150, 292; Bod. MS. A. 269 pp. 99–100; C. Realey, *The Early Opposition to Sir Robert Walpole* (Philadelphia, 1931).
48. Townshend to Walpole, 2 Oct. (ns) 1723, PRO. 43/5 f. 98; PRO. SP. 43/5 f. 111.
49. HL. Lo. 7628, 7667, 7664, 7608.
50. H.T. Dickinson, *Bolingbroke* (1970), p. 219.

51. RA. 97/110.
52. Black, 'Fresh Light on the Fall of Townshend', *HJ*, 29 (1986), pp. 41–64, and 'Additional Light on the Fall of Townshend', *Yale University Library Gazette*, 63 (1989), pp. 132–6.
53. G.H. Rose (ed.), *A Selection from the Papers of the Earls of Marchmont* (3 vols., 1831) II, 233; Beinecke, Osborn Shelves, Stair Letters, no. 51.
54. Wasner to Sinzendorf, 5 Oct. (ns) 1734, HHStA. Englische Korrespondenz 70; Ossorio to Charles Emmanuel III, 16 Jan. (ns) 1735, 26 Jan. (ns), 3, 10 May (ns) 1736, AST. LM. Ing. 42, 43.
55. BL. Add. 47033 f. 62; Ossorio to Charles Emmanuel, 4 May (ns) 1733, 18 Nov. (ns) 1734, AST. LM. Ing. 40.
56. Robert to Horatio, 6 Aug. 1736, BL. Add. 63749A f. 253.
57. C.S. Cowper (ed.), *The Diary of Mary, Countess Cowper 1714–1720* (1864), p. 164.
58. Newcastle to Earl of Carlisle, 7 Nov. 1727, Castle Howard J8/1/817; Ossorio to Charles Emmanuel, 6 Jan. (ns) 1738, AST. LM. Ing. 45.
59. Walpole to the Duke of Devonshire, 4 Dec. 1737, Chatsworth, Devonshire Mss. 1st series, Box 2, 114.9.
60. Lowther to Spedding, 18 Nov. 1740, Carlisle, Cumbria CRO. D/Lons./W; Robert to Horatio Walpole, 21 Aug. 1739, BL. Add. 63749A f. 320.
61. J. Russell, *Memoirs of the Affairs of Europe from the Peace of Utrecht* (1824) II, 401; P. Brent, *Liberal Anglican Politics: Whiggery, Religion and Reform, 1830–41* (Oxford, 1987), p. 45.
62. Earl Stanhope (ed.), *Miscellanies* (1863), pp. 67–9.

Chapter 4

1. M. Mack, *The Garden and the City* (1969), p. 339.
2. J.C. Beasley, 'Portraits of a Monster: Robert Walpole and Early English Prose Fiction', *Eighteenth Century Studies*, 14 (1981), pp. 406–31; J.A. Downie, 'Walpole, "the Poet's Foe"', in Black (ed.), *Britain in the Age of Walpole*, pp. 171–88; A. Pettit, *Illusory Consensus: Bolingbroke and the Polemical Response to Walpole, 1730–1737* (Newark, Delaware, 1996).
3. C. Gerrard, *The Patriot Opposition to Walpole: Politics, Poetry and National Myth, 1725–1742* (Oxford, 1995); B.A. Goldgar, *Walpole and the Wits: The Relation of Politics to Literature, 1722–1742* (Lincoln, Nebraska, 1976); J. Andrews, *A Comparative View of the French and English Nations* (1785), pp. 47–8.
4. P. Thicknesse, *Useful Hints to those who make the Tour of France* (1768), p. 130.
5. *Monitor*, 5 Aug. 1758, 9 July 1763; *Contrast*, 10 Aug. 1763; Cobbett, XVI, 1295.
6. *Walpole corresp.*, Walpole to Mann, 26 Aug. 1785; BL. Add. 23801 f. 481.
7. Lowther to Spedding, 18 May 1742, Carlisle, Cumbria RO. D/Lons/W.
8. Orrery to 'James III', 10 May 1724, RA. 74/58.
9. Townshend to Samuel Buckley, 16 Sept. [1735?], Bod. MS. Eng. Lett. c 144 f. 267; cf. Countess Cowper to Mrs Clayton, 21 June 1722, Beinecke, Osborn Shelves f c 110 2 f. 14; Thomas to Alan Brodrick, 16 Jan. 1725, Guildford, Surrey CRO. Brodrick Mss. 1248/6 f. 123; Charles, Lord Bruce to Pulteney, 24 Jan. 1731, Trowbridge, Wiltshire CRO. Savernake Mss. 1300 no. 1245.
10. NLS. MS. 14221 f. 186–7.
11. Sparre to Count Horn, Swedish first minister, 15 June 1733, PRO. SP. 107/13.
12. Sandon, Ryder Diary, 13 Feb. 1741.
13. Anon., *Letters from the Westminster Journal* (1747), iii–iv.

14. NAS. GD. 18/5245/4/14.
15. For Houghton in the context of country-house building elsewhere in Norfolk, A. Mackley, 'Country-House Building in Norfolk, 1700–1900', in P. Wade-Martins (ed.), *An Historical Atlas of Norfolk* (Norwich, 1993), pp. 108–9. For parks, cf. pp. 110–111.
16. Lady to Lord Burlington, 6 Nov. –, BL. Althorp B4.
17. BL. Add. 51345 f. 3. For his description in July 1731, Earl of Ilchester, *Lord Hervey and his Friends, 1726–38* (1950), pp. 70–2.
18. Bedford, CRO. L30/8/39/20.
19. HMC. *Portland*, VI, 160.
20. E.J. Climenson (ed.), *Passages from the Diaries of Mrs Philip Lybbe Powys* (1899), p. 6.
21. Proctor to Yorke, 15 July 1764, 13 Sept. 1772, Cambridge CRO. Yorke papers 408/F2.
22. Sandon, Ryder diary, 18 Oct. 1739.
23. Townshend to Walpole, 31 Aug. (ns) 1723, PRO. SP. 43/4; Walpole to Waldegrave, 21 Mar., 14, 21 Ap. 1735, Chewton; Waldegrave to Walpole, 7 Sept. (ns), 8 Oct. (ns) 1735, Robinson to Horatio Walpole, 29 Sept. (ns) 1736, BL. Add. 73815, 23854.
24. 'The Progress of Patriotism. A Tale', in *Collection of Poems published in the Craftsman* (1731), p. 48.
25. Delafaye to Waldegrave, 4, 11, 15 Nov. 1731, Chewton; Diemar to Landgrave of Hessen-Kassel, 9, 21, 24 Nov. (ns), 1, 11 Dec. (ns) 1731, Marburg, Staatsarchiv, Politische Akten nach Philipp d. Gr. England 204; Hervey to Stephen Fox, 2 Dec. 1731, Bury St Edmunds, West Suffolk CRO. 941/47/25/307. On [pre-biographical figures', L. Hughes, *Sophia, Regent of Russia 1657–1704* (New Haven, 1990).
26. HMC. *Carlisle*, p. 85.
27. Ossorio to Charles Emmanuel III, 2 Sept. (ns) 1733, AST. LM. Ing. 40.
28. Walpole to Townshend, 8 June, 6, 9 Aug.1723, PRO. SP. 43/66, 43/4 f. 203; Hervey to Stephen Fox, 30 Dec. 1731, Ilchester (ed.), *Hervey*, p. 129.
29. Harley, parliamentary diary, CUL. Add. 6851 f. 89–90.
30. Townshend to Buckley, 16 Sept. [1735?], Bod. MS. Eng. Lett. c. 144 f. 267.
31. P. Frowde, *Fall of Saguntum* (1727), iii; Fawkener to Walpole, 25 Oct. (ns) 1736, BL. Add. 74072.
32. BL. Egerton Mss. 1711 f. 184.
33. AE. MD. Ang. 6 f. 101; Coxe, *Orford*, III, 168.
34. BL. Add. 32686 f. 300, 312–13.
35. Robert to Horatio Walpole, 18 June 1736, BL. Add. 63749A f. 212.
36. PRO. SP. 43/4 f. 203, 211.
37. Plumb, *Sir Robert Walpole: The King's Minister* (1960), pp. 91–102.
38. BL. Althorp Mss B3, 14 Ap. 1726.
39. Lonsdale to Fleming, 30 Oct. 1737, Carlisle, Cumbria RO. D/Sen./Fleming 14.
40. NAS. GD. 248/48/1.
41. HL. Lo. 7902.
42. BL. Add. 63470 f. 154; Poyntz to Thomas Townshend, 23 Nov. 1740, BL. Althorp E5.
43. PRO. SP. 41/15 f. 272.
44. *Old England*, 9 Feb. 1745.
45. John Tucker to Samuel White, 19 July 1740, Bod. Ms. Don. C.112 f. 185; Henry Fox to Sir Charles Hanbury Williams, 30 Aug. 1740, 16 May 1741, Farmington, 48; B. Harris and Black, 'John Tucker, MP., and Mid-Eighteenth-Century British Politics', *Albion*, 29 (1997), pp. 18–20, 23.
46. HMC. *Egmont*, I, 46, 131, 244–68, 368; Cruickshanks, 'The Political Management of Sir Robert Walpole', in Black (ed.), *Britain in the Age of Walpole*, pp. 36–8.

47. Sarah Marlborough to Fish, 13 Mar. 1727, BL. Add. 61444 f. 110.
48. John to Pryse Campbell, 12 Feb. 1741, Carmarthen, Dyfed CRO., Cawdor Muniments, Box 138.

Chapter 5

1. RA. 55/67.
2. Stanhope to Sir Luke Schaub, 27 Ap. 1722, New York, Public Library, Hardwicke papers vol. 59.
3. BL. Add. 37388 f. 201–2, 32686 f. 152, 32689 f. 127; Deerhurst to Coventry, 24 Aug. 1740, Worcester, Hereford and Worcester, CRO. 705: 66 BA 4221/26; Holmes, *The Electorate and the National Will in the First Age of Party* (Lancaster, 1976); N. Landau, 'Independence, Deference and Voter Participation: The Behaviour of the Electorate in Early Eighteenth-Century Kent', *HJ*, 22 (1979), pp. 561–84; J.C.D. Clark, *English Society*, pp. 15–26; Speck, 'The Electorate in the First Age of Party', in Jones (ed.), *Britain in the First Age of Party*, pp. 45–62; Langford, 'Property and "Virtual Representation" in Eighteenth-Century England', *HJ*, 31 (1988), pp. 83–115; Dickinson, *The Politics of the People in Eighteenth-Century Britain* (1995).
4. Guildford, Surrey CRO. Brodrick Mss. 1248/7 f. 23; N. Hunt, 'The Russia Company and the Government, 1730–42', *Oxford Slavonic Papers*, 7 (1957), pp. 27–65; L. Sutherland, *The East India Company in Eighteenth-Century Politics* (Oxford, 1952).
5. Walpole to Townshend, 8 June 1723, PRO. SP. 43/66.
6. N. Rogers, 'Resistance to Oligarchy: The City Opposition to Walpole and his Successors, 1725–47', in J. Stevenson (ed.), *London in the Age of Reform* (Oxford, 1977), pp. 1–29, and 'The City Elections Act (1725) Reconsidered', *EHR*, 100 (1985), pp. 604–17.
7. L. Penson, 'The London West India Interest in the Eighteenth Century', *EHR*, 36 (1921), pp. 373–92; R. Sheridan, 'The Molasses Act and the Market Strategy of the British Sugar Planters', *Journal of Economic History*, 17 (1957), pp. 62–83.
8. Black, *Foreign Policy in the Age of Walpole*, pp. 93–117.
9. P.L. Woodfine, 'The Anglo-Spanish War of 1739', in Black (ed.), *The Origins of War in Early Modern Europe* (Edinburgh, 1987), pp. 185–209.
10. Cobbett, XIII, 272, 562, 564–5, 617.
11. R. Browning, *Political and Constitutional Ideas of the Court Whigs* (Baton Rouge, 1982).
12. J. McLachlan, *Trade and Peace with Old Spain, 1667–1750* (Cambridge, 1940).
13. A.J. Henderson, *London and the National Government 1721–42. A Study of City Politics and the Walpole Administration* (Durham, North Carolina, 1945); N. Rogers, 'Resistance to Oligarchy: The City opposition to Walpole and his Successors, 1725–47', in J. Stevenson (ed.), *London in the Age of Reform* (Oxford, 1977), pp. 1–29; Townshend to Newcastle, 29 June (ns) 1725, BL. Add. 32687 f. 87; NLS. MS. 7046 f. 38; Carew to Sydenham, 22 Ap. 1742, Taunton, CRO. Trollop-Bellew papers, DD/TB, box 16 OB8.
14. March, *A Duke and his Friends*, I, 165.
15. Black, 'The Medal as Political Propaganda', *Medal*, 10 (1986), pp. 8–10; NLS. MS. 7045 f. 92.
16. P. Corfield, *The Impact of English Towns 1700–1800* (Oxford, 1982); P. Clark (ed.), *The Transformation of English Towns 1600–1800* (1984); P. Borsay, *The English Urban Renaissance: Culture and Society in the Provincial Town 1660–1770* (Oxford, 1989).

17. BL. Add. 47028 f. 97.
18. BL. Add. 32688 f. 30; *Victoria County History. East Riding* I (1969), pp. 201–2; BL. Add. 47000 f. 116; *York Courant*, 20 Oct. 1741; L. Cust, *Records of the Cust Family Series* III (1927), pp. 32–3.
19. Plumb, *The Commercialization of Leisure in Eighteenth-Century England* (Reading, 1973); J. McKendrick et al., *The Birth of a Consumer Society* (1982).
20. Black, 'Grain Exports and Neutrality', *Journal of European Economic History*, 12 (1983), pp. 593–600.
21. BL. Add. 32688 f. 257, 35406 f. 140.
22. *York Courant*, 27 Oct. 1741.
23. A. Charlesworth (ed.), *An Atlas of Rural Protest in Britain 1548–1900* (1983).
24. Robert to Horatio, – Sept. 1736, BL. Add. 63749A f.263.
25. Cobbett, X, 249–50.
26. NLS. MS. 7046 f. 22.
27. BL. Add. 47028 f. 91.
28. E. Stockdale, *Law and Order in Georgian Bedfordshire* (Bedford, 1982), p. 11.
29. PRO. 30/29/1/11 f. 276.
30. HMC. *Egmont*, I, 220, 359.
31. PRO. SP. 105/282 f. 347.
32. Coxe, *Orford* I, 264–5, II, 340; Hervey, I, 135–43; Dickinson, *Bolingbroke*, p. 219.
33. Dickinson, 'Popular Politics in the Age of Walpole', in Black (ed.), *Britain in the Age of Walpole* (1984), p. 68.
34. PRO. SP. 78/290 f. 78; Liston to the Foreign Secretary, the Marquess of Carmarthen, 16 Ap. (ns) 1787, Waldegrave to Newcastle, 14 Oct. (ns) 1733, BL. Add. 34465, 32782.
35. Anon., *The Last Will and Testament of the Right Hon. Robert Earl of Orford* (1745).
36. G.H. Jones, *The Mainstream of Jacobitism* (Cambridge, Mass., 1954); Black, *Culloden and the '45* (Gloucester, 1990).
37. Plumb, *The Growth of Political Stability in England, 1675–1725* (1967).
38. HL. Lo. 7634.
39. Holmes, 'The Achievement of Stability: the Social Context of Politics from the 1680s to the Age of Walpole', in J. Cannon (ed.), *The Whig Ascendancy* (1981), pp. 1–22, reprinted in Holmes, *Politics, Religion and Society in England, 1679–1742* (1986), pp. 249–79; Holmes, *Augustan England: Professions, State and Society 1680–1730* (1982).
40. Kenyon, *Revolution Principles*, p. 204.
41. Colley, *Defiance of Oligarchy*, p. 21.
42. Cruickshanks, 'Religion and Royal Succession – The Rage of Party', in Jones (ed.), *Britain in the First Age of Party* (1987), p. 41.
43. D. Hay, P. Linebaugh and E.P. Thompson, *Albion's Fatal Tree: Crime and Society in Eighteenth-Century England* (1975); Thompson, *Whigs and Hunters: The Origin of the Black Act* (1975); Rogers, 'The Urban Opposition to Whig Oligarchy, 1720–60', in M. and J. Jacob (eds.), *The Origins of Anglo-American Radicalism* (1984), pp. 132–48.
44. PRO. SP. 43/4 f. 244.
45. Thompson, 'The Moral Economy of the English Crowd in the Eighteenth Century', *Past and Present* 50 (1971); Stevenson, *Popular Disturbances in England 1700–1870* (1979); Brewer and J. Styles (eds.), *An Ungovernable People: The English and their Law in the Seventeenth and Eighteenth Centuries* (1980); Rogers, 'Riot and Popular Jacobitism in Early Hanoverian England', in Cruickshanks (ed.), *Ideology and Conspiracy. Aspects of Jacobitism, 1689–1759* (Edinburgh, 1982), pp. 70–88.
46. Robert to Horatio, 29 July, 20 Aug., 30 Sept. 1736, BL. Add. 63749A f. 249, 256, 262.

Chapter 6

1. *Pasquin*, 13 May 1723; *Northampton Mercury*, 7 Oct. 1723.
2. *London Journal*, 9 Feb. 1723.
3. *London Journal*, 1 Aug. 1724.
4. *Weekly Register*, 4 Sept. 1731.
5. *Flying Post*, 21 Jan., 12 Aug. 1731; *London Journal*, 2 Aug. 1731; *Daily Gazetteer*, 24 July, 30 Oct. 1740.
6. *Whitehall Evening Post*, 6 Jan. 1728; *Hyp-Doctor*, 25 Jan. 1732.
7. *Free Briton*, 6 Jan. 1732.
8. *London Journal*, 12 Oct. 1728; *Free Briton*, 21 Jan. 1731; Anon., *Popular Prejudices against the Convention and Treaty with Spain Examined and Answered* (1739), pp. 28–9.
9. *Nonsense of Common-Sense*, 21 Feb. 1738; Anon., *Observations on a Pamphlet, entitled, an Answer to one Part of a Late Infamous Libel, etc. In a Letter to Mr P[ulteney]* (1731), Anon., *The True Principles of the Revolution Revived and Asserted* (1741), pp. 4–5.
10. *Daily Gazetteer*, 9 Dec. 1737.
11. *British Journal*, 9 Dec. 1727; *Daily Gazetteer*, 18, 29 Oct. 1740, 25 Feb. 1742.
12. Hervey, 1 Dec. 1740, Cobbett, XI, 739; Hervey to Stephen Fox, 25 Nov. 1729, Ilchester (ed.), *Hervey and his Friends*, p. 40; *Hyp-Doctor*, 2 Jan. 1733.
13. Anon., *Letter of Mr P.*, p. 44; Presentation of *Craftsman* and *Fog's* by Grand Jury for Middlesex, *Daily Courant*, 7 July 1731.
14. *Craftsman*, 9 Dec. 1726, 24 June 1727, 28 Sept., 2 Nov. 1728; Anon., *Memoirs of the Life and Conduct of William Pulteney* (1735), p. 33.
15. *Craftsman*, 16 Dec. 1726, 24 June, 23 Sept. 1727, 28 Sept., 26 Oct. 1728.
16. *Craftsman*, 23 Sept., 25 Nov. 1727, 9 Dec. 1726.
17. *Craftsman*, 31 July 1731.
18. *Champion*, 1 May 1740.
19. Chavigny to Chauvelin, 3 Mar. (ns) 1732, 28 Ap. (ns) 1733, Anon. memorandum, 27 June (ns) 1739, AE.CP. Ang. 376 f. 258, 380 f. 132, MD. Ang. 8 f. 202; Geraldino to St Gill, Spanish envoy in The Hague, 1 July (ns) 1738, PRO. SP. 94/246.
20. *Norwich Mercury*, 13 Mar. 1731, reprinting item from *Daily Courant*.
21. *London Journal*, 15 Sept., 6 Oct. 1722.
22. Tilson to Waldegrave, 6 Jan. 1730, Chewton.
23. Eg. Paxton to Newcastle, 29 Nov. 1733, BL. Add. 32689.
24. Townshend to Walpole, 12 July (ns) 1723, PRO. SP. 43/4.
25. Hanson, *Government and the Press*, pp. 113, 109. For the press wars: S. Targett, 'Government and Ideology during the Age of Whig Supremacy: The Political Argument of Walpole's Newspaper Propagandists', *HJ*, 37 (1994), pp. 289–318, and '"The Premier Scribbler Himself": Sir Robert Walpole and the Management of Political Opinion', *Studies in Newspaper and Periodical History* (1994), pp. 19–33. On Walpole's opponents, G.A. Cranfield, 'The *London Evening Post*, 1727–1744: A Study in the Development of the Political Press', *HJ*, 6 (1963); S. Varey (ed). *Lord Bolingbroke: Contributions to the Craftsman* (Oxford, 1982) and 'The *Craftsman*', *Prose Studies*, 16 (1993), pp. 58–77.
26. Delafaye to Waldegrave, 20 May 1731, Chewton.
27. Goodricke to Edward Hopkins, 16–17 Mar. 1732, BL. Add. 64929 f. 52.
28. Realey, 'The *London Journal* and its authors, 1720–1723', *Bulletin of the University of Kansas*, 36 (1935), pp. 28–9.

29. Poyntz to Delafaye, 25 Sept. 1723, PRO. SP. 43/5; *Mist's Weekly Journal*, 12 June 1725; Wharton's memorandum, 23 Aug. (ns) 1725, HHStA. England, Noten 2; *Norwich Mercury*, 2 May 1730; Delafaye to Waldegrave, 19 Oct. 1730, Chewton; *Craftsman*, 17 Oct. 1730, 27 Feb. 1731; Budgell, 'A Letter to every person in Great Britain who has the least regard for the foundation of our liberties, The Liberty of the Press', 21 May 1733, Bod. Mss. Hope f. 106.
30. *Craftsman*, 30 Nov. 1728, 6 Dec. 1729; Anon., *The Wooden Age* (1733), p. 3; [Marchmont], *A Serious Exhortation to the Electors of Great Britain* (1740), pp. 20–1.
31. Delafaye to Poyntz, 27 Feb. 1729, BL. Althorp E3.
32. *General Post Office Letter*, 19 May 1724; Walpole to Townshend, 28 June 1723, PRO. SP. 43/4.
33. Henry Dunster to Sir John Rushout, 11 Dec. 1729, Worcester CRO. 705: 66 BA 4221/26; Yorke to Newcastle, 14 July 1729, 29 June 1730, 15 Dec. 1733, Willes to Newcastle, 23 Dec. 1734, PRO. SP. 43/79, 36/19, 36/30, 36/33; Hanson, *Government and the Press*, p. 67.
34. Anon., *Observations on a Pamphlet . . . In a letter to Mr P-*, pp. 6–7.
35. Delafaye to Waldegrave, 31 Mar. 1732, Chewton.
36. A.D. McKillop, 'Thomson and the Licensers of the Stage', *Philological Quarterly*, 37 (1958), pp. 450, 452; L.W. Conolly, *The Censorship of English Drama 1737–1782* (San Marino, California, 1976), p. 10; V.J. Leisenfeld, *The Licensing Act of 1737* (Madison, 1984).
37. Delafaye's notes on examination of James Watson, – Mar. 1728, PRO. SP. 31/5.
38. Fagel to Hop, 14 Ap. (ns) 1739, PRO. SP. 107/26.
39. *Historical View . . . of the Political Writers*, p. 23.
40. Stair to Marlborough, 6 Feb. 1737, BL. Microfilm 687.
41. H. Barker, *Newspapers, Politics and English Society 1695–1855* (2000), pp. 138–41.
42. Warrants, 15 July, 18 Oct. 1739, Attorney General, Dudley Ryder, to Harrington, 8, 18 Oct., examination of printer Dr. Gaylard, 23 Oct. 1739, PRO. SP. 44/82, 36/50; Ryder's notes, 22 Sept. 1739, History of Parliament Transcripts.
43. Walpole, Cobbett, XI, 881–2.

Chapter 7

1. PRO. SP. 43/4 f. 119–20, 150, 227.
2. Anon. Memorandum, 1724, PRO. SP. 35/54 f. 361–2; Cruickshanks, *Political Untouchables: The Tories and the '45* (1979); P. Monod, *Jacobitism and the English People, 1688–1788* (Cambridge, 1989).
3. Cobbett, XI, 936–7; Macky to Walpole, 15, 25 Dec. (ns) 1723, Townshend to Walpole, 26 Oct. (ns) 1725, CUL. C(H) corresp. 1044, 1053, 1250; P. Fritz, *The English Ministers and Jacobitism between the Rebellions of 1715 and 1745* (Toronto, 1975); Black, 'British Intelligence and the Mid-Eighteenth Century Crisis', *Intelligence and National Security*, 2 (1987), pp. 209–29.
4. Walpole to Waldegrave, 10 Nov. 1733, 21 Jan. 1734, 1 Jan. 1735, Walpole to Thomas Pelham, 15 Nov. 1733, Chewton.
5. R. Freebairne to John Hay, 8 Jan. 1722, RA. 57/18.
6. Walpole to Townshend, 23 July 1723, PRO. SP. 43/4 f. 116.
7. HL. Lo. 8344.
8. Black, *British Foreign Policy in the Age of Walpole* (Edinburgh, 1985).
9. Bennett, *Tory Crisis in Church and State, 1688–1730*; R. Davis, 'The "Presbyterian" Opposition and the emergence of party in the House of Lords in the reign of Charles II', in Jones (ed.), *Party and Management in Parliament, 1660–1784*, pp. 1–35.

10. BL. Add. 62558 f. 80. For Whig Anglicanism, J.S. Chamberlain, *Accommodating High Churchmen. The Clergy of Sussex, 1700–45* (Urbana, Illinois, 1997); J. Gregory, *Restoration, Reformation and Reform, 1660–1828. Archbishops of Canterbury and Their Diocese* (Oxford, 2000), pp. 97–9.

11. T.F.J. Kendrick, 'Sir Robert Walpole, the Old Whigs and the Bishops, 1733–1736: A Study in Eighteenth Century Parliamentary Politics', *HJ*, 11 (1968), pp. 421–45; Taylor, 'Sir Robert Walpole, the Church of England, and the Quakers Tithe Bill of 1736', *Ibid.*, 28 (1985), pp. 51–77.

12. BL. Add. 47029 f. 132; RA. 103/80.

13. G.F. Nuttall (ed.), *Calendar of the Correspondence of Philip Doddridge* (1979), p. 355.

14. N. Hunt, *Two Early Political Associations: The Quakers and the Dissenting Deputies in the Age of Sir Robert Walpole* (Oxford, 1961).

15. N. Sykes, *Edmund Gibson, Bishop of London* (Oxford, 1926) and *Church and State in England in the Eighteenth Century* (Cambridge, 1934).

16. S.W. Baskerville, 'The Political Behaviour of the Cheshire Clergy, 1705–1752', *Northern History*, 23 (1987), pp. 74–97; Langford, 'Convocation and the Tory Clergy, 1717–61', in Cruickshanks and Black (eds.), *The Jacobite Challenge* (Edinburgh, 1988), pp. 107–22.

17. J.D. Walsh, 'Origins of the Evangelical Revival', in Bennett and Walsh (eds.), *Essays in Modern Church History* (1966); F. Baker, *John Wesley and the Church of England* (1970).

18. B.R. Kreiser, *Miracles, Convulsions and Ecclesiastical Politics in Early Eighteenth-Century Paris* (Princeton, 1978).

19. Hunt, *Political Associations*, p. 159.

20. *A Letter on a Proposed Alteration of the 39 Articles by Lord Walpole written 1751* (1863), pp. 5–6.

21. Townshend to Walpole, 8 Sept. 1723, PRO. SP. 43/4 f. 341.

22. Wellcome Institute, London, Mss. 5006, p. 34; *Walpole corresp.*, 4, 167.

23. Newcastle to Carteret, 3 June 1743, PRO. SP. 43/34. Borlase Warren died in 1747 and a Tory, Sir Charles Sedley, defeated a Whig in the subsequent by-election.

24. Newcastle to Waldegrave, 3 Mar. 1732, BL. Add. 32776 f. 156.

25. Cobbett,X, 31; RA. 103/80; Selwyn to Poyntz, 8 Jan. 1730, BL. Althorp Mss. E4.

26. E.R. Turner, 'The Excise Scheme of 1733', *EHR*, 42 (1927), pp. 54–7; Langford, *Excise Crisis*; M. Jubb, 'Economic Policy and Economic Development', in Black (ed.), *Britain in the Age of Walpole*, pp. 121–44; J.M. Price, 'The Excise Affair Revisited: The Administrative and Colonial Dimensions of a Parliamentary Crisis', in Baxter (ed.), *England's Rise to Greatness*, pp. 257–321; 'The honest Freeholders Resolution', Norwich, CRO. Hobart Mss.

27. D. Baugh, *British Naval Administration in the Age of Walpole* (Princeton, 1954); Dickson, *Financial Revolution*; J. Brewer, *The Sinews of Power: War, Money and the English State, 1688–1783* (1989).

28. W.R. Ward, *The English Land Tax in the Eighteenth Century* (Oxford, 1953).

29. Landau, *The Justices of the Peace 1679–1760* (Berkeley, 1984); S. Baskerville, 'The Management of the Tory Interest in Lancashire and Cheshire, 1714–47' (D.Phil., Oxford, 1976), appendix; Clavering to Lady Cowper, 26 Sept. 1719, Hertford CRO. Panshanger papers D/EP F196 f. 68.

30. Sedgwick, I, 33–50; Hill, *The Growth of Parliamentary Parties 1689–1742* (1976), pp. 189–226.

31. BL. Add. 47028 f. 7.

32. Kenyon, *Revolution Principles*.

33. Dickson, *Financial Revolution*, pp. 9–10, 80, 82, 209–10; Anon., *Outlines of a Plan of Finance* (1813), p. 1.

34. NAS. GD. 150/3474/56; Cobbett, X, 74–187; Dickson, *Financial Revolution*, pp. 212–15.

35. BL. Add. 74065. On wool smuggling, Benjamin Ward to Walpole, 27 Feb. 1730, CUL. C(H) corresp. 1687.

36. R. Wodrow, *Analecta* (4 vols., Edinburgh, 1842–3), III, 156.

37. Lowther to Spedding, 6 May 1740, Carlisle, Cumbria RO. D/Lons/W.

38. G.C. Gibbs, 'Newspapers, Parliament and Foreign Policy in the Age of Stanhope and Walpole', *Mélanges offerts à G. Jacquemyns* (Brussels, 1968), p. 293 and n.2, and 'The House of Commons in the Early Eighteenth Century', *Welsh History Review*, 7 (1974), p. 226; R. Lodge, book review *EHR*, 40 (1925), p. 440.

39. G.N. Clark, book review, *History*, 12 (1928), p. 79.

40. Chavigny to Morville, 20 Ap. (ns) 1724, Chammorel to Chauvelin, 13 July (ns) 1730, AE. CP. Ang. 347, 370; Palm to Charles VI, 13 Dec. (ns) 1725, CUL. CH. Corresp. 1379; Ossorio to Charles Emmanuel, 31 Mar. (ns) 1732, AST. LM. Ing. 39; Anon. Memorandum, 16 Nov. (ns) 1734, HHStA. Varia 8.

41. Waldegrave to Newcastle, 7 Feb. (ns) 1737, BL. Add. 32794; Memorandum for Cambis, 4 Mar. (ns) 1737, AE. CP. Ang. 394; Haslang to Törring, 24 Feb. (ns), 27 Mar. (ns) 1741, Munich KS. 17211.

42. BL. Add. 74065 no.1.

43. Delafaye to Poyntz, 8 Jan. 1730, BL. Althorp Mss. E4; Waldegrave to Newcastle, 31 Jan. (ns) 1731, extract in CUL. C(H) corresp. 1810; Newcastle to Walpole, 22 Oct. 1723, 22 June 1735, BL. Add. 32686 f. 358, PRO. SP. 36/35 f. 95.

44. Robert to Horatio, – Sept. 1736, BL. Add. 63749 f. 264.

45. Robert to Horatio, 28 Aug. 1730, BL. Add. 63749A f. 123–4.

46. E.g. Fawkener to Walpole, 8, 18 May (ns), 1 June (ns) 1736, BL. Add. 74072.

47. Delafaye to Tilson, 8 July 1729, PRO. SP. 43/79 f. 15.

48. Walpole to Newcastle, 25 July 1723, BL. Add. 32686 f. 285; Walpole to Townshend, 23 July 1723, PRO. SP. 43/4 f. 116–17, 43/66.

49. Walpole to Townshend, 9, 16 Aug. 1723, PRO. SP. 43/4 f. 211, 240–1.

50. Newcastle to Townshend, 20 May 1729, PRO. SP. 43/77.

51. Ossorio to Charles Emmanuel, 8 Dec. (ns) 1732, AST. LM. Ing. 39; Diemar to Eugene, 12 July (ns) 1734, 25 Jan. (ns), 1, 25 Mar. (ns), 24 May (ns), 3, 28 June (ns), 1735, HHStA. Grosse Korrespondenz 85a.

52. Newcastle to Keene, 12 Feb., 3 Ap., Newcastle to Horatio Walpole, 11 Ap. 1735, BL. Add. 32787 f. 10, 95, 121; Chavigny to Chauvelin, 1 Mar. (ns) 1735, AE. CP. Ang. 390 f. 290; Newcastle to Harrington, 11, 6 June, 8, 11 July, Harrington to Newcastle, 21 Aug. (ns) 1735, PRO. SP. 43/86–7; Ossorio to Charles Emmanuel III, 5 Mar. (ns), 17 June (ns) 1735, AST. LM. Ing. 43; *Daily Post Boy*, 9 July, *Thistle*, 9 July 1735. See also Ossorio to Charles Emmanuel, 20 May (ns), 24 Dec. (ns) 1734, 16 Jan. (ns), 13 Mar. (ns) 1735, AST. LM. Ing. 41–2; Haslang, Bavarian envoy to Charles VII, 7 Ap. (ns) 1741, Munich, Hauptstaatsarchiv, Kasten Schwarz, Britain 17211.

53. Couraud to Newcastle, 12 Dec. 1735, PRO. 36/37 f. 118–20; Newcastle to Waldegrave, 3 Oct., 6 Nov. 1735, Chewton.

54. Bonet to Frederick William, 29 Mar. (ns) 1718, Merseburg 41.

55. Chavigny to Chauvelin, 19 Jan. (ns) 1736, AE. CP. Ang. 393.

56. Walpole to Newcastle, 25 July, 31 Aug. 1723, BL. Add. 32686 f. 284–5, 320–1. cf. Cortanze, Sardinian envoy, to Victor Amadeus II, 22 Feb. 1723, AST. LM. Ing. 32.

57. Walpole to Newcastle, 7, 19 Sept., Delafaye to Newcastle, 19 Aug., 12, 25, 28 Nov. 1725, memorandum by Newcastle of meeting at Walpole's on 9 Sept. 1725, PRO. SP. 35/58 f. 25, 50, 35/59 f. 112, 168, 170–1, 182–3, BL. Add. 32689 f. 155–9; King, *Locke*, II, 21.
58. Palm to Charles VI, 13 Dec. (ns) 1726, CUL. CH. Corresp. 1379, deciphered and translated.
59. Walpole to Newcastle, 3 July 1730, BL. Add. 32687.
60. Cobbett, IX, 208, 19 Jan. 1734.
61. Cobbett, IX, 228, 25 Jan. 1734.
62. Ossorio to Charles Emmanuel, 21 Sept. (ns) 1734, 'avant la fin d'avril' [1735], AST. LM. Ing. 41–2; Chavigny to Chauvelin, 22 Ap. (ns) 1735, AE. CP. Ang. 391 f. 82.
63. Geraldino to the Spanish minister Torrenueva, 19 Dec. (ns) 1737, PRO. SP. 94/246.
64. Ossorio to Charles Emmanuel, 28 Ap. (ns), 12 May (ns), 2, 23, 30 June (ns), 14 July (ns), 11, 25 Aug. (ns), 1 Sept. (ns) 1738, AST. LM. Ing. 45.
65. Earl of Orrery, *Letters from Italy in the years 1754 and 1755* (1773), p. 155.
66. Cobbett XI, 1065, 1102, re Lords debate on 13 Feb. 1741.
67. Robert to Horatio Walpole, 18 June 1736, BL. Add. 63749A f. 214–15, cf. 6, 20 Aug., 3 Sept. 1736, f. 251–3, 255–7.

Chapter 8

1. P.D.G. Thomas, 'Party Politics in Eighteenth-Century Britain', *British Journal for Eighteenth-Century Studies*, 10 (1987), p. 205.
2. Lonsdale to Fleming, 30 Oct. 1737, 20 Sept. 1740, Carlisle, D/Sen/Fleming 14; Sedgwick, I, 377; HL. STG. Box 22 (9).
3. Reading, Berkshire CRO. D/E Hy04.
4. See e.g. for Newcastle and Norwich, K. Wilson, *The Sense of the People. Politics, Culture and Imperialism in England, 1715–1785* (Cambridge, 1995); P. Gauci, *Politics and Society in Great Yarmouth 1660–1722* (Oxford, 1996); P. Halliday, *Dismembering the Body Politics: Partisan Politics in English Towns 1650–1730* (1998); C. Estabrook, *Urbane and Rustic England: Cultural Ties and Social Spheres in the Provinces, 1660–1780* (Manchester, 1999).
5. S. Handley, 'Local legislative initiatives for economic and social development in Lancashire, 1689–1731', *Parliamentary History*, 9 (1990), pp. 14–37.
6. L. Glassey, 'Local Government' in Jones (ed.), *Britain in the First Age of Party*, p. 171.
7. Lowther to Spedding, 25 Aug. 1743, Carlisle, Cumbria RO. D/Lons/W2/1/104.
8. Harriet Fox to Catherine Countess of Egmont, 10 Oct. 1741, BL. Add. 47000 f. 116; Hertford, CRO. D/EP F196 f. 74.
9. Holmes (ed.), *Britain after the Glorious Revolution 1689–1714* (1969), p. 235; Thomas, 'Party Politics', p. 205.
10. Thomas, 'Sir Roger Newdigate's Essays on Party, *c.* 1762', *EHR*, 102 (1987), pp. 394–400.
11. BL. Add. 23825 f. 276–7.
12. Anon., *A Second Letter to Dr. Codex* (1734), p. 12; *Daily Gazetteer*, 1 Sept. 1735; BL. Add. 47021 B f. 55; *Old England*, 16 Feb. 1745.
13. Robert Freebairne to Hay, 8 Jan. 1722, Orrery to the Pretender, 30 June 1727, RA. 57/18, 107/150; Broglie to Morville, 30 Nov. (ns) 1724, AE. CP. Ang. 349.
14. BL. Add. 37366 f. 95, 47028 f. 207, Stowe 232 f. 51; Colley, *Defiance*, pp. 192–3; Duke of Chandos to Harcourt, 3 Nov. 1717, HL. ST. 57 vol. 13, p. 79.

15. BL. Add. 32686 f. 330, Stowe 242 f. 212; RA. 26/32; HL. ST. 57 vol. 13, p. 92.

16. Bod. Add. MS. A 269, pp. 74–5.

17. Newcastle to Townshend, 18 Aug. 1722, Beinecke, Osborn Files, Newcastle; BL. Add. 32686 f. 236.

18. BL. Add. 32686 f. 269.

19. Colley, *Defiance*, pp. 174, 50.

20. Browning, review of Colley, *Albion*, 14 (1982), pp. 311–12; Colley, *Defiance*, p. 55.

21. E. Gregg, *The Protestant Succession in International Politics 1710–1716* (New York, 1986), p. 297; Colley, *Defiance*, p. 208.

22. King, *Locke*, II, 49–50; Sedgwick, I, 201–2; Baugh, review of Hatton, *Journal of Modern History*, 53 (1981), p. 107.

23. Christie, 'The Tory Party, Jacobitism and the Forty-Five: A Note', *HJ*, 30 (1987), p. 931.

24. D. McKay, 'Bolingbroke, Oxford and the Defence of the Utrecht Settlement in Southern Europe', *EHR*, 86 (1971), pp. 264–84.

25. Delafaye to Poyntz, 26 Jan. 1730, BL. Althorp Mss. E4; Toland, *State Anatomy* (3rd edn., 1717), pp. 17, 25; Coxe, *Orford*, p. 128; HL. Lo. 7948.

26. Langford, *Excise Crisis*.

27. Black, *Convergence or Divergence? Britain and the Continent* (1994), pp. 123–6, 138–58; J.C.D. Clark, *English Society 1660–1832* (2nd edn., Cambridge, 2000) esp. pp. 19–26.

28. Hayton, 'The County interest and the party system, 1689–*c.*1720', in Jones (ed.), *Party and Management in Parliament*, pp. 65–6.

29. Clark, *The Dynamics of Change. The Crisis of the 1750s and English Party Systems* (Cambridge, 1982), p. 454, and 'A General Theory of Party, Opposition and Government, 1688–1832', *HJ*, 23 (1980), pp. 302–6.

30. Christie, 'The Changing Face of Parliamentary Politics, 1742–1789', in Black (ed.), *British Politics and Society from Walpole to Pitt, 1742–1789* (1990), pp. 108–110.

31. Clark, 'The Decline of Party, 1740–1760', *EHR*, 93 (1978), pp. 517–19; L. Namier, *England in the Age of the American Revolution* (2nd edn., 1963), pp. 192–5.

32. P.D. Brown and K. Schweizer (eds.), *The Devonshire Diary* (1982), pp. 57, 25, 52.

33. Namier and J. Brooke (eds.), *The History of Parliament. The House of Commons 1754–1790* (3 vols., 1964) II, 487.

34. Christie, 'Party in Politics in the Age of Lord North's Administration', *Parliamentary History*, 6 (1987), pp. 47–8, 62.

35. Brewer, *Party Ideology and Popular Politics at the Accession of George III* (Cambridge, 1976); Thomas, *John Wilkes: A Friend to Liberty* (Oxford, 1996).

36. J.E. Bradley, *Popular Politics and the American Revolution in England: Petitions, the Crown and Public Opinion* (Macon, Georgia, 1986); J. Sainsbury, *Disaffected Patriots: London Supporters of Revolutionary America 1769–1782* (Kingston, Ontario, 1987).

37. Mure to Elliot, 8 Feb. 1762, NLS. Mss. 11010.

Chapter 9

1. Tilson to Delafaye, 15 Nov. (ns) 1723, PRO. SP. 43/5 f. 248.

2. J.S. Gibson, *Playing the Scottish Card. The Franco-Jacobite Invasion of 1708* (Edinburgh, 1988).

Notes

3. C.A. Whatley, *'Bought and Sold for English Gold?' Explaining the Union of 1707* (Glasgow, 1994); HMC. *Egmont*, I, 220; BL. Add. 51417 f. 77; RA. 103/80.
4. Elliot to his father, Lord Minto, 15 Nov. 1755, NLS. Mss. 11001 f. 15.
5. BL. Add. 47028 f. 21.
6. Wodrow, *Analecta*, III, 280.
7. BL. Add. 61494 f. 4.
8. Townshend to Roxburgh, 24 Aug. (ns) 1725, PRO. SP. 43/6 f. 349.
9. Walpole to Newcastle, 20 Aug., Delafaye to Newcastle, 28 Nov. 1725, PRO. SP. 35/57, f. 250, 257, 35/59 f. 183.
10. Delafaye to Townshend, 22 Oct. 1725, PRO. SP. 43/75.
11. Carteret to Tweeddale, 22 Oct. 1740, NLS. Mss. 14420 f. 123.
12. J.S. Shaw, *The Management of Scottish Society, 1707–64* (Edinburgh, 1983).
13. Poyntz to Weston, 24 Sept. 1745, Farmington, Connecticut, Weston papers vol. 16.
14. PRO. SP. 43/6 f. 244, 282.
15. PRO. SP. 35/57 f. 250, 35/59 f. 183; Delafaye to Tilson, 17 Aug. 1725, PRO. SP. 43/75.
16. G. Elliot, *The Border Elliots* (Edinburgh, 1897), pp. 309–10.
17. Wodrow, *Analecta* III, 273.
18. H. Wickes, *Regiments of Foot* (Reading, 1974); BL. Blakeney Mss, p. 64.
19. Cobbett, XIII, 354.
20. *St James's Chronicle*, 17 Dec. 1771; Dalrymple to Gilbert Elliot, 26 Feb. 1763, NLS. Mss. 11016; A. Murdoch, *The People Above. Politics and Administration in Mid-Eighteenth-Century Scotland* (Edinburgh, 1980), p. 19.
21. PRO. SP. 63/393 f. 14.
22. RA. 94/54; AE. CP. Ang. 373 f. 233.
23. PRO. SP. 35/59 f. 182.
24. Craggs to Stanhope, 30 Oct. 1719, PRO. SP. 43/58.
25. Hertford, County Record Office D/EP F56 f. 33–6; D. Hayton, 'Walpole and Ireland', in Black (ed.), *Britain in the Age of Walpole*, p. 97.
26. *A List of the Absentees of Ireland* (Dublin, 1729); *The Present State of Ireland Considered* (Dublin, 1730), pp. 7, 19; *Some Observations on the present state of Ireland, particularly in relation to the Woollen Manufacture* (1971), p. 21.
27. *Some Observations*, p. 12; *Remarks on the English Woollen Manufactures* (1730).
28. Townshend to Walpole, 23 Aug. 1724, Beinecke, Osborn Files, Townshend; Newcastle to Horatio Walpole, 27 July 1724, BL. Add. 32739 f. 391; A. Goodwin, 'Wood's Halfpence', *EHR*, 51 (1936), pp. 647–74; R. Mahony, 'Protestant dependence and consumption in Swift's Irish writings', in S.J. Connolly (ed.), *Political Ideas in Eighteenth-Century Ireland* (Dublin, 2000), pp. 95–9.
29. Hertford CRO. D/EP F56 f. 17–19.
30. F.G. James, 'The Irish Lobby in the Early Eighteenth Century', *EHR*, 71 (1966), pp. 543–57.
31. BL. Add. 32687 f. 54.
32. Surrey CRO. Brodrick Mss. 1248/7 f. 17–18.
33. Hayton, 'Walpole and Ireland', esp. pp. 117–19.
34. Nathanael Clements to Sir Robert Wilmot, 20 Nov. 1741, Matlock, Derbyshire CRO. WH 3430, p. 102, cf. 3431, p. 523.
35. Colley, *Britons. Forging the Nation 1707–1837* (New Haven, 1992); C. Kidd, 'North Britishness and the Nature of Eighteenth-Century British Patriotisms', *HJ*, 39 (1996), pp. 361–82; Murdoch, *British History 1660–1832. National Identity and Local Culture* (1998).

Notes

Chapter 10

1. HMC. *Egmont*, III, 28–9, 31.
2. Cambis, French envoy, to Amelot, French foreign minister, 5, 12, 20, 26 Mar. (ns) 1739, AE. CP. Ang. 404 f. 148–50, 167, 178–9, 191–3.
3. Villettes, envoy in Turin, to Newcastle, 4 Ap. (ns) 1739, PRO.SP. 92/42.
4. London, Wellcome Institute for the History of Medicine, Mss. 5006, p. 17.
5. Woodfine, *Britannia's Glories. The Walpole Ministry and the 1739 War with Spain* (1998).
6. John Campbell to Pryse Campbell, 15 Nov. 1739, 26 Feb. 1740, Carmarthen, Dyfed CRO. Cawdor Muniments Box 138; Mackworth to Pleydell Courteen, 7 Jan. 1740, Swansea, University Library, Mackworth papers, no. 1301.
7. Wilson, 'Empire, Trade and Popular Politics in mid-Hanoverian Britain: the case of Admiral Vernon', *Past and Present*, 121 (1988), pp. 74–109; G. Jordan and Rogers, 'Admirals as Heroes: Patriotism and Liberty in Hanoverian England', *Journal of British Studies*, 28 (1989), pp. 201–24.
8. Lowther to Spedding, 1 Nov. 1740, Carlisle, Cumbria RO. D/Lons./W.
9. R.H. Harding, *Amphibious Warfare in the Eighteenth Century. The British Expedition to the West Indies 1740–1742* (Woodbridge, 1991), pp. 83–122.
10. Woodfine, 'The War of Jenkins' Ear: a new voice in the Wentworth-Vernon debate', *Journal of the Society for Army Historical Research*, 65 (1987), pp. 67–91.
11. I.G. Doolittle, 'A first-hand account of the Commons debate on the removal of Sir Robert Walpole, 13 Feb. 1741', *Bulletin of the Institute of Historical Research*, 53 (1980), pp. 125–40; Cobbett, XI, 1362; Coxe, *Orford*, I, 653; Pulteney to Tweeddale, 1 Mar. 1741, NLS. Mss. 7044 f. 158–9; Harley, 13 Feb. 1741, CUL. Add. Mss. 6851 II, f. 25–6.
12. Sandys to Rushout, 9 Ap. 1741, Worcester CRO. 705: 66 BA 4221/26.
13. Cobbett, XII, 168.
14. Ossorio to Charles Emmanuel, 5, 12 May (ns) 1738, AST. LM. Ing. 45. The best recent introduction is Woodfine, *Britannia's Glories*, pp. 213–23.
15. Newcastle to Pelham, 21 June, 12 July 1740, Nottingham UL. NeC 104, 107.
16. Tucker to Joseph Radcliffe, 11 Oct. 1740, Bod. Ms. Don. C. 112 f. 200; Lowther to Spedding, 30 Oct. 1740, Carlisle, Cumbria RO. D/Lons./W.
17. Lowther to Spedding, 6 Nov. 1740, Carlisle, Cumbria CRO. D/Lons./W.
18. BL. Add. 32693 f. 472; NAS. GD. 248/48/1.
19. BL. Add. 23810 f. 101; Morton to Duncan Forbes, 23 Jan. 1742, *More Culloden Papers* III (Inverness, 1927).
20. Keene to Waldegrave, 23 Mar. (ns) 1739, Chewton.
21. Sandon, Ryder Diary, 16 Feb. 1740.
22. St Clair to Ashe Windham, 14 Sept. 1738, Norwich CRO. Ketton-Cremer Mss. WKC 6/24 401X; Couraud to Waldegrave, 8 May 1739, Chewton.
23. *York Courant*, 24 Ap., *Weekly Courant* (Nottingham), 26 Ap. 1739.
24. Sarah Marlborough to Stair, 27 May 1740, Beinecke, Osborne Shelves, Stair Letters, no. 51.
25. Newcastle to Pelham, 12 July 1740, Nottingham UL. NeC 107.
26. HMC. *Egmont*, II, 150.
27. *St James's Chronicle*, 18 Ap. 1769.
28. Marburg, Staatsarchiv, 4f. England, report of 30 Jan. 1770.
29. Duke to Duchess of Newcastle, 10 Dec. 1741, BL. Add. 33073 f. 186.

30. George Harbin to Mrs Bampfyld, 19 Dec. 1741, Taunton, Somerset CRO. Dd/SAS FA 41 C 795.
31. Owen, *The Rise of the Pelhams* (1957), p. 26.
32. John to Pryse Campbell, 23 Dec. 1741, Carmarthen, Dyfed CRO. Cawdor Muniments, Box 138.
33. Zamboni to Haslang, 5 Jan. (ns) 1742, Munich, Bayerisches Haupstaatsarchiv, Gesandtschaft London 370.
34. Bishop of Oxford to Hardwicke, enclosing Prince of Wales' answer, 7 Jan. 1742, BL. Add. 35587 f. 2–5.
35. HMC. *Egmont*, III, 239.
36. Fox to Hanbury Williams, 15 Aug. 1741, Farmington, 48 f. 27; Newcastle to [Richmond], 13 Aug. 1741, Farmington, Miscellaneous Manuscripts.
37. John to Mary Campbell, 23 Jan. 1742, Cawdor Muniments, Box 138.
38. John to Pryse Campbell, 30 Jan. 1742, Cawdor 138.
39. Owen, *Rise of the Pelhams*, pp. 1–40.
40. Bod. MS. Eng. Lett. c.44 f. 58.
41. John to Mary Campbell, 4 Feb. 1742, Cawdor 138.
42. John to Pryse Campbell, 27 Feb., 24 Mar. 1742, Cawdor 138.
43. BL. Add. 63750 f. 34. For the burning of papers on behalf of others, see, e.g., Du Bourgay, envoy in Berlin, to Townshend, 28 June (ns) 1727, PRO. SP. 90/22 and Harrington to Keene, 30 Jan. 1730, BL. Add. 32765 f. 232–3.
44. Beinecke, Osborn Shelves, Stair Letters, no. 54.
45. John Drummond MP to Onslow Burrish, 28 May 1742, PRO. SP. 110/6.
46. Cobbett, XIII, 567.
47. *The Lives of Dr. Edward Pocock, Dr. Zacharay Pearce, Dr. Thomas Newton and the Rev. Philip Shelton* (2 vols., 1816), II, 49, 69–70.
48. Digby to John Ward, 6 Mar. 1742, Manchester, John Rylands Library, Bromley Davenport Mss. corresp. 4 (ii).
49. John to Richard Tucker, 1 Ap. 1742, Bod. MS Don c. 105 f. 55; John to Pryse Campbell, 1 Ap. 1742, Cawdor 138.
50. CUL. Add. 6851 vol. 2 f. 47.
51. NLS. 7046 f. 48.
52. John to Richard Tucker, 27 Ap., 13, 24 May 1742, Bod. MS Don c. 105 f. 94, 109, 122.
53. NAS. GD. 150/3485/46.
54. Harris and Black, 'John Tucker, MP', *Albion* (1997), pp. 20–1.
55. *Walpole corresp.* III, 34. For Horace's satires in defence of his father, *The original speech of Sir W-m St-pe, on the first reading of the bill for appointing the Assizes at Buckingham* (1748) and *The speech of Richard White-Liver Esq; in behalf of himself and his brethren. Spoken to the most august mob at Rag Fair* (1748).
56. Chichester, W. Sussex CRO. Goodwood Mss. 104 no. 276; T.J. McCann (ed.), *The Correspondence of the Dukes of Richmond and Newcastle 1724–1750* (Lewes, 1984), p. 124.
57. Sandon, 21 R. 144.
58. Coxe, *Orford*, III, 592.
59. PRO. 30/29/1/11, f. 285; Earl Gower to Pelham, 15 Oct. 1743, Nottingham UL. NeC 113.
60. Cobbett, XIII, 467; CUL. Add. 6851 vol. 2 f. 70.
61. Cholmondely to Walpole, 5 Nov., reply 7 Nov. 1744, BL. Add. 63749A f. 339–41.

62. Coxe, *Memoirs of the Administration of the Right Honourable Henry Pelham* (2 vols., 1829); J. Wilkes, *A Whig in Power: The Political Career of Henry Pelham* (New York, 1964).

Chapter 11

1. Beinecke, Osborn Shelves, Stair Letters, no. 3.
2. Lynch, *The Independent Patriot* (1737), p. 31.
3. AE. CP. Ang. 376 fol. 91.
4. Cobbett XI, 921, 1118.
5. HL. Montagu papers 4557.
6. HMC. *Carlisle*, p. 70; Weston to Poyntz, 29 Dec. 1729, BL. Althorp Mss. E3.

Further Reading

The best approach is to read documents from the period. Much material is in print, although a lot of it is in books published many years ago and thus only available in selected libraries. Particularly useful are W. Coxe, *Memoirs of the Life and Administration of Sir Robert Walpole, Earl of Orford* (1798) and R.R. Sedgwick (ed.), *Some Materials towards Memoirs of the Reign of George II by John Lord Hervey* (1931). Other useful collections include G.H. Rose, *A Selection from the Papers of the Earls of Marchmont* (1831), J. Graham, *Annals and Correspondence of the Viscount and the First and Second Earls of Stair* (Edinburgh, 1875); P. Yorke, *The Life and Correspondence of Philip Yorke, Earl of Hardwicke* (1913), B. Dobrée (ed.), *The Letters of Philip Dormer Stanhope, Fourth Earl of Chesterfield* (1932), and T.J. McCann (ed.), *The Correspondence of the Dukes of Richmond and Newcastle 1724–50* (Lewes, 1984). Many volumes of the Historical Manuscripts Commission reports are of great importance. Particularly noteworthy are the Carlisle, Onslow, Polwarth, Portland, Stuart, Townshend, Trevor and Weston papers and the Egmont Diary. A very helpful collection of documents has been edited by Stephen Baskerville as *Walpole in Power, 1720–1742* (Oxford, 1985).

The press of the period offers much of interest. The major collection, that of the British Library, has been microfilmed, while many other newspapers can be read in the reference or local studies departments of major public libraries. There are important accessible collections in many towns, including Bristol, Bury St Edmunds, Canterbury, Chester, Derby, Edinburgh, Exeter, Gloucester, Ipswich, Leeds, Newcastle, Northampton, Norwich, Nottingham and Reading. Modern editions include S. Varey (ed.), *Lord Bolingbroke: Contributions to the Craftsman* (Oxford, 1982) and W.B. Coley (ed.), *The Jacobites Journal* (Oxford, 1982). The press is approached in G.A. Cranfield, *The Development of the Provincial Newspaper, 1700–1760* (Oxford, 1962), J.M. Black, *The*

English Press 1621–1861 (Stroud, 2001) and H. Barker, *Newspapers, Politics and English Society 1695–1855* (Harlow, 2000).

Excellent modern editions of Defoe, Fielding, Gay, Johnson, Pope and Swift have made the literature of the period readily accessible. For a good recent overview, W.A. Speck, *Literature and Society in Eighteenth-Century England. Ideology, Politics and Culture, 1680–1820* (Harlow, 1998). Important studies of the period include J.M. Black (ed.), *Britain in the Age of Walpole* (1984), J.M. Black, *Eighteenth-Century Britain 1688–1783* (2001), J.C.D. Clark, *English Society 1660–1832* (2nd edn., Cambridge, 2000), T.M. Devine and J.R. Young (eds.), *Eighteenth Century Scotland: New Perspectives* (Edinburgh, 1999), G. Holmes and D. Szechi, *The Age of Oligarchy. Pre-industrial Britain 1722–1793* (Harlow, 1993), P. Langford, *A Polite and Commercial People: England, 1727–1783* (Oxford, 1989), F. O'Gorman, *The Long Eighteenth Century. British Political and Social History 1688–1832* (1997), W. Prest, *Albion Ascendant. English History 1660–1815* (Oxford, 1998), R. Price, *British Society 1680–1880* (Cambridge, 1999). Other studies can be followed through the footnotes of this book.

It is always interesting to read other approaches. One of the best is H.T. Dickinson, *Walpole and the Whig Supremacy* (1973). J.H. Plumb, *Sir Robert Walpole. The Making of a Statesman* (1956), *Sir Robert Walpole. The King's Minister* (1960), and *The Growth of Political Stability in England, 1675–1725* (1967) are still of value but need to be read in the light of more recent work. C. Jones (ed.), *Britain in the First Age of Party 1680–1750* (1987) is a collection containing much of interest. Among recent detailed studies, one of the best is P.L. Woodfine, *Britannia's Glories. The Walpole Ministry and the 1739 War with Spain* (Woodbridge, 1998). A visually engrossing coverage is provided by Paul Langford's *Walpole and the Robinocracy* (Cambridge, 1986) in the series *The English Satirical Print* edited by Michael Duffy.

Index

Note: RW refers throughout to Sir Robert Walpole

Index

Index

risings (1685, 1715, 1745) 9, 97, 125, 147, 155, 156, 157
Secretary of State 154, 176
Squadrone 155
Secret Office of the Post Office 68
Secretaries of State 8, 27, 61, 131–2
  dual roles 59, 132
  for Scotland 154, 176
Septennial Act (1716) 13, 39, 45, 88, 89, 96, 175
Settlement, Act of (1701) 57
Seven Years War (1756–63) 18, 67, 156, 161, 166
Seville, Treaty of 51
Shippen, William (Jacobite MP) 11, 12
Shorter, Catherine (1st wife of RW) 4, 40
Sinking Fund 11, 127–8
Skerrett, Maria (Molly) (2nd wife of RW) 40–1
Societies for the Reformation of Manners 117
society: eighteenth-century culture 89, 125, 181–2
  development of consumer society 90
  disturbances and riots 91–3, 97–9, 125, 156
  education and culture 89–90
  hierarchical nature of 124
  literary figures 66
  public opinion and debate 81, 83, 95, 104–6
  and religion 93, 118
  stability and strife 94–9, 118, 180–2
  urban–rural differences 88–90, 98
Soissons, Congress of 32
South Sea Company (Bubble) 19–20, 32, 60, 134, 165
Spain 16
  Convention of the Pardo 85, 89, 91, 136, 164, 165
  and trade issues 85, 91
  War of Succession (1701–14) 4, 55, 126, 150
  wars with England (1718–20, 1739–48) 15, 48, 130–1, 166
spy network 115
Stage Licensing Act (1737) 111

Stair, John, 2nd Earl of 14, 112
Stamp Acts (1712, 1725) 111
Stanhope, Charles 20
Stanhope, James 4, 10, 20
  alliance negotiation with France (1716) 9
  as Secretary of State 8, 52, 53
Stanhope, Philip *see* Chesterfield
Stanhope, William (Lord Harrington) 36, 82, 134, 135, 168
Stanhope–Sunderland ministry 44, 48, 117, 121, 124, 125, 127, 150
State Anatomy of Great Britain (Toland) 145
Steele, Richard 7
Stuart, Prince Charles Edward 147, 155, 156, 168
Suffolk, Henrietta Howard, Countess of 30
Sugar Act (1739) 84
Sunderland, Charles, 3rd Earl of 10, 26, 27, 44, 52, 53, 60, 125
Supplement to the Freeholder's Journal 127
Sweden 10, 11, 132–3
Swift, Jonathan 7, 66
Sydney, Thomas, 1st Viscount (Townshend's grandson) 34–5

taxation issues 33, 36–7, 91, 93, 116, 121–3, 128–31
  import/export duties 130
  income tax introduction 128
  and Irish Treasury 161
  land tax 36, 90, 122, 125
  Malt tax disturbances 154, 156
  unfairness of system 123
  see also Excise Bill crisis (1733); excise duties
Test Act (1673) 13, 117
Thicknesse, Philip 67
Tithe Bill (1736) 40, 118, 121
Toleration Act (1689) 3, 117
Tories 13, 39–40, 41, 42, 116–21, 140–2
  alliance with opposition-Whigs 13, 14, 26–7, 102, 125–6
  foreign policies 14–15, 112, 115–16

and Jacobitism 114–15, 144–5
  leadership 44–5
  and the monarchy 41, 55–6
  purging from Commissions 124–5
Tower of London: RW's imprisonment (1711) 7, 169
Townshend, Charles, 2nd Viscount (RW's brother-in-law) 18, 45, 56
  and Anglo-French alliance 27–8
  ill-health 32, 35
  on Ireland 160
  letters to RW 106, 114, 120
  partnership/dispute with RW 10, 29, 33–5, 136
  resignation 34–5, 52, 61
  on Scotland 155, 157
  as Secretary of State 8, 20, 52
trade issues
  as election policies 84, 90
  India and Far East 129
  international relations 83–5
  policy disputes 42, 48
  West Indies/Spanish 48, 84, 85, 87, 136, 139
Treasury (RW's appointments) 8–9, 20, 43, 127
Triennial Act (1694) 45, 96
Trinitarian Dissenters, licensing of ministers 3
True Briton 108, 110, 111
Turner, Charles (RW's brother-in-law) 4, 18, 28, 48

Union, Act of (1707) 13, 91, 152, 153
Universal Spy 105
urban–rural politics and culture 89–90
Utrecht, Treaty of (1713) 7, 8, 33, 44, 55, 128, 142, 145

Vernon, Admiral Edward 165–6
Vienna, Second Treaty of 36, 125

Wake, William (Archbishop of Canterbury) 14
Wales 162, 163

211